COOKING WITH THE CUISINART™ FOOD PROCESSOR

Other books by Roy Andries de Groot

Revolutionizing French Cooking
Feasts for All Seasons
The Auberge of the Flowering Hearth
Esquire's Handbook for Hosts

COOKING
WITH THE
CUISINART™
FOOD
PROCESSOR

ROY ANDRIES DE GROOT

McGRAW-HILL BOOK COMPANY
New York   St. Louis   San Francisco
Düsseldorf   Mexico   Toronto

8 9   DODO   7 9 8

Design by Judith Michaels.

Library of Congress Cataloging in Publication Data

De Groot, Roy Andries,
Cooking with the Cuisinart food processor.

Includes index.
1. Cookery. 2. Kitchen utensils. I. Title.
TX652.D43   641.5'89   76-46586
ISBN 0-07-016273-5

To Katherine

who is so devoted to her Cuisinart
that now we have to have two
"Hers" and "His"

Contents

CONTENTS

3: Our Twenty-One Favorite Recipes with the Cuisinart Chopper-Churner, 31

4: Cream Soups Almost without Cream – Velvet Sauces Almost Instantly, 67

5: Easy, Fast, Simple Casseroles and Everyday Family Dishes, 81

6: Easy Basic Breads, Brawny Breakfast Elegance, 95

7: Juicy, Flavorful Chopped (Not Ground) Beef – Ideas from around the World, 101

8: Super Sandwiches and Their Fancy Fillings, 115

9: Salads at Speed and Vegetables with Vitamins, 125

10: Three International Menus for Prestigious Parties, 137

11: The Chopper-Churner Cuts Costs with Lively Encore Entrees, 157

12: The Chopper-Churner Can Also Cut Calories, 175

13: Fun with Home-Made Natural Aromatic Herb Salts, 189

14: More Fun with Off-Beat Pastries, 193

15: The Proper Ending for a Meal (or a Cookbook) Is a Memorable Dessert, 201

CONTENTS

Introduction

THE PHENOMENAL FRENCH
CHOPPER-CHURNER

It was in Paris, about five years ago, that we discovered this extraordinary kitchen machine, which was then called *Le Robot Coupe*, The Robot Cutter. We were immediately so impressed by its multipurpose efficiency and versatility that we spent almost all of the next three days playing around with it in the apartment kitchen of a Paris friend. With unbelievable speed and astonishing precision, it chopped raw meat, mashed potatoes, minced unpeeled garlic and tomatoes, whirled up satiny sauces and soups, grated and shredded anything from the hardest cheese to the softest cucumber, crushed ice cubes, mixed bread dough, converted smoked salmon into a heavenly smooth spreading paste . . . in short it was as miraculous a servant as Aladdin's Slave of the Lamp.

At the end of the first series of tests, an interview was arranged with Pierre Verdun, the French industrial designer who had developed the small home version of the machine, soon to be renamed Le Magimix. After many questions, the last one had in it a faint tinge of wickedness: "Monsieur Verdun, can it be truly possible that every single one of these multitudinous functions of your machine was precisely planned into the design? Surely, one or two of the things it can do came about accidentally?" Monsieur Verdun drew himself up to his fullest height and turned on a look of such sub-zero disdain as is only possible to a furiously aroused Frenchman: "M'sieur! This is not a machine! It is a phenomenon!"

That was how and why, when Le Magimix came to the United

States and was rechristened the Cuisinart, it was headlined in magazines and newspapers from the *New York Times* to the *San Francisco Herald and Examiner* and back again to the *Village Voice* as "The Phenomenal Cuisinart." In France, we have also heard it called "La Nouvelle Révolution Française." Great French chefs have told us that it is as much a turning point in gastronomic history as the invention of the fire grill rack, the turning spit, the enclosed oven, the pressure cooker, the electric grape pitter, the potato chip, the popsicle, or deepfrozen TV dinners. It is quite inaccurate, we think, to call this machine a "super-blender." It is about as far ahead of any old-fashioned blender as the moon space rocket was from the Wright Brothers' biplane. The Cuisinart unit is, quite simply, a pair of supersharp chef's knives, a blender, a grater, an electric mixer, a dough-maker, a nut grinder, a stone mortar and pestle, and a fine sieve all rolled into a single unit.

Yet, above all of these marvelous capabilities, perhaps the most important phenomenon of the Cuisinart is that once you become familiar with its working, it invites you to experiment in your cooking. All of us, these days, are surely trying to provide lighter, less expensively rich, less fattening yet imaginatively satisfying family and party meals. This is the new movement – the new Low-High Cuisine – which is sweeping across France as fast as it is into the home kitchens of America. But, let us face it, the new cuisine recipes – even those invented by the great French chefs – have been made possible largely by the new kitchen machines, chief among them the Cuisinart. Using it at home, you will gain a new perspective on the taste of avocado, or watercress, when you whip them into the fluff of an almost-instant mayonnaise (pages 53–54). You will feel as if you had really never tasted the true nuttiness of chestnuts until you whirl them into a velvety, savory purée (page 68). Your cream soups will take on a new dimension of naturalness of flavor when you make them without cream or artificial thickening with flour (Chapter 4). You will serve your tomatoes, spinach, broccoli or zucchini as concentrated mousses or purées, with the flavor of each vegetable magnified (page 130). You will churn up, in a few seconds, low-calorie salad dressings, savory garnishes, soups, snacks and other diet concoctions (Chapter 12). You will make an airy cake from ground nuts instead of flour (page 62) and silky sherbets almost without sugar (pages 204–206). You will prepare, for your most lavish parties, superb specialties

2

of the great chefs, Mousse of Salmon, Gâteau of Foie Gras with Oysters, or Glacéed Chestnuts in Croquettes – dishes that perhaps you have never dared to tackle before, but that are now miraculously fast and easy (pages 138, 140 and 142).

In short, dishes that once were within the range only of the professional cooks are now – by means of the same Cuisinart machine that is used by the professionals – simplified to the average ability of any intelligent amateur cook. Because of its fantastic speed, it allows you to do more, to experiment in new directions, and still spend less time in the kitchen. These recipes will show you ways with food that are faster and lighter, healthier and more precisely cooked, with more respect for the inherent qualities of the fresh ingredients – an altogether better, easier and simpler home cuisine.

1

The Hows and Whys of the Cuisinart Chopper-Churner

HOW DID IT ALL COME ABOUT?

The beginning was in France, about twenty years ago. A man named Pierre Verdun was calling regularly on all the major restaurants and selling them various types of large, professional cutting and slicing machines. Pierre watched his machines in operation in the kitchens. He could clearly see the faults in the design of many of them. Although he had had no engineering training, he had the audacity to go back to the makers of the machines with advice on how they might be made to work better. His employers thought he had the damnedest cheek and promptly fired him. He was so convinced he was right that he sold some family property, borrowed from the banks, mortgaged himself up to the hilt, hired a group of design engineers and launched the company that is now called Le Robot Coupe, The Robot Cutter. First, he made some large restaurant models, ranging up to an enormous 60-quart machine. By about 1970, Verdun's restaurant equipment was considered to be the best and most durable in France.

By this time, Pierre Verdun was deep into his next dream. He could sell only a few thousand big machines to restaurants. But if he could redesign it down to a much smaller scale, he could put it into millions of home kitchens around the world. This small machine – a fairly exact replica with the same relative power, solidity and strength as the professional equipment – was christened Le Magimix. It was seen at a Paris trade fair by a visiting American named Carl Sontheimer, a retired consulting engineer, who instantly saw great possibilities for Le Magimix in the U.S. His retirement was forgotten. He

5

tested the unit for six months, he adapted its design slightly for the American market, he signed a contract to become the U.S. distributor and launched it in 1973 as the Cuisinart machine. Its American success was so instantaneous and so immense that Carl has been running hell-for-leather ever since and never has a moment to look back.

WHAT ARE THE SECRETS OF ITS EXTRAORDINARY U.S. SUCCESS?

The first secret is in the rotating, scythe-shaped stainless steel double blades, razor-sharp and serrated, which cut cleanly through anything in their path in the bowl at a steady rate of 60 slashes per second. This is, in fact, rather a slow speed compared to the standard electric blender, which often turns at up to 6,000 revolutions per minute. The Cuisinart runs at one single speed of 1,800 revolutions per minute – this gives the powerful Cuisinart blades an immense cutting force. The machine is not geared up to high speeds. It is a direct, solid, power drive. Its blades are very large – almost 4½ inches along the serrated curve, compared to the average blender blades of about 1¼ inches, and they are thin and razor-like. They cut and slice as if they were the sharpest of chef's knives. A blender has relatively thick, blunt blades, chisel-shaped. At their high speed, they tend to grind and mash. Mashing squeezes the juice from the food, leaving it dry. Cutting holds in the juice. A blender tends to mash everything to a paste. The Cuisinart blades cut and re-cut into smaller and smaller bits. A standard meat grinder squeezes the tiny bits of meat through the grid of the disk. The Cuisinart blades chop and cut the meat as if with a chef's knife.

The second secret is in the angle and shape of the Cuisinart blades – one is set lower than the other and almost scrapes the floor of the bowl. The tips of the blades, as they turn, almost touch the circular sides of the bowl. This means that not even the smallest amount of food can escape. Unlike most other kitchen machines, the Cuisinart works with equal efficiency on a minimum load and on a maximum – it can chop a half pound of beef just as well as a half ounce. Underneath the blades of an average blender, there is often a space up to a half inch in which food can hide. The tips of the blender blades are often about an inch from the clover-leaf walls of the jug. The average blender jug is about 3½ inches across and tapers toward the bottom where the blades are – the Cuisinart work bowl is a uniform

6 inches in diameter. The superior efficiency of this wide work bowl is obvious. More of the food is constantly in contact with the serrated, razor-sharp blades.

The third secret is the placement of the upper Cuisinart blade. It is designed to throw the already cut bits of food outwards and upwards – up the sides of the bowl, then back down to the center for the next series of cuts. While the blades are whirling, the circulating food looks almost exactly like a constantly revolving doughnut – coming up on the outside and going back down at the center. For this basic reason, there is very little pushing down to be done in the work bowl. This is a big contrast to the often rather uncertain circulation in a standard blender. In the latter, an immovable canopy is often formed over the whirling blades, so that the food has to be continually and dangerously pushed down while the blades are actually turning. This danger is eliminated from the Cuisinart chopper-churner, which is designed so that the motor is instantly switched off the moment the cover is opened.

WHAT DOES THE CUISINART CHOPPER-CHURNER DO BEST IN MY OWN KITCHEN?

To begin with, it *chops and cuts* with extraordinary precision and speed. It is virtually the equivalent of having, as your constant kitchen helper, a skilled chef armed with two super-sharp chef's knives and a cutting board. Beyond this, it can also produce all the results achieved by a stone pestle and mortar. It can *tenderize* any tough ingredients by slashing and reslashing their fibers, just as if they were pounded for an hour in a mortar. As with the constant hammering by a pestle, ingredients can be reduced to a smooth paste or *purée* (see, for example, the recipe for a smoked salmon pâté on page 144), and ingredients that are not easily marriageable can be forced to *amalgamate* perfectly. (Mayonnaise, for example, is so totally mixed and whipped in the Cuisinart work bowl that it virtually never separates, even in a very cold refrigerator. Hand-beaten mayonnaise, on the other hand, can easily separate at low temperatures.)

The machine will *mince* whole cloves of garlic or shallots and chunks of ripe tomatoes without your having to peel them. The whirling blades disintegrate almost all kinds of peel and skins to the point at which they will be absorbed during the cooking. The same goes for spinach stalks, which will be so finely minced that they will be just as smooth as the creamed spinach leaves. And the Cuisinart blades are unequaled for the fast, precise *slicing* of anything from raw meat to a stick of butter (see the Basic Techniques for slicing beginning on page 23). For paper-thin slicing this machine can almost entirely replace the cleaver in Chinese cooking. You can cut cucumbers so thin that you can read the newspaper through them – for whatever that is worth – and you can make thin lengthwise slices of carrot or white turnip to use in place of toast for low-calorie canapés.

As for *mixing fluffy and light pastry doughs,* the Cuisinart machine is more efficient at almost instantly blending all kinds of flours with all kinds of fats and liquids than any other unit we have ever known. (It cannot, of course, make flaky pastry, which will always have to be buttered and turned by hand.)

You can have a ball of dough ready in about 30 seconds.

CAN THE CUISINART CHOPPER-CHURNER HELP WITH MY FOOD BUDGET?

Yes, by quickly converting any kind of leftover fish, meat, poultry, etc., cooked or raw, into a smooth pâté or spread for serving as an appetizer. It will do the same for any fruit or vegetable, cooked or raw, for serving as a garnish or sauce. These will certainly enrich your gastronomic life. But, in our opinion, the revival of a leftover does not really save you money unless you bring it back as a main dish. Let us be specific. Let us assume that you have some cold, cooked pork chops. You cut away the bone and fat from the lean meat, chunk it into one-inch cubes, coarsely chop it in the Cuisinart machine and use it to add body, texture and protein nutrition to a sauce for a spaghetti supper. You may add to it some aromatic herbs, garlic, onions and tomatoes, also coarsely chopped by the Cuisinart blades. It is a matter of a few seconds. You can adapt our recipe for spaghetti sauce on page 57, using the pork in place of some of the beef. Or, if you have a supply of cold, grilled steak, you can chunk it, coarsely chop it and use it, with some added fresh raw meat, in a main dish meat loaf. Chapter 6 contains recipes for main-dish leftovers, but you can also adapt many other recipes in this book to use whatever you happen to have in the refrigerator. Try, for example, the Super

Meat Loaf in the Style of Middle Eastern Kibbee, page 39, or the Ancient French Stuffed Cabbage, page 111.

HOW MUCH FOOD CAN I PUT IN THE WORK BOWL AT A TIME?

The amount will vary according to the hardness and thickness of the ingredient. We achieve the best results with these amounts:

> Raw meat: up to ½ pound.
> Hard grating cheeses: up to ½ cup of small chunks.
> Shelled nuts: up to 1 cup.
> Raw hard vegetables: up to 1½ cups.
> Raw soft vegetables: up to 2 cups.
> For thin soups: up to 2½ cups.
> For thick soups, including purées of vegetables: up to 3½ cups.
> For thick, pouring batters such as crêpe, etc.: up to 4 cups.

Since very few operations take longer than 30 seconds in the Cuisinart machine, including emptying the bowl, you can easily run many batches one after another in a very short time. When chopping raw beef, for example, we find that it takes just 30 seconds to load the bowl with a half pound, whirl the blades, and empty the bowl. This way you can chop at a steady rate of one pound per minute. (For detailed instructions, see the various recipes for a supper party menu for a crowd of 50 people, beginning on page 149.)

DO THE BLADES EVER JAM UP?

Very rarely. Although the blades will gradually chop even relatively hard things and will shave a full load of ice cubes into a crushed bed, it is possible for a solid lump of something accidentally to jam itself into such a position that it stops the blades. No problem. When the motor is forced to a stop with the power on, a thermostatic overload switch operates to turn off the electricity. The moment there is a jam, simply unplug the machine and lift out the blades. Within about a minute, the motor will have cooled down and you can resume your operations.

This is not to say that a Cuisinart machine cannot be damaged by flagrant misuse. There was the sad case of the woman who had just received one as a Christmas present. After joyously playing with it for a few hours, she called her husband into the kitchen and proudly extolled its virtues. "Look," she said, grabbing a long, hard, salami sausage as if it were a night stick and pushing it down into the machine: "this marvel will slice absolutely anything!" Perhaps the wife's voice, expressing so much love for her new toy, aroused some subconscious feeling of jealousy in the husband. After she had gone upstairs, he tiptoed into the kitchen, turned on the appliance and, precisely imitating her technique with the salami, stuck the long, oak broom handle into the machine to see whether it, too, could be neatly sliced. It could not. He had to buy his wife a new Cuisinart machine.

This is an extreme case. If a piece of meat in the work bowl, for example, accidentally has a hidden bone in it, you will hear an immediate loud clatter and should at once turn off the machine. The chances of any damage from such an incident are extremely remote. The blades are much too strong to be dented.

Sometimes there is a problem with yeast doughs. If you add a bit too much liquid while the blades are whirling, the dough suddenly becomes extremely sticky and rubbery – so much so, in fact, that the motor begins to slow down and you have to turn it off at once. The solution to this problem is to have standing ready on your work surface a spare ¼-cup measure of flour. The moment you hear the motor slow down, dump in the flour through the cover chimney. Instantly the motor will speed up again and all will be well.

HOW DO I CLEAN MY CUISINART APPLIANCE?

We wipe the motor box with a damp cloth and then dry it with a clean towel. If there is any spillage of liquid on top of the box, wipe it off immediately. The motor shaft opening and switch button are fully sealed against any entry of liquid into the case. The work bowl, the cover and all the accessories, except the pusher, may be loaded into the dishwasher. (The shape of the pusher might be distorted by the hot water in the dishwater, so that it would no longer slide easily into the chimney. It should be washed in warm soapy water in the sink.)

WHAT WON'T THE CUISINART MACHINE DO?

It is not a beater. It will not beat air into, say, whites of eggs. Its force will solidify them into a meringue, but without increasing their volume. The Cuisinart unit will not replace the hand or electric rotary beater, the coffee grinder, or the butter churn.

HOW CAN I GET HELP IF I HAVE PROBLEMS IN UNDERSTANDING OR WORKING THE MACHINE?

Write to Cuisinarts Inc., 1 Barry Place, Stamford, Connecticut 06902, or phone (203) 324-6900.

HOW CAN THE CUISINART, OR ANY AUTOMATIC MACHINE, PREPARE FINE FOODS AS WELL AS THE SKILLED USE OF ONE'S HANDS? SURELY SUPERB HANDWORK WILL ALWAYS BE THE BEST IN LUXURY COOKING?

Yes, this old theory may still be true in terms of a very few, extremely detailed, high kitchen techniques. We do not believe, for example, that the cutting of raw vegetables into the tiny, matchstick *julienne* can be done in any machine, nor could you cut the perfectly uniform, miniature cubes of variously colored, cooked vegetables for the superb appearance of a classic, high cuisine, *Salade Russe*. But, you must remember, that there have been enormous economic changes in the professional practice of high cooking. Labor costs no longer permit even the most luxurious restaurant to have sixty assistant chefs working side by side in its kitchen. More of the professional jobs have to be done by machine and, since more and more chefs are using the Cuisinart, there is less and less difference between what they do with the machine and what you can do with it. Once you have mastered its operation, you will do exactly the same work with it as the great chefs. The skill of the individual hand is no longer the most important factor in cooking.

And this is not to say that the Cuisinart chopper-churner, in a great majority of its uses, is any kind of compromise from the best handwork. You could not produce a smoother purée of vegetables by laboriously forcing them through a fine sieve. You could not chop beef by hand with a chef's knife on a wooden board any better than the blades do in the Cuisinart work bowl. You could not grate hard cheese any better by hand. You could not even prepare mayonnaise as well in a copper bowl with a hand balloon whisk. You could not, with the sharpest knife, slice cucumber more evenly, more finely, more thinly. As to Japanese and Chinese cooking, the Cuisinart machine will chop, shred, produce paper-thin slices of meats and vegetables, and purée shrimp into paste just as well as a skillfully used sharp cleaver. With all these jobs, the Cuisinart unit saves you so much time and work that it will give you the opportunity if you wish to do some fancy hand cutting and sculpturing for the decorative aspects of your party dish. The Cuisinart chopper-churner is the wave of the future, and the future is with us now, especially in the professional kitchens.

2

The Basic Techniques of the Cuisinart Chopper-Churner

PLAYING ALADDIN IN YOUR OWN KITCHEN WITH THE MACHINE AS YOUR SLAVE OF THE LAMP

THE MOST BASIC OF ALL THE RULES

The Cuisinart is different from almost every other kitchen machine. It has no fancy controls. No line of pushbuttons. No knobs, levers or switches for different modes of operation. Everything you do – every result you want – is under your control by the precise timing between the starting and the stopping. Your success with the machine depends entirely on your learning about the timing.

And that is the problem! None of us seems to be able entirely to comprehend, at first, the lightning speed of the Cuisinart chopper-churner. We are all used to the slower timing of other appliances. In an electric beater, it may take 2 or 3 minutes to whip a bowl of egg whites. In the old type of electric blender, it may have taken 60 seconds to purée a soup. Passing a half pound of beef through a meat grinder usually took 3 or 4 minutes. We chop a half pound of beef with our Cuisinart blades in 4 seconds flat. We mince parsely, garlic, mushrooms, onions, shallots, tomatoes, in 1 or 2 seconds. The average job is done in 5 seconds in the Cuisinart machine. The longest job (apart from a very few quite special things) is about 10 seconds. So – when you switch the motor on, you have to be there, preferably with your hand on the controlling cover. You have to watch carefully through the clear plastic walls of the work bowl. You simply cannot switch on the Cuisinart machine and then go over to the ice box and pour yourself a glass of ginger ale.

In the recipes in this book, we give "from-to" indications of the expected timing of each Cuisinart operation. They have to be "from-to" because much depends on the original texture of the ingredients. Meat can be tender or tough. Vegetables can be hard or soft. Fruits vary in their ripeness. So you must watch – and YOU MUST LEARN TO COUNT SECONDS ACCURATELY. Our system is to switch on and instantly start counting to a steady beat: one chimpanzee, two chimpanzees, three chimpanzees, and so on. Any word of about the same length will do. Pick your own, if you like. One armadillo, two armadillos . . . or one elephantiasis, two elephantiases . . . . We remain loyal to our friends the chimpanzees. This is the first, absolutely essential lesson in your effective control of the power of the Cuisinart chopper-churner.

Mistakes in timing can lead to the waste of a lot of good food. Several years ago, at the first Christmas after we got our first Cuisinart machine, we gave one as a present to a friend whose absolutely favorite food was chopped beef. We promised her that, if she would chop fresh meat in the machine, she would have the best quality and texture she had ever known. Two days later, she called us: "Your machine is a bust at grinding beef. It simply won't work." We were flabbergasted. We began asking questions to smoke out the problem. "What sort of ground beef comes out?" She said that it was a kind of slimy, sticky paste, totally inedible. Remembering that we chop our beef for 4 seconds, we asked: "How long did you keep the machine running?" The answer: "Seven minutes." Even if she had said 90 seconds, her disaster would have been equally complete.

In the early days of the Cuisinart unit, a professional chef called us from a restaurant in Philadelphia. He said what a great machine the Cuisinart was, but bemoaned the fact that it would not chop beef. Again, we were staggered. We shot out our probing questions: "How long did you run the beef through the machine?" He said: "I tried for 15 minutes, but nothing would go through." "Go through what?" we asked. He replied: "Through the holes in the grating disk." He had been treating the beef as if it were cheese, instead of putting it into the work bowl with the steel blades. We could only suppose that he thought it was somehow un-American to read an instruction book.

THE ONE-SECOND START-STOP TECHNIQUE

When you chop beef, or purée a soup, you run the motor for the requisite number of seconds and then stop. But when you are doing dry chopping – of, let us say, green scallions, or walnut halves – continuous operation can run you into a problem. As the chopped bits grow smaller, quite a number of them begin bouncing, in rhythm, on the tops of the blades, thus cleverly avoiding the cutting edges. The result is that your chopped bits will be quite uneven in size. The way to avoid this is not to run the motor continuously, but to start and stop it in short, one-second bursts. Stopping the blades after the first second allows the recalcitrant bits to fall to the botton of the work bowl, so that they will be in the path of the knives when the motor is restarted. Thus everything continues to be chopped evenly. Also, the stopping allows you to remove the cover and look inside to see how everything is going. You will get precisely the degree of chopping fineness you want – from coarse chunks to the finest mincing. We suggest this stop-start technique all through the recipes in this book. It is a basic principle of effective Cuisinart operation. Never be afraid to stop the motor at any time, remove the cover and look inside the work bowl. It will help you to get precisely the result you want. The motor cannot be harmed even if you start it and stop it in a sequence of, say, 20 one-second bursts. THERE IS NO SINGLE OPERATION OF THE CUISINART MACHINE WHICH CAN IN ANY WAY BE HARMED BY STOPPING THE MOTOR AND THEN RESTARTING IT.

THE SIZE OF THE PIECES YOU LOAD INTO THE WORK BOWL

If you are chopping and churning ingredients to a complete purée, the shape and size of the pieces you load into the work bowl is not important. You simply keep on whirling the blades until everything is mashed. But if you want to chop foods down in even bits, you must start by loading the bowl with even chunks. Otherwise, you will find yourself ending up with some large bits surrounded by gobs of mash. This is, obviously, because the blades work faster on the smaller pieces. You can save innumerable hours of your kitchen time by always chopping your onions in the machine. If you want a fine mince, you can start by quartering medium peeled onions. But if you

15

want them coarsely chopped, you had better begin by chunking them in roughly 1-inch pieces.

The size of the starting chunks, or cubes, also depends on the hardness of the ingredients. Again, obviously, too large a piece of too hard a substance will overload and slow down the motor. The largest solid cube that the blades will accept is about 1½-inches square. Pieces larger than that will not fit down between the blades and, therefore, will not be effectively cut. We find, in general, that the ideal size is about 1-inch square. We cut our beef, for example, into 1-inch cubes. We also chunk soft vegetables (for example, cooked beets, green beans, broccoli tops, cucumber and zucchini) into roughly 1-inch chunks. But harder vegetables (raw carrots, raw cauliflower, raw potatoes, raw turnips), as well as tougher meats, or anything quite hard, had better be evenly cut into, say, ½-inch cubes. Develop and use your judgment in deciding on the starting size. For example, very hard and old Parmesan cheese had better be cut into considerably smaller chunks. (Incidentally, very hard cheese should not be grated with the disk, but should be ground up in the bowl by the steel blades.) The simple, general rule is that the softer the ingredient, or the finer it is to be chopped, the larger it can be at the start, always provided that it is not so large that it will fail to be cut by the serrated edges. This principle applies mainly to dry ingredients. When the chunks in the work bowl are surrounded by liquid, the circulation problem is nonexistent, as the churning motion will bring everything in turn down in front of the blades.

BASIC ORDER FOR ADDING TO THE WORK BOWL

Generally, all the ingredients of a recipe (up to the limit of the load) are put into the bowl at once. But in a few cases (for example, pastry doughs), there is a necessary sequence for bringing the ingredients together. The basic rule for almost all pastry recipes is: first put in the measured flour with all the other dry ingredients and let the machine sift them together, next add the soft fatty ingredients, finally the liquids. (See Mixing Bread and Pastry Doughs, page 21.)

For some cake batters, the order is reversed. In general, the Cuisinart works well with any cake recipe that begins "Cream the butter and sugar together . . ." You put the slices of butter into the bowl first, add the measured sugar, then whirl the blades for a second or two to accomplish the creaming. Next, add, all at once, the eggs and other required liquids, mixing them in with 1 or 2 more one-second bursts. Finally, add, all at once, the flour and all other dry ingredients, working them in with 3 or 4 more one-second bursts. Check carefully. You just want the flour to disappear. Then stop at once. Your job is done. If you whirl the blades longer than that, your cake may be heavy, too solid, and tough in texture.

THE VARIOUS CUISINART TOOLS

The Stainless Steel Blades

This is the most important of all the tools. You will use it for at least 90 per cent of your jobs. These curving serrated blades are the modern equivalent of the old technique of chopping on a wooden board with a super-sharp chef's knife in each hand. They move so fast – with 60 deadly slashes per second – that you must hold them under precise control in each of their different functions.

To Chop Raw Beef for Hamburger or Beef Tartare: Cut the entirely lean meat into 1-inch cubes. Put them into the work bowl, not more than ½ pound at a time (but you can put in less, down to a single cube). Whirl the blades for no more than 4 to 6 seconds, for the coarseness or fineness you used to prefer in your store-bought hamburger. (Recipes on pages 101, 107–111, and in Chapter 7.)

Chopping Other Raw or Cooked Meats for Meat Loaves and Terrines: The techniques are exactly the same as for the above, but the times will vary by a second or two, more or less, according to the texture and toughness of each meat.

Smoothing Cooked or Raw Foods into Appetizer Pâtés or Dips, Sausage Stuffings, Mousses, or Quenelles, etc.: Simply put the cubed or chunked meats or fish, with the aromatic herbs and other ingredients all at once into the work bowl. No more than 2 cups total for each batch. Simply whirl the blades until everything is amalgamated into a paste of the degree of smoothness you want – usually somewhere between 5 and 15 seconds, according to the texture. Stop the motor about every 3 seconds to check progress and taste. Finally, if you need to adjust the seasonings, you can work in the last additions with 1 or 2 extra one-second bursts (see page 15). (Recipes on pages 144, 150, 158, and 132 and 140.)

Coarse or Fine Chopping of Onions, Mushrooms, Scallions, and Other Soft Vegetables: For the average, fairly coarse bits, peel and cut the onions into roughly 1-inch chunks. The same with mushrooms or other vegetables. Cut scallions into 1-inch lengths. Start and stop the motor in one-second bursts, checking after each, until you get the bit-size you want – usually in about 1 to 3 bursts.

For much finer mincing of onions or other soft vegetables, you can load the bowl with larger chunks. Cut peeled medium onions into quarters. Medium mushrooms and other vegetables, about the same. Scallions into 2-inch lengths. Use exactly the same technique, but with more one-second bursts – say 5 to 8.

For a purée of onions or other soft vegetables, follow exactly the

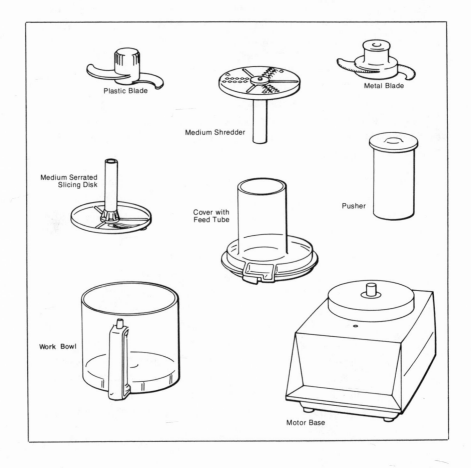

same techniques, but after the preliminary chopping bursts, whirl the blades continuously for about 3 to 6 seconds more. Stop the motor every 3 seconds, remove the cover, check and taste, until you have exactly what you want.

Fine Mincing of Garlic, Fresh Herbs, Parsley, Lemon Rind, Shallots, etc.: Garlic and shallot cloves can be put into the work bowl whole and unpeeled. The blades completely disintegrate the skins. Fresh herb leaves should be pulled off their stalks. Parsley in sprigs, lemon rind in 1- or 2-inch slivers. Start and stop the motor in one-second bursts, checking after each. Usually one or two bursts will do the job.

Mixing and Smoothing Garlic, Anchovy, Parsley, or Other Aromatic Herb Butters: Work with the same technique as above. When you have fairly finely minced the garlic and/or anchovies and/or other herbs, remove the cover and add to the bowl the sliced butter at room temperature (or, for a low-calorie version, some low-fat cottage or pot cheese), with any other ingredients, plus seasonings. Whirl the blades continuously, stopping and checking every 3 seconds, until you have it all perfectly amalgamated and completely smooth – usually in about 4 to 5 seconds. The garlic, anchovy, or herb bits will be almost completely puréed. While the blades are whirling, if the butter starts crawling up the sides of the bowl, stop the motor and, with a spatula, scrape the butter back down to return it to the action. Finally, check and taste, adding lemon juice and adjusting seasonings. Work in any last additions with a final, one-second burst of the blades.

Chopping, Grinding, Mashing, or Mincing Raw Carrots, Potatoes, or Other Hard Vegetables: The techniques are exactly the same as for soft vegetables, but the starting chunks should be a good deal smaller. Begin the chopping with one-second bursts. Then, to move into finer grinds, whirl the blades continuously for 3 seconds at a time, checking after each run. These chewy-grainy grinds of hard vegetables make an excellent texture contrast in a mousse of soft vegetables. For this purpose, we use (all raw) carrots, Chinese water chestnuts, Jerusalem artichokes, salted or unsalted peanuts, white turnips, or other hard vegetables ground to the texture of, approximately, coarse cornmeal. Then, when the soft mousse is made, we stir into it, spoonful by spoonful, some of the crisp grinds, until we achieve the perfect balance of texture contrasts. (See recipe on page 132.) Most of these texture grinds should be freshly prepared, but you can, for example, pre-grind a supply of peanuts and keep them ready in a covered jar in the refrigerator. They will add a crispy texture to all kinds of savory or sweet mixes.

Grinding Old, Hard, Parmesan, Romano, or Other Very Tough Cheeses: With these very hard types, do not use the grating-shredding disks. They may be bent or distorted by the extreme pressure. Chunk the cheese into the bowl (sometimes we use a chisel) in quite small pieces roughly the size of walnut halves, no more than 1 cup at a time. Start with one-second bursts, checking each time, until the cheese is fairly finely chopped. Then whirl the blades continuously, 3 seconds at a time, until you have exactly the fineness of grating you want. (Medium-firm cheeses can be put through the grating-shredding disks (see page 22).

Chopping or Grinding Nuts: In general, use the same techniques as for chopping hard vegetables, above. Begin by starting and stopping the motor in one-second bursts, checking after each, until you have the bit-size you want. Then, for much finer grinds, whirl the blades 3 seconds at a time, continuing to check carefully. In this way, you can get very fine grinds of nuts for delicate cakes. (See recipe for a cake entirely without flour, using instead, a superfine grind of hazelnuts, on page 62.)

Grinding and Smoothing Home-Made Peanut and Other Nut Butters: See the basic recipe on page 115.

Churning and Puréeing Creamy Soups Without Cream: The Cuisinart blades will produce marvelously rich and luxuriously thick soups, hot or cold, with no artificial thickening by butter, cream or flour. The trick is simply to cook a group of vegetables (usually including potatoes, which give a memorable texture) until they are quite soft, then to purée them, in batches, in the work bowl. (Or you can use raw avocado, or cooked chestnuts – see recipes on pages 68 and 74). When the moment comes for puréeing the soup, the important point to remember is to avoid overfilling the work bowl. It does have a central opening, through which the drive shaft comes up and it is possible, under certain limited circumstances, for liquid to trickle down and spread out, under the bowl, on top of the motor case. This is not dangerous for the motor, since the case is sealed watertight, but it may cause a general mess on your work surface.

If the liquid is water, or a very thin bouillon, do not put in more than 2½ cups per load. But why put in thin liquids at all? Churning in the Cuisinart does nothing to a bouillon. It is far better to sieve out the solids from the soup and purée them separately, batch by batch, returning each completed batch to the liquid in the soup kettle and stirring it in. This technique, also, allows you to control the precise final thickness of your soup. Since these solids are much thicker than water and will, therefore, not leak down the tube so easily, you can load the bowl with as much as 3½ cups at a time. In fact, with very thick soup, or crêpe batters, you can safely go up to about 4 cups per load.

As an added safeguard, always lift the bowl off the machine immediately after each batch is puréed and leave the blades in position. As you lift the bowl, the blades drop down about a quarter inch and help to seal the central opening. When you pour the purée back into the soup kettle, it is desirable to avoid pouring in the steel blades also.

Mixing, Working and Smoothing Sauces: See basic recipes, beginning on page 76.

Whipping Up Various Kinds of Mayonnaise: One of the great French chefs recently told us: "I will never go back to beating mayonnaise by hand. The power of the Cuisinart motor forces the ingredients so tightly together that they never separate, even at very cold temperature in the refrigerator. I could never make mayonnaise as well as this by hand." The machine also allows us to vary the colors, flavors and textures of our mayonnaise, by adding avocado, spinach, tomato, watercress . . . (See basic recipes on pages 53, 54, and 77–79.) This unique, amalgamating force of the Cuisinart motor can also be used for shotgun weddings of all kinds of different ingredients which would never get together except by force. (See the recipe for A Smooth Pâté of Parmesan and Romano Cheeses on page 150.)

Mixing Bread and Pastry Doughs: Flour never needs to be sifted before the measured amount is put into the work bowl. First spread it evenly around the bottom, add whatever other dry ingredients are called for in the recipe (salt, baking powder, dry yeast, sugar, etc.), then just flash the blades on and off in a one-second burst and you will find that everything is completely fluffed up and amalgamated. Next, add the butter or other fats and whirl the blades in about 2 or 3 one-second bursts to amalgamate it to the "niblet corn" stage. Finally, add the liquids – eggs, ice water, milk, etc. – and whirl the blades again. The machine signals you that the job is done, in a most dramatic way: the ball of finished dough rides up onto the top of the blades and simply has to be lifted out and transferred to the pastry board. It is as if the machine is handing you the finished job. (See the various recipes on pages 26, 86, 169, and 106, 193.)

Grinding Dry Bread or Cracker Crumbs: See basic instructions, beginning on page 22.

Mixing Various Types of Off-Beat Pie Shells: See basic recipes, beginning on page 193.

Chopping and Crushing Ice: Remove the pusher from the chimney in the cover. Start the motor with, of course, the steel blades in place. Drop the ice cubes quickly one after another, down the chimney. Don't be scared by the roar of the noise. Work very fast. If you let the motor run too long, you will just get a mash. Stop when you have the texture you want.

The Medium Grating-Shredding Disk
With this or the other discs to be described later, the machine is an entirely different operation. The medium-shredding disk rides and turns at the top of the work bowl, so that the rest of the bowl becomes the receptacle for the grated or shredded food. You have to watch to see that it does not overfill and jam up. Empty it as often as necessary. Timing is no longer a precise problem. No more need to count chimpanzees. You work with the motor running all the time and you push the food down through the chimney in the cover. NEVER, NEVER push things down with your fingers – unless you want the tips of your fingers grated into the bowl! The plunger-pusher is there for the pushing-down job. Remember that, when you remove the cover, the momentum of the motor may keep the disk turning for an extra second or two. NEVER touch the disk while it is turning. You may cut your hand quite badly. To empty the bowl, lift it up off the motor and then pull the disk up and off.

Grating Medium and Soft Cheeses: Cut the cheese into pieces of a size to run easily, yet snugly, down the cover chimney. With the grating-shredding disk in place and the motor running, press the cheese down the chimney with the pusher. Remember that if you push hard you will get thick shreds – if gently, thin shreds. Your hand has considerable control. Everything works very fast. You can grate vast quantities of cheese in a very short time.

Shredding Mozzarella for Pizza: Pretty well the same technique as above, but with slight variations. Cut the mozzarella into chunks that will fit snugly into the chimney. Fill up the chimney completely and have the pusher in your hand, then start the motor. Push down gently for long, thin strands, harder for shorter, thicker strands.

Making a Quick Imitation of a Julienne of Vegetables: Cutting a true, matchstick *julienne* of vegetables is a long and tedious hand job. But with the grating-shredding disk, you can do a quick imitation. Scrape some carrots and cut them into lengths just long enough to fit sideways into the chimney. Peel and do the same with some cucumber, green pepper and, perhaps, some yellow parsnip and white turnip. Finally, some well-shaped mushroom caps of a good color. Choose your own balance of colors and flavors. Now, with the grating-shredding disk in place and the motor running, press these pieces, lying sideways, down the chimney. They will be cut into 2- or 3-inch long, narrow shavings, which can be used for multicolored decoration of dishes, or, when tumbled together, make a very pretty, crisp, refreshing and edible display. For a closer approximation of *julienne* strips, see page 26.

The Medium Serrated Slicing Disk
There are several available slicing disks. This one is for medium-sized medium-thick slices and, because it has an extremely sharp, serrated cutting edge it is, in our opinion, the most useful general purpose slicer. It is the one that normally comes with the machine. For basic rules for using it, see the introduction to the grating-shredding disks, above. WARNING: Since the cutting edge of this slicer is exceedingly sharp, it must be used with greater caution than all the other disks. NEVER use your fingers down the chimney. Do not remove the cover until the disk has stopped turning. When you stop the motor, the overrun of the momentum is only about 1 second, but even in that short time, if you were to place your hand on the disk, you would be quite sorry.

Slicing Carrots, Cucumbers, Mushrooms, Onions and Other Vegetables:
With the serrated slicing disk in place and the motor running, push
the vegetables down through the chimney. It will be easier to keep
them standing up straight if you pack them fairly tightly into the
chimney. Use as many carrots as necessary, side-by-side, to fill the
space. If the cucumbers are thin, use two side-by-side. Push down
mushroom caps on their back for round slices, or on their sides for
hammer-head slices. Remember that the harder you push down, the
thicker the slices will be. Push very gently for very thin slices. As the
slices fall through into the bowl, watch it to see that it does not overfill and jam up. Empty it as often as necessary.

Slicing Green Beans French Style: Trim and cut the green beans in
lengths exactly to fit, sideways, down the chimney. Have the serrated
slicing disk in position, but do not yet start the motor. Entirely fill
the chimney with the beans, not standing up, but lying down sideways. Arm yourself with the pusher and start the motor. Keep a
steady, firm pressure on the beams. They will be perfectly and thinly
cut into "French beans."

The Best Method for Home-Made Coleslaw: Choose a firm young head
of green cabbage and cut out all its tough core. Now stand it on its
base and, with a very sharp knife, cut it downwards into "columns,"
each wide enough to fit easily yet snugly down the chimney. They
should pack the chimney fairly tightly. With the serrated slicing disk
in position, start the motor and firmly push the cabbage downwards.
Before you can say "coleslaw," the work bowl will be full of perfectly
shredded cabbage.

Slicing Cooked Meat or Sausages: This is basically, exactly the same
technique as for the soft vegetables above.

Slicing Raw Meats: For some Chinese or Japanese recipes, or for any
special purpose you may choose, it is sometimes necessary to cut thin
slices of raw meat. This is virtually impossible when the meat is
flabbily soft at normal room temperature. The trick is, first, to cut
the meat into pieces of a size to fit easily and snugly down the
chimney. Then partly freeze (or fully freeze and partly thaw out) these
pieces, so that they are quite stiff and yet not rock hard – usually in
about 1½ to 2 hours. In this happy state, they can be pushed down
the chimney and will slice easily and perfectly with the serrated

slicing disk. They will not slice very happily – in fact, not slice at all – with the vegetable slicing disk that does not have a serrated edge (see below).

OTHER AVAILABLE TOOLS

There are several other tools that either come with the machine or can be specially ordered as extras. We have to say, quite frankly, that we are not totally enthusiastic about their possible uses.

The Non-Cutting Plastic Blades:
These are exactly the same shape and size as the steel blades. They fit into the work bowl in exactly the same way. But they have no cutting edges. They come free with the machine. What are their uses? A friend of ours, a professional chef, said the other day, "Their only use is to keep you awake at night, wondering what they are for." Frankly, we are inclined to agree with him. We have never, in absolute truth, found a special use for them in which they shine noticeably above the steel blades.

We have been told that the plastic blades give a coarser texture to some meat or fish pâtés. We can produce better coarse textures using the steel blades, by simply whirling them for a slightly shorter time. We have been told to use them for whipping up cream or mayonnaise. We find that the steel blades do both of these jobs slightly better. In France it is maintained that the sole purpose of the plastic blades is to whip egg whites. But since the Cuisinarts people do not claim that their machine can whip egg whites . . . what can we say?

A Fine-Shred Grating Disk:
Same as the other one, but has many more, smaller holes, placed closer together. Thus it gives much finer shredding.

A Vegetable Slicing Disk:
The edge, of course, is not nearly so sharp. So it can be used only for slicing soft vegetables. No good for meats. Nor for any harder foods.

A Fine-Cut Serrated Slicing Disk:
Produces slices half as thick as those from the medium-serrated slicing disk. But – do we have to be able to read our *New York Times* through

our cucumber slices? It may also be used to cut fine *julienne* vegetable strips.

Cutting Fine Julienne Vegetable Strips: Cut any firm vegetable (e.g., thick carrot, celery root, parsnip, white turnip, zucchini, etc.) into a solid block that fits snugly down the chimney. First slice it with the fine serrated disk, pushing down firmly with the plunger. Then remove the cover, turning it upside down to use the chimney with plunger partially withdrawn as a bowl. Next remove the disk and reassemble the cut slices inside the chimney with edges downward. Fill this container snugly so that the slices will not fall over or drop out when you put the cover over the replaced disk. Turn on the machine, push down the plunger, and the *julienne* strips will appear instantly in the bowl below. If you want thicker *julienne*, use the medium slicing disk.

An Extra-Thick Serrated Slicing Disk:
This is now being delivered with new models of the Cuisinart machine. You can easily test to see whether or not you have it by slicing a cucumber or carrot. If you get eight slices to an inch you have this slicer. If not, this extra-thick slicing disk may be ordered from the company. There are at least two excellent uses for this disk: slicing cooked meats and bread.

Slicing Leftover Cooked Meat: Since cooked meats have firm textures they do not have to be chilled, as do raw meats. (See above.) You can, for example, prepare the sliced beef, ham, or other meats for the Main Dish Salad from Provence (page 52) or Leftover Beef or Veal in Red Wine Sauce (page 160).

Preparing Very Thin Home-Made Melba Toast: With the extra-thick serrated disk in place and the motor running, push down the chimney with the pusher an extra-narrow, firm, day-old loaf of French bread. Dry the cut slices in a 250° F. oven for about 10 minutes for a supply of lovely, thin, tender Melba toast.

A Stainless Steel Disk for French-Cutting Potatoes:
This is a new addition to the collection of tools and it works extraordinarily well. Peel and trim the potatoes so that they slide easily yet snugly down the chimney. Do not push down on the potatoes with the plunger but let them drop of their own weight. As the pieces fall

down the chimney they are cut into fairly thin lengths for French *pommes allumettes.*

THE DO'S AND DON'T'S OF THE CUISINART

The extraordinary speed and efficiency of the Cuisinart chopper-churner are due to its powerful motor and extra-sharp, sturdy cutting tools. Such a machine always involves some dangers. Shall we say that the Cuisinart unit is about as dangerous or as safe as an automobile. Either can be a dangerous machine if it is handled incorrectly or carelessly. Any powerful motor attached to sharp blades is potentially dangerous to the human body. To help you avoid problems while cooking with the Cuisinart, here are some precautions to keep in mind.

DO handle the blades and disks carefully, just as you would sharp knives.

DON'T ever leave the steel blades resting near the edge of a counter where they might fall off onto your foot, cutting right through the shoe and bringing human blood to flow.

DON'T ever leave them where children can get at them.

DO proceed in the following order when assembling the Cuisinart for use:
1. Fit the bowl on the base.
2. Place the blades or disk on the motor shaft.
3. Make sure the blades or disk are all the way down – if they aren't, the machine could be seriously damaged.
4. Then go ahead with the food preparation.

DON'T ever start the blades with a single large piece of something very hard (say, a ¼-pound chunk of Parmesan cheese) in the work bowl. It could jam the blades. If you ever hear the motor laboring, DO turn it off at once.

DO remember, when using the Cuisinart appliance close to the stove, to watch the electric power cord and make sure that it does not fall onto any of the heating elements. This might melt the rubber covering and cause a short circuit, or even a small fire.

DON'T use the vegetable slicing disk for meat – you may damage both the disk and the motor. Use only the medium-slicing disk with the serrated cutting edge.

DO always use the pusher – never your fingers – when putting food down the cover chimney.

DON'T overfill the bowl beyond the amounts clearly stated in each recipe. See page 9 for information about the capacity of the bowl for different ingredients.

DO always remember to check the progress of the food being chopped and churned in the work bowl. The motto is: Stop and Look, Stop and Look. In that way, you will always get precisely the result you want. There is absolutely no operation done in the machine that suffers by stopping and looking. Absolutely no sequence has to be continuous. Nor can the starting and stopping in any way hurt the motor.

DO WAIT UNTIL THE BLADES OR DISKS HAVE REACHED A DEAD STOP BEFORE REMOVING THE COVER! It will take only a second. Even if they are turning slowly they can still cut you.

DON'T ever place your palm on a spinning disk to stop it. You may get sliced.

DO lift the work bowl (when emptying it) off the base before removing the blades. This will form a seal between the hub of the blades and the bowl and prevent possible leakage. And DON'T pour the blades into your soup! Remember that they are not attached to the bowl.

DO remember to wash out the work bowl thoroughly as soon as possible after you have finished using it to avoid any clinging odors. Often just rinsing with water is enough. After chopping ingredients of a tenacious aromatic quality, such as garlic, onions, shallots, or strong spices, it is best to leave the bowl uncovered and open to the air after washing it, so that the odors can completely dissipate.

DON'T set the blades or a disk on the motor shaft without the bowl. The small red depressed dot in the front of the base is the switch that is activated by a spring mechanism in the bowl, and it could be accidentally pressed.

DON'T store the machine with the cover locked in the ON position. This could wear out the spring and make it difficult, eventually, to turn the machine off.

As you follow the recipes in this book, make these precautions a part of your kitchen routine, and using the Cuisinart machine will indeed be as safe and effortless as rubbing a magic lamp.

3

Our Twenty-One Favorite Recipes with the Chopper Churner

In our kitchen we find the Cuisinart machine valuable for at least one step in every recipe. There are some recipes, however, that can hardly be done well at all without its extraordinary efficiency, ease and speed. The very ease of the work – combined with the speed, which prevents the ingredients from wilting – seems to contribute to the memorable total quality of the dish. In this chapter are the recipes that are most often demanded by our family and close friends, that are most consistently useful in day-to-day menu-planning, that are quick and simple to prepare and are relatively low in the cost of the basic ingredients. There isn't a fancy preparation, a spoonful of caviar, or a cube of foie gras anywhere in this chapter. Later, perhaps, we may try to prove that the Cuisinart blades can also chop truffles – but not here! These are our twenty-one most memorable everyday recipes.

ONE-DISH FRENCH BEEF STEW FROM PROVENCE WITH VEGETABLES, AMERICAN RED WINE AND CALIFORNIA BRANDY

(for 4 to 6)

This is a little bit of Provincial France – the Sunday evening beef stew prepared by Grandmère in a thousand country kitchens, the pot releasing a glorious scent and giving off the sound of a bubbling spring – all of which we have modernized and speeded up with the help of the Cuisinart machine. What goes into it, apart from the meat, can be almost any vegetables you have on hand. You can cook it, as slowly as possible, in any kind of pot-enameled cast iron, ceramic,

31

tinned copper, earthenware, stainless steel or even an electric slow crock cooker. A wide pot rather than deep is preferable, about 2 to 3 quarts capacity with a tightly fitting lid. The stew is simply assembled and then left alone to bubble gently until it is time to serve it. You can also cook it the day before – the taste is better when you reheat it. This is the original one-dish, trouble-free, meal-in-a-pot combination.

Salt pork, streaky, fairly lean, sliced ¼ inch thick (½ lb)

Pork rind, unsmoked, cut into inch squares (¼ lb)

Tomatoes, red and ripe (3 medium)

Olive oil, first quality (2 Tbs)

Carrots, scraped and diagonally sliced (4 medium)

Yellow onions, peeled and sliced (3 medium)

Pig's feet, fresh, cut lengthwise by butcher (2)

Salt, coarse crystal, to taste

Black pepper, freshly ground, to taste

Beef, lean, cross-rib or sirloin or top round or rump, cut into small steaks about 3 by 3 inches, 1 inch thick (2 to 3 lbs)

Garlic, whole cloves, peeled and sliced (2)

Bay leaves, crumbled (2)

Parsley (large bunch)

Rosemary (2 tsps dried or 2 Tbs fresh)

Thyme (2 tsps dried or 2 Tbs fresh leaf)

Orange rind, thin outer skin (2 1½-inch slivers)

Red wine, perhaps California Petite Sirah or Zinfandel (1 bottle)

California brandy (½ cup)

For a Garnish:

Anchovies, canned, flat fillets (6)

Capers, drained (2 Tbs)

Black olives, stoned (about 16)

Preparation in About 30 Minutes of Active Work, Plus Almost 3 Hours of Entirely Unsupervised Simmering
One of the most boring and time-consuming first jobs of this recipe used to be the dicing of the salt pork. We now do it in 3 seconds in the Cuisinart machine. With the steel blade in place, neatly pack into the bowl the entire ½ pound of salt pork slices, standing vertically on their ends between the blades. Then whirl the blades for not a flash more than 2 seconds and the pork will be diced. If it isn't done completely, give it 1 or 2 one-second bursts more. Transfer the dice

to a bowl and hold. Next, repeat this operation with the squares of pork rind: without rinsing out the Cuisinart bowl, put in the pork rind squares and in 2 seconds of whirling the blades you will have diced pork rind. Transfer them to a second bowl and hold. We used to have to skin the tomatoes. No more – with the Cuisinart machine we simply quarter the raw tomatoes, pack them all at once into the bowl and whirl the blades for 8 to 10 seconds. The skins are disintegrated and disappear, while the tomato flesh is neatly and finely minced.

Now begin assembling the pot. Spread across the bottom the 2 tablespoons of olive oil, then, as the first layer, the diced salt pork. On top of this, spread the sliced carrots and onions, the minced tomatoes, half the dice of pork rind and the pig's feet, with salt and pepper to taste. Now carefully arrange on top the small beef steaks, neatly overlapping them and interspersing them with the sliced garlic, the crumbled bay leaves, several sprigs of parsley, the rosemary, the thyme and the slivers of orange rind. When all the beef is in, cover it with the remaining dice of pork rind and more salt and pepper to taste. Start the pot cooking, uncovered, over medium frying heat, so that the bottom layers just begin to sizzle gently. Heavy frying or burning is to be absolutely avoided. Let this continue for 10 minutes.

Pour the bottle of red wine into a quart saucepan and bring it up just to the first bubbling of boiling. (This gets rid of all the alcohol, which evaporates off.) Add the wine to the pot of meat and vegetables. Then heat the ½ cup of brandy in a small saucepan to just above blood heat and set it on fire. Pour the flaming brandy into the main pot, and when the flames die down, cover the pot tightly (putting a sheet of aluminum foil under the lid if the latter is not absolutely secure) and reduce the heat to gentlest simmering. (You can hear the bubbling if you place your ear about an inch away from the side of the pot.) Or, if you prefer, you can do the cooking in the center of an oven at 300°F. Leave the pot entirely alone – do not open it even once – for 2½ hours. Then, it will be ready to serve on very hot, deep plates or in wide gumbo bowls.

While the simmering is in progress, you can prepare an optional garnish – what Provençal cooks call a *persillade* – to spoon into the plates of stew at table. Put into the Cuisinart bowl a good handful of the remaining parsley leaves (no stalks), the 6 anchovy fillets, and the 2 tablespoons of capers. Chop and churn them into a smooth paste – usually in 5 to 7 seconds. Hold it in a small covered serving bowl to be brought later to table. Fill a second, small serving bowl with the black olives.

When you first open the lid of the pot, you will find a thin layer of fat on top. Skim this off with a large shallow spoon. The gelatinous flesh of the pig's feet will have fallen off the bones and we like to cut it into small cubes, to vary the texture of the stew. Or, if you prefer, you can simply discard the flesh with the bones. As the stew is ladled into the plates, sprinkle some of the *persillade* on top and garnish each plate with 3 or 4 olives.

This stew is ideal for an evening when you will be coming home late and still want to serve a party dinner with minimum time and work. Prepare the stew the day before. Simmer it for only an hour and a half, then let it cool and set it in the refrigerator. The next evening, the moment you come home, set the pot over simmering heat, allow half an hour for it to warm up and one hour more of cooking. You will then sit down to a party dinner with no preparation at all – at least for the main dish. Any leftover stew can be reheated again later – and the dish is also excellent cold, when the sauce is a savory jelly.

ONE-PAN ONE-DISH PORK CHOPS WITH CHERRIES AND POTATOES IN GINGER-CREAM SAUCE

(for 4)

There is only one thing you have to do in advance – the day before, if you like: boil or pressure cook the potatoes in their jackets and hold them in the refrigerator.

Olive oil (1 Tbs)

Pork chops, about ¾ inch thick, most fat trimmed off (4)

Salt, coarse crystal, to taste

Black pepper, freshly ground, to taste

Mustard, dry English (about 1½ tsp)

Sage, ground (about ¼ tsp)

Thyme, ground (about ½ tsp)

Cherries, pitted, fresh or canned, unsweetened (about ½ lb)

Porto wine, Ruby (up to 4 Tbs)

Cinnamon, ground (¼ tsp)

Clove, ground (¼ tsp)

Sugar (perhaps 3 tsp)

Scallions, bulbs and stalks, cut into 1½-inch pieces (4)

Garlic, whole clove (1)

Caraway seed, whole (¼ tsp)

Marjoram (½ tsp dried, or 2 tsp
   fresh)
Oregano, dried (½ tsp)
Rosemary (½ tsp dried, or 2 tsp
   fresh)
Lemon rind (about 6 slivers)
Ginger root (1-inch slice fresh,
   or 1 tsp dried ground)

Sour cream (1½ cups)
Potatoes, preboiled in their
   jackets (6 to 8 medium)
Peas, fresh or frozen, latter
   thawed out (10 to 12 oz or
   1¼ to 1½ cups)

Assuming the Supply of Preboiled Potatoes, Preparation, from Start to Serving, in About 1 Hour

Both the preparation and the cooking can be done in a 12-inch sauté pan with a well-fitting lid or a reasonably deep frypan. Put the table-spoon of oil in the pan and set it on a top burner over medium-high frying heat. (If you have a calibrated control or are using an electric frypan, set the temperature at 360°F.) While the pan is heating up, pound into and rub onto the 4 pork chops some salt and pepper, 1 tea-spoon of the dry mustard, the sage and thyme. When the oil is hot, put in the chops and fry them until they are lightly gilded – usually about 6 to 8 minutes on each side. Move them around once or twice on each side to make sure they are not sticking.

While the chops are frying, prepare the cherries. Put them into a mixing bowl and stir in 2 tablespoons of the Porto and the ¼ teaspoon each of cinnamon and clove. Taste. The mixture should be very lightly sweet. If the cherries are still sour, stir in another tablespoon or two of Porto. Then, if you have still not achieved the gentle sweet-ness, stir in, teaspoon by teaspoon, some of the sugar, tasting after each addition. Hold, covered.

Next, chop the aromatic ingredients. Put into the Cuisinart bowl: all the pieces of cut scallion, the whole garlic clove, the ¼ teaspoon caraway seeds, the marjoram, oregano, rosemary and the pieces of lemon rind; then mince everything finely – usually in 3 to 5 one-second bursts of the steel blades. Sprinkle this mixture over the pork chops during the last 3 or 4 minutes of frying.

Now mix the sour cream sauce. There is no need to rinse out the Cuisinart bowl. If you are using fresh ginger root, put the slices plus the remaining ½ teaspoon of dry mustard into the Cuisinart and whirl until it is finely minced – usually in 4 to 5 seconds. Now spoon in the

1½ cups of sour cream. (If you are using dried ginger, add it after the sour cream.) Whirl the blades again, until the sour cream is lightly and nicely flavored all through with ginger and mustard. Taste it and stir in a pinch more of this or that until you have it precisely to your taste.

When the chops are ready, turn down the heat under the pan to simmering temperature (about 230°F) and cover the chops with a layer of half the sour cream sauce, then a layer of the cherries, then the rest of the sour cream. Cover the pan and let everything gently simmer while you finish preparing the already-cooked potatoes. Skin them and slice them evenly about ¼-inch thick. Now lay them on top of the sour cream in the sauté pan, slightly overlapping them all across the top surface as if they were the top crust of a pie. Lightly salt and pepper them, put back the lid and keep everything simmering for another 25 minutes. Put in the peas, spreading them around into all the odd corners. Recover and continue the simmering for 5 minutes longer. Then serve at once on very hot plates.

THE ABSOLUTELY FAIL-SAFE METHOD FOR BAKING, FLAVORING AND DECORATING A FESTIVE WHOLE HAM

(for a big party, or constant family use)

This is a magnificent main dish for a feast or a handsome center-piece for a party buffet. It can also be made and stored in the refrigerator tightly covered for any of dozens of different family meals. This revolutionary baking method – as safe and sure as the Rock of Gibraltar – was taught us by our friend Jim Kite, who cures superb Virginia hams at his Wolftown smokehouse.

Allspice berries, whole (2 tsp)	**Madeira, slightly sweet Bual**
Bay leaves, whole (2)	**(2 Tbs)**
Mustard, dry English (1 tsp)	**Ham, uncooked, country-style,**
Maple syrup, pure (2 Tbs)	**all bones in (about 13 to**
(or honey, or brown sugar)	**15 lbs)**

Less Than 1 Hour of Work, Plus 23 Hours of Totally Unsupervised Baking
The principle of this method is perfectly simple. You put your ham into the oven about 24 hours before you want to sit down at table

to eat it. The 24 hours includes about 20 minutes at the beginning for the preparation of the ham, plus about 40 minutes at the end for its decoration. So – if you want to place your ham on the table at 7:00 P.M. tomorrow, at about 7:00 P.M. today preheat your oven to 170°F. The temperature never rises above this and therefore, the ham could not overcook even if you left it in the oven for a week. It loses not a drop of its juices and the pink flesh comes out as tender as spring lamb.

First, prepare the aromatic mixture for the inside of the ham. Put into the Cuisinart bowl: the 2 teaspoons allspice, the 2 bay leaves and the teaspoon of dry mustard. Run the steel blades until these are fairly finely powdered – usually in 10 to 15 seconds. Then add the 2 tablespoons of maple syrup and 1 tablespoon of the Madeira, whirling the blades again for 2 or 3 seconds to blend everything thoroughly together. Now check for thickness. The mixture should be slightly syrupy, but not honey-thick or it won't spread through the ham flesh. To thin it, add, teaspoon by teaspoon, more of the Madeira, running the machine for a second or two after each addition, until you have a syrupy but runny mix. Hold it for the moment.

Next, clean up the ham, as needed. Any first-class, properly aged ham will usually have some dark smoke patches and perhaps some bits of penicillin-type mold here and there. Scrub off any surface blemishes with a stiff wire brush and cut away any crusty patches with a knife. Place the ham on a cutting board, skin side down. Now, using a very sharp, small knife at the center of the skinless side of the ham, cut a cone-shaped hole – about 1½ inches in diameter at the top, but narrowing to a point where the tip of the knife reaches the central bone. Pull out the cone-shaped piece that you have now cut away. At the bottom of the hole, the bone must be exposed, since it is along the bone that the aromatic syrup will run to flavor the flesh during the baking. Fill the cone-shaped hole with the aromatic mixture from the Cuisinart bowl. Get in as much as you can, pushing it and working it down toward the bone. Now, turn back to the cone-shaped piece you removed. Cut a ⅜-inch slice at its widest circumference and use this slice as the plug for the hole in the ham. Now completely wrap the ham in extra-wide aluminum foil, set it (of course, with the hole upward) on a baking tray in the center of the oven and forget it completely for exactly 23 hours. (For the final decoration of the ham, see the next recipe.)

37

CUISINART GLAZE FOR DECORATING A WHOLE HAM

(for 1 baked ham)

Cloves, whole, for decorating
(at least 50)
Orange Curaçao liqueur (¼ to
½ cup)
Mustard, prepared, preferably
imported strong German
(½ cup)

Molasses, dark unsulphured
(½ cup)
Mustard, dry English (1 tsp)
Brown sugar (1 Tbs)
Porto wine, Ruby (1 Tbs)
Tabasco (½ tsp)

Preparation During the Final 40 Minutes Before the Ham Is To Be Served

Take the ham out of the oven (see previous recipe) and at once turn the temperature control up to 425°F. Unwrap the ham from its foil. At 170°F, it will not burn your fingers. Using a small, sharp-pointed knife, remove the skin from the ham and score the dome of fat with diagonal straight lines, about an inch apart, first one way then the other, making a diamond-shaped pattern. The cuts should be fairly deep, almost down to the flesh. Into the center of each diamond stick a whole clove with a good, round head on it. Set the ham back in the oven until the fat is slightly browned and the cuts have opened up, so that the diamonds are now separated – usually in 20 to 25 minutes. During this period, baste the top of the ham repeatedly with the Curaçao liqueur.

Meanwhile, mix the glaze in the Cuisinart bowl, putting in the ½ cup each of made mustard and molasses, the 1 teaspoon of dry mustard, the 1 tablespoon each of brown sugar and Porto plus the ½ teaspoon of Tabasco. Whirl the steel blades until they are all perfectly blended – usually in 4 to 6 seconds. Hold until the ham is ready.

As soon as the surface effect on the ham is achieved, take it out and reduce the oven heat to 350°F. Using a small ladle, dribble the glazing mixture thickly over the top of the ham. Never mind if some glaze dribbles down, but a thick coating should remain. Put the ham back in the oven until the glazed surface is set and beautifully shiny – usually in about 15 minutes. Bring it at once to table for the carving and the expectant gasps of the guests.

OUR SUPER MEAT LOAF OF BEEF AND LAMB WITH NUTS IN THE STYLE OF A MIDDLE EASTERN KIBBEE

(for 4 to 6)

Around the eastern and southern shores of the Mediterranean, *kibbee* is virtually a national dish. In the old days, the perfect smoothness of the meat was achieved by pounding it for hours in a huge stone mortar with a two-hand wooden pestle. Now all that is changed. More Cuisinart machines per capita are in use in the Middle East than in any other part of the world — all because it can grind the meats for a *kibbee* so much faster and with so much more smooth tenderness.

Cracked wheat grains, sold in ½ lb
  boxes as "wheat pilaff," or
  "buckwheat groats" or
  "Bulghur wheat," etc. (¾ cup)
Dry white wine (1 cup)
Yellow onions, peeled and
  chunked (4, medium)
Lamb, entirely lean, 1-inch cubes
  cut from leg (1 lb)
Salt, coarse crystal, to taste
Black pepper, freshly ground to
  taste

Beef, entirely lean, 1-inch cubes
  cut from bottom round or chuck
  (½ lb)
Peanuts, salted, shelled (¼ lb)
Parsley (small bunch)
Allspice berries, whole (1 tsp)
Coriander seed, whole (1 tsp)
Raisins, golden seedless (½ cup)
Butter, salted (¼ lb)

Best Flavor When Prepared Ahead and Reheated, with Active Preparation About 30 Minutes and Unsupervised Baking About 1 Hour

First, soak and expand the wheat grains, according to the directions on the package, using the white wine, heated, instead of hot water. The grains usually expand to double or treble their dry volume, so ¾ cup of the dry grains will at least provide the 1½ cups required for the *kibbee*. During the 15 minutes or so of soaking time, start preparing the meats.

Put half the chunked onions into the Cuisinart bowl and run the machine until the onions are chopped to the size of white haricot beans by starting and stopping the machine in 1 second. Now add the pound of lamb, spreading the cubes evenly around the bowl, and sprinkle on 1 tablespoon of salt and a good grinding of pepper. Whirl the steel blades until the lamb is so fine and smooth that it is almost, but not quite, a paste – usually in somewhere between 10 and 15 seconds. Watch it closely. Do not overrun the blades. Empty the lamb out into a covered bowl and hold it.

Now put into the Cuisinart bowl the remaining onions and chop them exactly as you did the first lot. Evenly spread in the beef cubes and this time run the blades only until the meat is quite coarsely ground – usually in no more than 4 seconds. The beef must be chopped much more coarsely than the lamb, to provide the essential texture contrast of the layers of the *kibbee*. Transfer the mixture to a fair-sized covered bowl and hold it.

Now do a series of very quick operations with the Cuisinart machine. Rinse out the bowl and dry it. Put in the ¼ pound of peanuts and chop them for no more than 2 to 3 seconds. They should be quite coarse. Transfer them to a covered dish and hold. Without cleaning the Cuisinart bowl, put in a handful of parsley leaves pulled away from the stalks and mince them fairly coarsely – whirling the steel blades for about 2 seconds. Transfer the chopped parsley to a small covered dish and hold it. Again without cleaning the Cuisinart bowl, put in the 1 teaspoon each of allspice and coriander seeds, 1 teaspoon of salt and a few grinds of pepper. Whirl until they are coarsely powdered – usually in 5 to 7 seconds. Transfer them to a small covered dish and hold.

Now begin assembling the parts of the *kibbee*. Preferably with your fingers, gently and lightly work into the beef – lifting and folding rather than pressing and squeezing – half of the peanuts, the ½ cup of raisins, half of the minced parsley, and all of the aromatic allspice-coriander powder. Now set a 10- or 12-inch sauté pan over medium-high frying heat and melt in it 4 tablespoons of the butter, taking care that it does not brown. Spread the beef mixture into the hot butter, stirring it around, just until the meat is crumbly and lightly brown – usually in 3 to 4 minutes. Turn off the heat and hold the sauté pan, uncovered. Preheat the oven to 350°F.

Drain the wheat grains, measure 1½ cups of them and lightly blend this (again preferably with fingers) into the lamb. Choose a shallow baking tin or ceramic casserole, not more than 2½ inches deep, which must be large enough to hold both the beef and the lamb without spilling the melted butter that is going to be poured over the top. It should be around 2 quarts capacity. Liberally butter its bottom and sides. Divide the lamb into two halves. Spread the first half on the bottom of the pan as a smooth, even layer about ½ inch thick. Spread the entire beef mixture on top as a middle layer. Put in the remaining lamb as a top layer. Using a 4-pronged fork and pushing it in each time about ⅜ inch deep, prick parallel lines of holes across the top surface of the *kibbee*, to encourage the absorption of melting butter. Neatly sprinkle the remaining peanuts over the top and dot with the remaining butter. Bake in the center of the oven until the top shows the first signs of light browning – usually in about 50 minutes to an hour. Finally, just before serving, brown the *kibbee* more thoroughly under a grill for about 2 or 3 minutes.

Kibbee is one of the most flexible dishes in all the world. You can stop the cooking halfway, wrap it tightly in foil, and refrigerate it for reheating another day. Or you can freeze it for lengthy keeping. The flavor seems to improve and mellow with time. After complete cooking, it is excellent sliced, cold (at room rather than refrigerator temperature). As a variation, serve it with our Neapolitan tomato sauce (page 59). A *kibbee* is a marvelous dish for a picnic. Obviously, you can make a *kibbee* in any shape of your choosing, so long as you always keep the beef mixture as the central filling of the lamb mixture. You can also use different kinds of nuts for variations in texture. There is no end to the flexible wonder of *kibbee*!

BARCELONA-STYLE ONE-DISH FISH FILLETS WITH ALMOND SAUCE IN A CHINESE WOK

(for 4)

We do it in our electric wok, but you can equally well use a 12-inch covered sauté pan, or a sufficiently deep covered frypan. When they served this lovely fish to us in Barcelona, the chef made the sauce quite memorable with a traditional touch of semisweet chocolate. It is included in this recipe and you should try its extraordinary effect. Then, if you absolutely do not like the faint flavor of chocolate, you can simply leave it out. The recipe also works well without it.

Olive oil, first quality (½ cup)
Yellow onions, peeled and
   quartered (3 medium)

Garlic, whole cloves (3)
Tomatoes, Italian plum (16-oz
   can)

Dry white wine (1 cup)
Bay leaves, whole (2)
Salt, coarse crystal, to taste
Black pepper, freshly ground, to
   taste
Almonds, shelled and blanched
   (1 cup)

Semisweet chocolate bits (up to
   3 Tbs)
Fish fillets, fresh, or frozen and
   thawed; flounder, lemon sole,
   ocean perch, sole, etc. (4)

**Prepared in About 1¾ Hours from Start to Serving, with About
30 Minutes of Active Work, Plus 1¼ Hours of Unsupervised
Simmering**

We heat up our electric wok to medium-high frying temperature and
put in it the ½ cup olive oil. While it is getting hot, put the onion
quarters into the Cuisinart bowl and mince them fairly finely – about
4 to 6 one-second bursts. When the oil in the wok is hot, add the
minced onions and stir them around until they are lightly gilded. As
soon as they begin to color, drop in the 3 garlic cloves. Meanwhile,
without rinsing the Cuisinart bowl, put into it the 2 cups of tomatoes
and the cup of white wine. Whirl the blades for hardly more than 2
or 3 seconds, just to cut up the tomatoes and blend them with the
wine. Then, the moment the onions are the right color, stop the frying by pouring in the tomato-wine blend. Also add to the wok the
2 bay leaves, plus salt and pepper to taste. The mixture should taste a
little bit peppery, but don't overdo it. Now reduce the heat to gentle
simmering, cover the wok, and keep it bubbling, stirring occasionally, until all the flavors are thoroughly blended and the texture is
very smooth – usually in about an hour.

Meanwhile put into the Cuisinart bowl the cup of shelled and
blanched almonds and whirl the blades until the nuts have been
chopped and churned into a completely smooth paste – usually in
about 2 minutes. When the sauce has completed its simmering,
pick out and discard the bay leaves. Also pick out the 3 cloves of
garlic and squeeze them so that their inside flesh, which is now a soft
mush, drops back into the liquid and can be smoothly blended in.
Discard the garlic skins.

When the tomato mixture is thoroughly smooth and its flavors
completely blended, you should aim to achieve a creamy texture
by removing the cover and turning up the heat slightly so that the
mixture bubbles quite merrily, thus boiling off the water to reduce

the volume and concentrate the flavors. Now work in the almond paste, tablespoon by tablespoon, using a wooden spoon to amalgamate it completely into the liquid until the sauce has a creamy consistency. Break up any lumps by squeezing them, with the back of the spoon, against the sides of the wok. Turn down the heat slightly, so that the liquid is no longer bubbling, and then smoothly work in 2 teaspoons of the semisweet chocolate bits. You should end up with a delicately faint flavor of chocolate and the sauce should be slightly thickened and very smooth. Until you achieve this effect, keep on working in more chocolate bits, a few at a time, taking care not to go too far. Taste as you go. We usually find that up to 1 tablespoon is about enough, but it is strictly a matter of personal taste.

Return the liquid sauce in the wok to gentle simmering. Taste it once more and, if necessary, finally adjust the seasonings. Then carefully slide the fish fillets into the bubbling liquid. Let them simmer, uncovered, until the flesh is just opaque and flaky when tested with a fork – usually in about 7 to 10 minutes. Our simple rule of thumb for fish fillets is to cook them 10 minutes for every inch of thickness. In Barcelona, they serve the fish on a bed of saffron rice with plenty of the simmering sauce ladled over the top.

CHINESE-STYLE GLAZED SPARERIBS WITH 20-SECOND BARBECUE SAUCE

(for 4)

This is a speeded-up version of a very authentic recipe from a Chinese friend who is a most excellent cook. If you have a Chinese food shop near you, you can use the authentic flavorings and spices. If not, we give you Western alternatives.

Pork spareribs, uncut (4 lbs)
Chinese *heung new fun* five-
   flavor spice powder (1 tsp)
   If not available, replace with
    with the following:
    Star anise, whole (3)
    Fennel seed, whole (½ tsp)
    Black pepper (2 or 3 grinds)

Cloves, whole (4)
Cinnamon, ground (½ tsp)
Salt, coarse crystal (2 tsp)
Chinese *naam yu* bean curd sauce
   (¼ cup)
   If not available, replace with
    the following:

Tabasco (¼ tsp)

Worcestershire sauce
(2 Tbs)

Ginger root, fresh or dry
ground (1-inch piece
fresh, or 1 tsp ground)

Vinegar, tarragon wine
(2 Tbs)

Soy sauce, light (¼ cup)

Sugar (1 tsp)

Honey (¼ cup)

Garlic, whole clove, unpeeled (1)

Optional Garnish:

English mustard

**Preparation in About 1 Hour from Start to Serving, with
About 20 Minutes of Active Work, Plus About 40 Minutes
in the Oven**

Preheat your oven to 325°F. We believe in cooking spareribs
slowly, to melt off a good part of the fat, to absorb the sauce, and
to give them crispness and a shiny glaze. Place each sheet of ribs
on a cutting board and with a sharp-pointed knife, cut halfway
through between each bone so that the ribs are almost separated,
but still hang together. Now put all the remaining ingredients into
the Cuisinart bowl: the teaspoon of Chinese spice powder (or the
5 alternatives), the 2 teaspoons of salt, the ¼ cup of brick-red bean
curd sauce (or the 4 alternatives), the ¼ cup of soy sauce, the
teaspoon of sugar, the ¼ cup of honey and the unpeeled clove of
garlic. Whirl the steel blades until all these ingredients are completely pulverized and churned into a smooth sauce – usually in
about 15 or 20 seconds. Rub this sauce thoroughly into all sides of
the ribs and place them on a baking pan (deep enough to hold the
released fat) in the center of the oven. Rub on more sauce at
10-minute intervals. Bake the ribs for 20 minutes on one side, then
20 minutes on the other. Finally, pour off the released fat from
the pan, turn up the oven to 450°F to brown, crisp and glaze. The
ribs should become a rich brown, thoroughly crisp and nicely
glazed. Just before serving them, cut the bones completely apart,
so that each diner can pick up each rib separately with his fingers.
We like to serve them with a strong English mustard.

MORAVIAN SPICED POT ROAST OF BEEF

(for 4 to 6)

A big pot roast is a wonderful party dish. It seems to expand the hos-
pitality with the feeling that there is unlimited plenty for everyone.

We think the best cut is the tip of the rump, but obviously you can also use the bottom or heel of the round, the brisket, or the arm or blade of the chuck or shoulder. We always leave the bone in, since it helps to conduct the heat evenly to the center of the roast, making it well worth the slight extra trouble in carving. We have adapted this old recipe from one given us many years ago by our hostess at a farm in the Central Moravian valley of Czechoslovakia that lies between Bohemia and the Carpathian mountains, where the beef grow lean and tender from cropping the lush grasses, and the herbs grow wild along the edges of the woods.

Salt, coarse crystal (1 tsp or more, to taste)

Sage, dried or fresh (1 tsp dried, or 1 Tbs fresh leaf)

Thyme, dried or fresh (1 tsp dried, or 1 Tbs fresh leaf)

Black pepper, freshly ground, to taste

Cloves, whole (2 tsp)

Allspice, whole berries (2 tsp)

Bay leaves (2 whole)

Lemon, whole (1)

Beef bouillon (2½ cups)

Beef pot roast, see above (about 3½ lbs)

Butter (2 Tbs)

Olive oil, first quality (2 Tbs)

Carrots, scraped and sliced (½ cup)

Yellow onions, peeled and sliced (½ cup)

Start It the Day Before, with Only About 15 Minutes of Active Work, Plus About 2 Hours of Simmering in the Pot

Peel the thin yellow rind from the lemon as the first step in the preparation of the aromatic cooking liquor. Put into the bowl of the Cuisinart: 1 teaspoon of the salt (perhaps more later), the sage, thyme, about ½ teaspoon of the ground black pepper (perhaps more later), the whole cloves, the whole allspice, and 2 whole bay leaves, and the lemon rind. Then mince them finely by whirling the steel blades for about 3 to 5 seconds. Now roll the skinned lemon around on a cutting board or the counter top, pressing down on it hard with your hands to loosen and soften the interior flesh. Cut it in half and squeeze out 3 tablespoons of its juice. Add this, with the 2½ cups of beef bouillon, to the Cuisinart workbowl and run the blades for a couple more seconds, just to mix everything thoroughly. Taste once more and add, if necessary, more salt and/or pepper and/or lemon juice. When it is dead right, transfer it to a 1-quart saucepan and heat it up just to boiling. Put the piece of beef into a refrigerator storage jar large enough to hold it comfortably and pour the boiling aromatic liquor over it, turning the meat so that all sides are thoroughly wetted. Let it marinate in the refrigerator, covered, for about 24 hours, turning the meat over and around several times.

When you are ready to begin cooking the pot roast, take it out of its marinating liquor and dry it thoroughly, saving the liquor. Choose a heavy Dutch oven or enameled iron casserole large enough to hold the meat and set it over fairly high frying heat on a top burner. Lubricate its bottom with the 2 tablespoons each of butter and olive oil and, when they are quite hot but not yet smoking, sear the meat on all sides to a good dark brown color. Turn off the heat under the Dutch oven and hiss in the aromatic liquor. Spread around the meat the ½ cup each of sliced carrots and onions. The pot roasting can be done on a top burner, keeping the liquid merrily bubbling to provide enough steam within the Dutch oven. Or you can set it all in the center of an oven at 325°F. The timing will be about the same both ways. It should end up meltingly tender, with its central interior temperature at 130°F. This usually takes about 2 hours.

When the beef is perfect, keep it warm in an oven at 175°F, while you deal with the magnificent gravy. We prefer not to use flour for thickening, since it dilutes the flavor. Much better to pass it once more through the Cuisinart machine, thickening the liquid by puréeing the vegetables in about 3 or 4 seconds. If this does not provide quite enough thickness, we usually keep in the refrigerator a supply of boiled and mashed potatoes, and some can be added to the pot roast gravy in the Cuisinart workbowl, tablespoon by tablespoon, until you achieve the exact thickness of the sauce to suit your taste. Adjust the seasonings, reheat briefly, and serve over the sliced beef.

AN ARABIAN-STYLE PILAFF OF RICE AS A VARIATION FROM SPANISH RICE

(for 4)

This is an extremely good and highly flexible way to cook rice. You can make it either bland and simple in flavor or highly aromatic with all kinds of exotic bits and pieces in it. Generally, it is a side dish to accompany the main course. But it can also be so richly flecked with meat, poultry, fish, bits of melted cheese or fruits and nuts, that it becomes a main supper dish in its own delectable right. Here is a simple version to show you the basic principle. After this, let your imagination take off on other variations.

Rice, long-grained white
  (1½ cups)
Beef bouillon (2¼ cups)
Butter (2 Tbs)
Golden raisins, seedless (about
  ⅓ cup)

Salt, coarse crystal, to taste
Black pepper, freshly ground, to
  taste

As to other garnishes, almost anything goes: chopped scallions, green pepper, watercress leaves, other greens, bits of tomato, cooked leftover vegetables, chopped nuts, lightly sautéed mushroom slices, any kind of leftover meat or fish – all of these coarsely chopped for a second or two in the Cuisinart.

Preparation from Start to Serving in About 50 Minutes
First half-cook the rice in boiling, slightly salted water for exactly 7 minutes. (An aluminum rice ball is most convenient for this.) While it is boiling, preheat your oven to 150°F keep-warm temperature and set in it to warm up a 1½-quart Boston-style, lidded, earthenware bean baking pot. In a saucepan, heat up the 2¼ cups of beef bouillon and keep it, covered, just at the boiling point. While waiting, do any necessary chopping of the garnishes in the Cuisinart machine.

When the 7-minute timer rings, drain the rice, take the beanpot out of the oven and at once turn the oven temperature up to 350°F. Liberally butter the inside of the beanpot and pack the rice in loosely. Now, preferably using a rubber spatula or wooden spoon, gently and lightly blend into the rice the ⅓ cup of raisins, plus all the other chopped garnishes planned for the occasion. Keep it all light and loose. Gently pour in the hot bouillon, then taste and add salt and pepper, as needed. Dot the surface of the rice with the remaining butter. Stretch a piece of folded cotton cloth (a white handkerchief does very well) across the opening of the beanpot and press it down with the lid. This trick helps to seal in the steam and prevents condensation, improving the expansion of the rice and helping to dry it as it completes its cooking. Set the beanpot in the center of the oven and leave it there for 25 minutes.

Then taste the rice for doneness and check that all the liquid has been absorbed. The rice should be perfectly done at the very moment when the pot has dried out. If a small amount of liquid remains in the bottom, put the pot back in the oven, now uncovered, until all the liquid has boiled off – usually in 5 to 7 minutes. Finally, gently fluff the rice in the pot, using a wooden fork, then serve at once in the covered beanpot. (Incidentally, this rice is the near-perfect accompaniment both to our Barcelona-Style Fish Fillets on page 41 and our Provençal Beef Stew on page 31.)

FRY-BAKED CHICKEN WITH ANCHOVIES, OLIVES AND TOMATOES IN THE STYLE OF PROVENCE

(for 4)

This is a memorable example of how a most unusual sauce can be whipped up by the Cuisinart steel blades in literally a few seconds.

Roasting chicken, cut up in fair-sized pieces for fricasseeing (3 to 3½ lbs)

Lemon, fresh (half)

Garlic, fresh, unpeeled (2 to 4 cloves)

Basil (about 3 tsps dried or 3 Tbs fresh)

Thyme (about 3 tsps dried or 3 Tbs fresh)

Salt, coarse crystal, to taste

Black pepper, freshly ground, to taste

Flour (2 to 3 Tbs)

Olive oil, first quality (about 4 to 5 Tbs)

Anchovy fillets (2 or more to taste)

Red ripe tomatoes, peeled, seeded, and coarsely chunked (4 medium-large)

If your market does not currently have good fresh tomatoes, it is better to use canned Italian plum tomatoes, drained and coarsely chunked (about 8 from a 2-lb can).

Marjoram (2 tsps dried or 2 Tbs fresh)

Dry Vermouth (about ¼ cup)

Black olives, pitted and drained (about 3 doz or contents of 6-oz can)

From Start to Table in About 40 Minutes

You will need a tightly lidded casserole, about 10 to 11 inches across and about 3 inches deep, that can be used first for frying on top of the stove and then for baking in the oven. Adjust the shelves of your oven so that the casserole will be at the center and preheat it to 325°F.

Clean and refresh each large piece of chicken by rubbing it with the cut side of the half lemon. (It looks much better, on the serving plate at table, to offer one large, well-shaped piece rather than several small, almost unrecognizable pieces.) Now peel and sliver 1 clove of garlic and work one or two slivers (to your taste) plus a pinch or two of basil and thyme under the skin of each chicken piece. Lightly pat each piece with salt and pepper and dust with flour. Lubricate the bottom of the casserole with about 4 tablespoons of olive oil, place it over medium-high frying heat and, when the oil is quite hot but certainly not smoking, fry the chicken pieces two or three at a time, until they are golden on all sides. Take out the pieces as they are done (adding a bit more oil, if necessary) and, when all have been gilded, pack them into the casserole, cover and set in the oven to bake to perfect doneness – usually in 25 to 30 minutes.

Meanwhile, prepare the sauce in the Cuisinart work bowl. Put in 1 to 3 whole unpeeled cloves of garlic to your taste and turn the motor on and off twice, for less than one second each time. This is the perfect way to chop garlic. Now add the flat fillets of anchovies. How many will really depend on how salty and strong they are. Nibble a tiny bit and judge. If very salty, 2 fillets may be enough. But sometimes the anchovies are relatively so bland that we have had to add a whole 2-ounce can to achieve the salty, tangy, true Provençal flavor in the sauce. Whirl the blades until you have a coarse anchovy-garlic paste – usually in 5 to 7 seconds. Stop the blades, add the chunked tomatoes, the basil, marjoram and thyme and whirl again until all this is a not-too-smooth purée – usually in 10 to 12 seconds. Taste it and work in more anchovies or herbs, if you like. Transfer this sauce to an 8-inch sauté pan and set it over medium-high heat, letting it bubble fairly strongly to reduce, thicken and concentrate its flavor. Stir regularly and work in the ¼ cup of dry vermouth (or a little more, to your taste). The sauce should achieve the right consistency just about at the moment when the chicken is done. If the sauce is finished before the chicken, cover the sauté pan and keep it warm over very low heat. A couple of minutes before serving, add the olives to the sauce and stir them around just long enough so that they become warm. You are not trying to cook them. Taste and adjust the seasonings. Now serve in the modern French "new cuisine" way, which requires that the sauce be served under instead of on top of the chicken. Have ready 4 hot serving plates. Spread each with the bright red sauce speckled with the black olives. Then place in the center a piece of the bright gold chicken – its color seeming to symbolize the sunshine of Provence. If you add a circle of sparkling vegetables, you will have contrasts of color and tastes to make a memorable party dish. Link with this a rosé from Provence or a Zinfandel rosé from California.

LUXURIOUS SAUTÉ-PAN CHICKEN IN CHAMPAGNE FROM THE THREE-STAR RESTAURANT LASSERRE IN PARIS

(for 4)

Here is proof that a recipe from a chef of one of the greatest restaurants in the world can still be perfectly easy to prepare, perfectly simple in concept while at the same time being quite wonderful to eat – worthy of one of your most important party dinners.

Salt pork, sliced ¼ inch thick
  (¼ lb)
White onions, smallish, peeled
  (about a dozen)
Mushrooms, wiped and sliced
  (¼ lb)
Chicken or capon, roaster-fryer,
  cut up for fricasseeing (about
  3 to 3½ lbs)
Salt, coarse crystal, to taste
Pepper, freshly ground, to taste
Shallot cloves (about 6, according
  to size)

Parsley (small bunch)
Thyme (1 tsp dried or 1 Tbs
  fresh leaf)
Butter (4 Tbs)
Flour (about 1 Tbs)
Bay leaves, crumbled (2)
Rosé champagne, can be
  California or New York State
  (about 1¾ cups)
Heavy cream (1½ cups)

Preparation in About 1 Hour from Start to Serving

First dice the salt pork with the Cuisinart blades using the technique described on page 32. Transfer the dice to an 8-inch sauté pan, add the dozen onions, then just cover them with cold water and bring it quickly to the boil. As soon as it begins bubbling, turn off the heat and drain off the water. Now set the pan over medium frying heat and sauté the dice and the onions until the pork is just beginning to brown and the onions are flecked with spots – usually in about 5 to 6 minutes. Then add the sliced mushrooms and continue sautéeing, now more gently, until the mushrooms have expelled their water and the sizzling begins to die down – usually in about 10 more minutes. Shake the pan occasionally and stir its contents around to encourage the blending of the flavors. When they all look to be perfectly done, turn off the heat and hold the pan, uncovered.

Now turn to the chicken, which is to be gently poached in a 10- or 12-inch sauté pan with a well-fitting lid. Pat and rub the chicken pieces with salt and pepper and hold them. This is the moment to chop the shallots and herbs with the Cuisinart blades. First do the unpeeled shallots separately, coarsely chopping them in about 1 second. Then remove the shallots and put in the parsley and any fresh leaves of thyme, again minced fairly coarsely by whirling the blades for a second or two. Place the larger sauté pan over medium-high frying heat and melt in it the 4 tablespoons of butter. As soon as it is thoroughly hot but not browning or smoking, put in the chicken pieces skin side down, sprinkle in the shallots, then sauté until the chicken shows the very first signs of gilding – usually in about 6 to 8 minutes. Turn the pieces and repeat the process – usually in about 5 to 6 minutes longer. Now very lightly sprinkle over the pieces, on both sides, the tablespoon of flour. At this point, spread around and between the chicken pieces the crumbled bay leaves, 4 tablespoons of the mixed parsley and thyme, the mushrooms, onions and pork dice and sprinkle over all the first ¼ cup of champagne. At this point, it is best to pour the remaining 1½ cups of champagne to be held for the later cooking so that the bottle can be recorked and kept cold in the refrigerator for serving at table. Reduce the heat to gentle simmering and put on the lid. Continue this poaching, sprinkling on small extra doses of champagne as it boils off, until the chicken is perfectly done – usually in 30 to 40 minutes.

Set your oven to keep-warm temperature, 175°F, and warm up in it the platter on which the chicken is to be served. When the chicken is done, using a slotted spoon, set the pieces on the serving platter in the oven, sprinkling on the pork dice and garnishing the chicken with the mushrooms and onions. Cover with foil and keep warm in the oven while you complete the sauce.

Quickly skim off the fat from the sauté pan and add the rest of the champagne, bring it quickly to the boil and deglaze the pan by firmly scraping its bottom with a wooden spoon to detach and dissolve all the flavorful browned bits. Boil the champagne hard to reduce it to

about ⅓ cup, then, lifting the pan off the fire for the moment, carefully and gently blend in the 1½ cups of cream. Put it back on the
heat and continue a gentle but steady bubbling, now stirring continuously, until the sauce is just thick enough to coat the spoon –
usually about 5 minutes longer. Taste and adjust the seasonings, then
pour the sauce over the chicken, sprinkle on the remaining parsley
and thyme mixture, and serve at once, all very hot. Accompany it
with a pilaff of rice (page 46) and drink with it the rest of the champagne, plus, if you are feeling festive, a second bottle.

A MAIN-DISH SALAD FROM PROVENCE WITH HAM, PINEAPPLE AND AN EXOTIC BLEND OF VEGETABLES

(for 4)

This is quite perfect at a table on a terrace above a French sandy beach
overlooking the Mediterranean. It is extraordinarily good as the principal supper dish on a dining table anywhere. Although ham is probably the ideal meat for this salad and is always served in Provence,
you can substitute slices or strips of other meats or sausages or cheeses
(for example, roast beef, corned beef, pastrami, pepperoni, salami,
summer sausage, Gruyère, etc.). Most of them can be sliced with the
Cuisinart extra-thick serrated slicing disk.

White celery, washed (small head)
Watercress, stalks removed
    (1 bunch)
Parsley, stalks removed
    (small bunch)
Orange peel, outer rind (3 good
    slivers)
Garlic, whole clove, unpeeled (1)

Ham, cooked, cut into 2-inch
    strips (1 lb)
Pineapple cubes (½ lb)
Rosy mayonnaise, for the dressing
    (page 77)
Tomatoes, sliced (2 medium)
Black olives, stoned (2 dozen)

Preparation in About 15 Minutes from Start to Serving
Remove the Cuisinart steel blades and put into place the grating and
shredding disk. With the machine running, feed the whole head of
white celery down the cover chimney, pressing the last of it down with
the pusher. It will be perfectly grated. Transfer it to the salad serving
bowl. Remove the grating disk, put back the steel blades, and put into
the bowl the watercress leaves and half the parsley leaves, running the

52

blades until the green herbs are coarsely chopped – usually in 1 to 2 seconds. Add to the salad bowl. Without rinsing the Cuisinart bowl, put into it the 3 slivers of orange rind and the whole unpeeled clove of garlic, mincing them finely – usually in 8 to 10 seconds. Add to the salad. Also add the strips of ham and the cubes of pineapple. Toss the salad with 5 or 6 tablespoons (to your taste) of our Rosy Mayonnaise (see page 77). Finally, decorate the top with the tomato slices, parsley and the black olives. Serve quite cold on chilled plates.

QUICK HOME-MADE MAYONNAISE FLAVORED WITH AVOCADO

(about 2 cups – keeps, refrigerated, at least 1 week)

This is one of the most magical of all the tricks of the Cuisinart. Unlike hand-beaten mayonnaise, which tends to separate under refrigeration, this mayonnaise is virtually inseparable. We have adapted the brilliant flavor variation from the original recipe which came to us from one of the most famous of the young revolutionary chefs of Paris, Alain Senderens at his restaurant, l'Archestrate. As to the making, we have a secret trick. We think the machine works better if you start with 3 egg yolks instead of the standard 2.

Egg yolks, large (3)
Avocado, fully ripe, peeled and
    chunked (about 14 oz)
Salt, fine-grind (about ½ tsp)
Black pepper, freshly ground, to
    taste
Red cayenne pepper (a pinch)
Mustard, English dry powdered
    (about 1 tsp)
Mustard, French Dijon
    (about 1 tsp)

Paprika, Hungarian sweet
    (about ¾ tsp)
Lemon juice, freshly squeezed
    (about 1 tsp)
Vinegar, French tarragon white
    wine (about 1 tsp)
Peanut oil (⅔ cup)
Olive oil, best quality (⅓ cup)

Preparation in About 5 Minutes from Start to Serving
Without breaking them, carefully place the 3 yolks in the Cuisinart work bowl with the steel blades in position. Then add half the

chunked flesh of the avocado, the ½ teaspoon of salt, a few grinds of pepper, a pinch of red cayenne pepper, the 1 teaspoon each of dry English mustard and Dijon French, the ¾ teaspoon of sweet paprika, plus the 1 teaspoon each of lemon juice and tarragon white wine vinegar. Now, just switch the motor almost instantly on and off to break the egg yolks and roughly blend the ingredients. Even 1 second is too much. If the yolks are churned at this point, they may disintegrate. Fill a 1-cup measure with the ⅔ cup of peanut oil and ⅓ cup of olive oil. Remove the pusher from the chimney of the Cuisinart cover, start the steel blades whirling, and immediately begin pouring in the oil in a slow, steady stream. After you have poured in a half cup, you can pour considerably faster. The moment it is all in, stop the motor. Taste the mayonnaise and adjust its flavor and thickness to your pleasure. You may add small extra quantities of any or all of the aromatic ingredients: avocado, mustard, paprika, lemon juice, vinegar, salt, pepper, or cayenne. Blend in each addition by just starting and stopping the steel blades. Another secret trick is quickly to boil a little water and add 1 tablespoon of it to the mayonnaise through the chimney while the blades are whirling. This helps to smooth out the mayonnaise and prevent it from separating.

QUICK HOME-MADE MAYONNAISE FLAVORED WITH WATERCRESS

(about 2 cups – keeps, refrigerated, at least 1 week)

This is an adaptation of an original recipe from one of the supreme restaurants of Paris, Le Grand Véfour, owned and run by the gastronomic star of French television, Raymond Oliver. You can prepare it, exactly as in the previous recipe, in under 5 minutes, substituting a large bunch of watercress for the avocado. First, however, cut away all tough stalks from a large bunch of watercress, leaving only the crisp, fresh leaves. Pack these into the Cuisinart work bowl and run the steel blades until the cress is chopped and churned almost to a purée – usually in about 6 to 12 seconds. Then add to this all the ingredients of the previous recipe (except, of course, the avocado) and follow exactly the same procedure.

OUR SUPER CUSTOM-CHOPPED HAMBURGER

(for 4)

We are often asked the question, "Can a hamburger provide noble eating worthy of a true gourmet?" Our answer is always, "Yes, if . . ." Here, now, we offer the documentation of what we mean. First, of course, the beef must be of the very top quality and it MUST be freshly custom-chopped at home. Note that we say "chopped" rather than "ground." Putting the beef through the squeezing action of an old-fashioned meat grinder presses out a good part of the juice. The razor-sharp blades of the Cuisinart actually chop the meat almost exactly as the professional chefs do it with two knives, one in each hand. The beef to buy, in the solid piece, absolutely without a speck of fat, is top round, sirloin, tail of porterhouse, or T-bone. Our ideal choice of meat is a mix, half chuck and half sirloin. Then, also, there are one or two other "secret tricks". . .

Beef, completely lean, solid pieces to be chopped at home (2 lbs)

Anchovies, flat fillets (2 2-oz cans)

Butter, sweet, farm-fresh, top quality (up to ¼ pound)

Eggs, large, farm-fresh, grade A (2)

English-style round crumpets or muffins (4)

Tabasco (up to 8 drops)

Lemon, ready to squeeze (½)

Sea salt, coarse crystal, to taste

Chinese Szechuan whole peppercorns, ground in a hand grinder, to taste

Parsley, fresh leaf only (enough to fill 4 Tbs after fine chopping)

Since Nothing Superb Can Ever Be Done Quickly, This May Take 15 Minutes

Chunk the beef into 1-inch cubes and divide them into four ½ pound portions. For absolute tightness of control, pass each of these separately through the Cuisinart work bowl, using the steel blade. Pack the meat lightly around the bowl. Whirl the blades only until the meat is fairly coarsely chopped – never more than 3 or 4 seconds per load. Now, with your fingers (but touching the meat as lightly as possible), work each ½ pound portion into an oval or round hamburger patty, roughly 1 inch thick. Keep it all very loose – lift and fold rather than press and squeeze. Never mix anything with the meat, on pain of instant execution. Hold the patties at room temperature to ripen.

All this business about frying in salt, or sautéeing in butter, is the purest nonsense. The perfect hamburger must be cooked without fat or salt, by dry heat, under a very hot grill. Preheat your grill to its maximum temperature.

While waiting for the heat to develop and the hamburgers to ripen, we prepare a batch of our "secret" anchovy-butter dressing. Rinse and dry the Cuisinart bowl. Put into it the entire contents (including the oil) of the two 2-ounce cans of anchovies. (If you can get the Spanish top quality variety, or the Greek fresh anchovies, your hamburgers will be uplifted almost to greatness!) Add to the bowl 6 tablespoons of the butter, then whirl the blades until they have produced a perfectly churned, creamy-smooth anchovy paste – usually in 5 to 8 seconds. Hold the butter in the Cuisinart bowl.

Place a shallow soup bowl over a saucepan of gently simmering water as a sort of make-shift double boiler. As it heats up, transfer to it the anchovy butter from the Cuisinart bowl. Stir it around gently with a wooden spoon as it gets warm. Have ready alongside, the 2 eggs in two separate bowls, each egg lightly beaten with a few strokes of a fork. Now – as in all great cooking – everything must be brought to the point of perfection by instantaneous timing of multiple activities.

First, set the hamburger patties under the hot grill, with their top surfaces about 5 inches below the fire. We cannot tell you how long to leave them. This must be your own personal calculation. It isn't for us to decide your taste in the rareness of the meat. At the particular temperature of our grill, we do our ½ pound patties until they are just lightly browned – for about 3 minutes on the first side and 2 minutes on the other.

The second simultaneous job is to toast and lightly butter the English crumpets and have them ready to be the pedestal for the hamburgers. It is our personal opinion that the standard hamburger bun, with a solid thickness of bread both above and below the meat, provides altogether too much starch in relation to the beef. We, therefore, insist on serving our hamburgers without a roof of bread over them.

The third simultaneous job is the rapid completion of the anchovy-butter dressing. Gently work into the warm butter, one by one, the 2 eggs, prodding and stirring them around with a wooden spoon until they show the first signs of thickening. Then incorporate a drop or two, to your taste, of Tabasco. At the precise moment when the hamburgers are done to perfection, the anchovy butter should have reached the consistency of whipped cream. Lower the hamburger onto the crumpet, spread it with about a tablespoon of the bright-yellow anchovy balm, spritz it with lemon, dust with salt and a couple of turns of freshly ground Szechuan pepper, give it a touch of greenery with a sprinkling of parsley and serve it instantly. This, to us, is the finest hamburger in the world.

FAST PRESSURIZED SUPER-RICH BEEF AND TOMATO SAUCE FOR SPAGHETTI

(for 4)

We all know that Italian cooks achieve the superb unctuousness and thickness of their spaghetti sauce à la Bolognese by at least 24 hours of barely simmering it in a huge copper pot. We approach the same degree of luscious luxury without greasiness in not much more than 15 minutes by bringing out the trusty pressure cooker. This recipe demonstrates, again, the extraordinary facility of the Cuisinart machine for freshly chopping chunks of lean beef without squeezing out the juices as the old-fashioned meat grinder normally does — this is the secret of the success of this recipe.

Parmesan cheese, coarsely
  chunked (½ lb)
Yellow onions, peeled and
  chunked (3 medium)
Garlic, whole cloves, unpeeled (2)
Parsley, fresh leaf only (enough to
  fill ⅓ cup)
Basil, dried or fresh (1 tsp dried,
  1 Tbs fresh)
Tomatoes, Italian peeled plum
  (28-oz can)

Tomato paste, preferably imported
  Italian (6 oz can)
Olive oil, preferably first-grade
  Italian (4 Tbs)
Beef, all lean, bottom round or
  chuck, coarsely chunked (1 lb)
Golden raisins, seedless (½ cup)
Salt, to taste
Black pepper, to taste

Preparation in About 15 Minutes,
Plus 15 Minutes of Pressure Cooking

First, grind the Parmesan with the Cuisinart steel blade. Put the chunks into the bowl, then start and stop the machine in one-second bursts until the cheese is ground to a fairly coarse texture – usually in 12 to 16 seconds. Empty the grated Parmesan into a serving dish to be brought to table. Next, chop the vegetables and herbs. Put into the Cuisinart bowl the 3 chunked onions, the 2 unpeeled garlic cloves, the ⅓ cup of parsley, and the basil; then run the steel blades until they are finely minced – stopping and starting if necessary to allow the larger lumps to fall down in between the blades – usually in 5 to 8 seconds. Now add about 2 cups of the tomatoes and blend with the minced vegetables by running the machine for another 4 or 5 seconds. Pour the mixture into a jug and hold. Blend the remaining tomatoes and the 6 ounces of tomato paste in the Cuisinart machine by running the steel blades for 3 to 5 seconds, then stir this into the vegetable mixture. Rinse and dry the Cuisinart bowl and put in half the pound of chunked beef. Whirl the blades only 3 or 4 seconds. Remove the meat and chop the other ½ pound in the same way. Count the seconds and watch carefully or the meat will become a sticky paste.

Choose a 2½- to 3-quart pressure cooker and set it on a top burner over medium-high frying heat. Lubricate its bottom with the 4 tablespoons of olive oil, then put in the beef, spreading it around and breaking it up with a wooden spoon until it has just lost its redness – usually in 3 to 4 minutes. At once add the tomato mixture and bring it up to gentle simmering, stirring to incorporate it with the beef. Also add the ½ cup of raisins, 6 tablespoons of the grated cheese, plus salt and pepper to taste. As soon as it is all simmering, put on the lid, and cook at 15 pounds of pressure for 15 minutes, then cool the cooker immediately. In the meantime you can cook your spaghetti in the normal way, leaving it nicely chewy or *al dente*, as the Italians say. Also, if you are having them, you can sauté the Curried Meat Balls (page 60), then plop them into the sauce as soon as the pressure cooker is opened. We serve all this with the remaining Parmesan sprinkled over, a green salad, a long loaf of Italian bread and a good, strong, peasanty red wine.

AN EVEN QUICKER ALTERNATIVE NEAPOLITAN SAUCE FOR SPAGHETTI

(for 4)

This quick sauce requires no pressurizing – and it is quite inexpensive since it involves no meat. It improves if it is made several hours ahead, allowed to develop flavor as it stands at room temperature, and then reheated just before serving.

Garlic, whole, unpeeled (2 cloves)
Yellow onions, peeled and
  chunked (2 medium)
Carrot, scraped and chunked
  (1 medium)
Green bell pepper, cored and
  chunked (1 medium)
Parsley, fresh leaf (enough for
  2 Tbs, chopped)
Basil (1 tsp dried or 1 Tbs fresh)
Oregano, dried (1 tsp)

Marjoram (1 tsp dried or 1 Tbs
  fresh)
Thyme (1 tsp dried or 1 Tbs fresh)
Tomato sauce, preferably imported
  Italian (3 8-oz cans)
Olive oil, first-quality Italian
  (⅓ cup)
Salt, coarse crystal, to taste
Black pepper, freshly ground,
  to taste
Parmesan cheese (5 oz)

Prepared in About 30 Minutes
First, let the Cuisinart machine do the chopping. Put into its bowl: the 2 cloves of garlic, the 2 chunked onions, the chunked carrot and green pepper, the parsley, and the herbs, if you are using whole leaves that need chopping. Start and stop the steel blades in one-second bursts until everything is finely minced – usually in about 7 to 10 bursts. Now pour in 2 cups of the tomato sauce and again whirl the blades until everything is just smoothly blended, no more than that – usually in 3 to 5 seconds.

Heat the ⅓ cup of olive oil in a sauté pan over medium frying temperature and as soon as it begins to get hot, add the contents of the Cuisinart bowl. At this point, stir in any of the herbs that are dried, the remaining cup of tomato sauce, plus salt and pepper to taste. Adjust the heat to a merry bubbling so that the sauce reduces, blending and sharpening its flavors. Keep it bubbling, stirring quite often, until it begins to thicken – usually in about 20 minutes. Taste once more and finally adjust the seasonings, adding the chopped leaves of any of the herbs that are fresh. Then blend with the spaghetti and plenty of Parmesan cheese, freshly ground in the Cuisinart work bowl as described in the previous recipe.

OUR MOST UNUSUAL CURRIED MEAT BALLS FILLED WITH PEANUTS

(for 4)

We sometimes serve these with our spaghetti – or they can be grilled over charcoal at a barbecue and served as appetizers on individual small skewers, such as Italian *spiedini* or Japanese bamboo *kushi*.

Beef, top round, entirely fatless, coarsely chunked (1 lb)
White beef fat, corasely chunked (3 oz)
Cardamom pods, white (6 whole)
Coriander seeds, whole (1 tsp)
Flour, whole wheat, or – preferably – Indian chick pea (2 Tbs or more as needed)
Caraway seeds, whole (½ tsp)
Cinnamon, ground (¼ tsp)
Cloves, ground (¼ tsp)
Turmeric, ground (1 tsp)
Black pepper, freshly ground, to taste

Salt, coarse crystal, to taste
Yellow onions, peeled and chunked (2 medium)
Watercress, small bunch (⅓ cup chopped leaves)
Lemon juice (2 Tbs or more as needed)
Ginger, ground (1 tsp)
Chili powder (1 tsp)
Large egg (1)
Unsalted peanuts (about 3 oz or about ⅓ cup)
Plain yoghurt (about 4 Tbs)

Prepared, in Advance If Necessary, in About 20 Minutes

Divide the pound of beef and the 3 ounces of white fat into 2 equal portions. Put one batch at a time of combined beef and fat into the Cuisinart work bowl – whirl the steel blades until it is coarsely chopped and thoroughly mixed – never for more than 4 or 5 seconds per batch. Be most careful not to overrun. The Cuisinart machine works so fast that even a few seconds too long can turn the meat into a sticky paste. Transfer to a mixing bowl. Clean and dry the Cuisinart work bowl and put into it all the ingredients to be chopped and ground: the 6 cardamom pods, the 1 teaspoon of coriander seeds, the 2 tablespoons of flour, the ½ teaspoon caraway seeds, the ¼ teaspoon each of cinnamon and cloves, the 1 teaspoon of turmeric, a few grinds of pepper, about 3 teaspoons of the salt, the 2 chunked onions, the ⅓ cup of watercress leaves, the 2 tablespoons of lemon juice, the 1 teaspoon of ground ginger and the 1 teaspoon of chili powder. Use the start and stop technique until everything is finely minced and thoroughly mixed – usually in 8 to 10 one-second starts and stops. Then crack the egg into the Cuisinart bowl and whirl the blades 1 or 2 seconds more just to blend it in. Add this aromatic mixture to the beef in the bowl and, preferably with your fingers, thoroughly knead and work it all together. Do not press down or squeeze the meat – rather, lift it and fold it, to keep it all quite light while working it into a firm, smooth paste. If it needs to be stiffened slightly, work in a bit more flour; if it gets too stiff, add a bit more lemon juice.

Preheat your grill. Now detach a small handful of the beef mixture and, again using your fingers, work it into a ball about the size of a small plum. Punch a hole in one side and press into the center of the ball about 4 peanuts. Repeat this operation until you have used up all the beef mixture, which should give you about 12 to 15 balls. Using a pastry brush, paint them with the yoghurt, then grill the balls, turning them every minute or two, until they are nicely browned on all sides – usually in 4 to 6 minutes. Finally, if we are using these meat balls with one of our spaghetti sauces, we drop them into the sauce for a final 2 or 3 minutes (no more than that) of reheating in the bubbling sauce. If we are going to serve the meat balls as appetizers, we spear them on the baby skewers.

SPAGHETTI CASSEROLE WITH CANNED SALMON OR TUNA AND LEMON-CREAM SAUCE

(for 4)

Our children never tired of this. They loved it hot. They loved – equally – the remains of it, cold, the next day.

Spaghetti, thin spaghettini (¾ lb)
Scallions (1 small bunch)
Sour cream (2 cups or 1 pint)
Butter, melted (½ cup or a ¼-lb stick)
Lemon juice (up to 6 Tbs)

Salt, coarse crystal, to taste
Black pepper, freshly ground to taste
Butter, unmelted (1 Tbs)
Salmon or tuna, canned, drained and coarsely flaked (4 cups)

Prepared in 40 Minutes from Start to Serving
Preheat your oven to 400°F. Cook the spaghetti in fast-boiling salted water in the normal way until it is just tender, but still, as the Italians say, *al dente* – a bit chewy. While it is bubbling, prepare the sauce in the Cuisinart. Top and tail the scallions, cut them into 2-inch lengths and put them into the Cuisinart bowl. Chop the scallions into bits the size of large peas, stopping and starting the machine at one-second intervals – usually 2 or 3 one-second bursts will be enough. Now remove the cover and add to the bowl the 2 cups of sour cream, the ½ cup of melted butter and 4 tablespoons of the lemon juice. Whirl the blades until these are thoroughly mixed – usually in about 3 seconds. Now taste the sauce, add salt and pepper as you please, plus, if you like a lemon flavor, a few more dashes of the lemon juice. Run the motor for one more second to mix. Then taste again. Choose a 4-quart heatproof, lidded casserole and warm it up under running hot water. Then dry it and thoroughly butter its bottom and sides.

As soon as the spaghetti is perfectly done, lift it out into a colander, rinse it under running hot water, and drain it thoroughly. Then put it into the baking casserole, spreading it out and loosening it as much as possible, so that the sauce will run into it. Spread the salmon or tuna in a neat layer on top of the spaghetti. Pour the sauce from the Cuisinart bowl over everything, cover the casserole, set it in the center of the oven to bake for 30 minutes. Then serve it at once on very hot plates. Any leftover part, kept well covered in the refrigerator, will become an almost solid "spaghetti pie," quite different in texture but equally attractive to eat.

EASY AND FAST LEMON-NUT SOUFFLÉ CAKE ENTIRELY WITHOUT FLOUR

(10-inch cake, about 8 servings)

This wonderfully light cake rises without benefit of baking powder or yeast. It should be made the day before serving.

Hazelnuts or filberts, shelled (1 lb)	**Sugar, white granulated (about**
Lemons (2)	**2¼ cups)**

Egg yolks (10, large)

Vanilla extract, 100 % pure
  (2 tsp)

Butter (1 Tbs)

Sugar, fine-grind white (½ cup)

Egg whites (12, large)

Heavy cream for whipping, as an
  optional garnish (2 cups)

**Prepared in About 2½ Hours, Including at least 2 Hours
of Entirely Unsupervised Baking**

First chop the pound of nuts. Put half of them into the bowl of the
Cuisinart and run the steel blades, stopping and restarting them every
3 or 4 seconds until the nuts are quite finely ground, but still dry and
not pasty – usually in about 15 to 17 seconds. Empty them into a
bowl, then repeat the operation with the rest of the nuts and hold
these separately from the first. Now thinly peel off the yellow outer
rind of the 2 lemons, preferably using a French lemon-zest scraper or
a very sharp potato peeler, and put all the bits into the Cuisinart bowl.
Finely mince the peel, usually in about 5 to 7 seconds, and then, without stopping the motor, steadily pour in through the lid chimney 2
cups of the granulated sugar. Continue whirling the blades until
lemon and sugar are thoroughly blended – usually in about 10 to 15
seconds. Transfer this mixture to a third storage bowl and hold it.
Without necessarily washing the Cuisinart bowl, set it back on top of
the motor and put in five of the egg yolks. Run the blades for 3 seconds, just to break up and mix the yolks. Then add half the lemon-
flavored sugar, the first half of the nuts and one teaspoon of the
vanilla extract, and whirl the blades until everything is thoroughly
mixed – usually in 18 to 23 seconds. Transfer to a large mixing bowl
and hold. Repeat the operation with the remaining five egg yolks plus
the rest of the lemon-sugar and nuts with the other teaspoon of
vanilla. Add to the first part of the mixture in the large bowl. Preheat
your oven to 300°F. ·

For this cake we use our 10-inch diameter tube pan with a removable bottom. Lightly grease the bottom and sides of the pan with the
butter, then thinly coat the buttered surfaces with fine-grind sugar.
Beat the egg whites in a round-bottomed bowl or with an electric
rotary beater until they stand up in stiff peaks. Then, using a rubber
spatula, gently and lightly fold them into the nut mixture. Pour at
once into the tube pan and set in the center of the oven. It takes
longer than the average soufflé – usually a little more than 2 hours.

Do not open the oven door during the first 2 hours because a sudden draft of cold air may cause the soufflé to fall. At the end of the time, gently stick in a shiny knife. When it comes out dry, the cake is done. It should be light golden brown and springy to the touch. Let it cool completely before taking it out of the pan.

Roll the 2 lemons around on a wooden board, pressing down hard with your hand to loosen and soften the interior flesh. Cut them in halves and squeeze out all the juice, putting it into the Cuisinart bowl. Add the ½ cup of fine-grind sugar and run the machine for not more than 2 seconds. Spoon the mixture thickly, without smoothing it, onto the top of the cake until it is all used up. The surface should be crinkly and rough. It is best to let the cake set for 24 hours before cutting and serving it. If you want it to be very rich, you can mound the inside of the cake with stiffly whipped cream, but you don't have to.

ONE-DISH BUTTERED APPLES WITH GINGER AND VANILLA

(for 4)

One of our favorite desserts – made easy and fast with the help of the Cuisinart.

Baking apples, peeled, preferably Rome Beauties (4 fairly large)
Sweet butter, coarsely chunked (¼ lb stick)
Sugar, granulated white or unrefined (½ cup)
Vanilla bean, split lengthwise in 4 strips (1 whole; or vanilla extract, 2 tsps)

Ginger wine, English (Merrydown or Stone's, or a domestic ginger liqueur) (4 Tbs)
Orange marmalade (about 8 Tbs)

Prepared on Top of the Stove and in the Oven in About 50 Minutes
Core the apples from the stem end but do not cut all the way through, so that the insides will be like cups to hold the fillings. Stand the apples, openings upward, in a lidded, heatproof casserole that can be used both on top of the stove and in the oven. Preheat the oven to 350°F. Put the chunks of butter into the Cuisinart work bowl and add the ½ cup of sugar. Whirl the steel blades until the butter and sugar

are smoothly creamed together – in hardly more than 12 seconds. Push 2 tablespoons of this mixture down into the core cavity of each apple. Drop the remainder of the mixture in bits and pieces across the bottom of the casserole and set it, uncovered, on a top burner at quite gentle heat until the butter is melted. Meanwhile, cut each strip of vanilla bean crosswise into four parts. Stick four of these pieces into each apple. (If you have no vanilla bean, put ½ teaspoon of pure vanilla extract into each apple.) As soon as the butter is melted, put on the lid, turn up the heat to gentle simmering and let the apples cook for 10 minutes.

Now uncover the casserole, gently pick up each apple with a pair of tongs, empty each cavity into the bottom of the casserole and replace the apples now with the holes downwards, so that the steam will cook them evenly inside. Re-cover the casserole and continue the simmering for another 10 minutes.

Again, uncover the casserole and, now treating the apples very gently because they are beginning to become soft, turn them over again and put the pieces of vanilla bean back inside. Now add to each cavity 1 tablespoon of the ginger wine and fill up each cavity with the juices from the bottom of the casserole. Thickly spread the top of each apple with a couple of tablespoons of the orange marmalade. Then cover the casserole and set it in the oven for the final poaching, until the apples are beautifully glazed and perfectly soft but not mushy or beginning to lose their shape – usually in 20 to 30 minutes.

When you serve the apples, spoon plenty of the fragrant pan juices over them. You can, if you like, remove the pieces of vanilla bean, but we prefer to leave them in place to give off their lovely scent as the apple is placed before the diner. Vanilla beans, of course, are not to be eaten, but the pieces can later be washed, dried and reused.

4

Cream Soups Almost Without Cream -
Velvet Sauces Almost Instantly

The ancient, traditional rules for thickening soups and smoothing sauces have had to be rewritten with the coming of the Cuisinart chopper-churner. In France today, the soup and sauce departments have perhaps been more completely revolutionized by the machine than any other part of the kitchen. The use of the classic *roux* – the thickening blend of butter and flour – seems to have gone forever. Instead, any desired degree of creamy thickness can be achieved in a hot or cold soup with a purée of soft vegetables produced in 2 or 3 seconds. And the smoothness of a sauce is no longer dependent on laborious, slow stirring over the hot fire, but rather on the perfect amalgamation of its ingredients in advance, before it is heated up. Then, over the fire, the sauce turns to velvet within a few seconds. Even cold sauces – including mayonnaise – can be given dramatic new flavors with aromatic vegetables whipped smoothly into them.

HOT CREAM SOUPS FOR FALL AND WINTER

IDEAS FOR 4

The basic principle is completely simple and entirely flexible. In a few seconds you can make an excellent soup from leftover cooked vegetables. Cooked potatoes, especially, will give a fine smoothness and texture. No need to worry about the exact proportions. But you should always try to include some onion, a sprig or two of parsley, a small amount of dried or fresh herbs, plus, for freshness of flavor, a few chunks of raw vegetables: green celery, green pepper, tomato . . .

Put no more than 1½ cups of these mixed vegetables at one time into the Cuisinart bowl, fitted with the steel blades. Whirl them only until the vegetables are smoothly puréed, not yet a sticky paste –

67

usually in about 4 to 8 seconds. Transfer the purée to a saucepan and add an equal amount of liquid: beef, chicken, or veal bouillon, left-over gravy or sauce diluted with dry white wine, or, if you must, fresh cold water. As it all heats up, season it to your taste. If it becomes too thick, work in more liquid. If too thin, quickly purée and add more vegetables, especially potatoes.

Another version of this basic soup starts with raw vegetables. Simply chunk into the Cuisinart bowl, say, a medium carrot, first scraped, the white part of a small leek, first washed and desanded (or a scallion instead), and a small handful each of parsley, young spinach leaves and watercress. At first, start and stop the steel blades in one-second bursts, until the mixture is evenly chopped – usually in about 5 or 6 bursts – then run them continuously until everything is finely minced – usually in about 3 to 4 seconds more. Now add a couple of medium-size boiled potatoes, first peeled and sliced, plus 3 tablespoons of tomato paste. Run the machine again until everything is coarsely puréed – usually in about 3 to 5 seconds longer. Quickly bring to the boil a pint of beef or chicken bouillon. Start the steel blades again and, while they are whirling, pour the boiling liquid in a steady stream into the bowl through the chimney of the cover. Leave the motor running until the soup is now smoothly creamed and quite thick – usually in about 15 to 20 seconds more. Now transfer everything to a saucepan and heat it up to gentle simmering, at the same time flavoring and thinning it to your taste by stirring in salt, pepper and up to 1 more cup of hot bouillon. As soon as this creamy soup is thoroughly hot, serve it at once in hot bowls. Any leftover part of it can be refrigerated, covered, then reheated a day or two later, when it is likely to taste even better than on the first day.

For attractive variations of these cream soups, try adding lightly steamed asparagus or green beans, broccoli tops, raw cucumber or mushrooms, or boiled young white turnips, either puréed as above or incorporated into one or another of the recipes which follow.

HOT CREAM OF CHESTNUT

(for 4)

This is the soup *par excellence* for a cold winter's night of rain and storm. It is one of the most luxurious of all soups and the Cuisinart seems to have a special way of perfectly puréeing chestnuts to a satiny cream (as we prove again on page 142, with our Sweet Glacéed Chestnuts in Croquette Balls). As a first course, it is so attractive on the tongue, so filling and so rich, that you would be wise to follow it with a light main course and a fluffy dessert. See the recipe on page 143 for advice on shelling and skinning fresh chestnuts in season, or, out of season, replacing them with the preshelled and skinned imported Italian dried chestnuts which must be soaked overnight. You can break up most of the nuts as you skin them but keep 8 whole.

Fresh chestnuts, shelled and
  skinned - or imported Italian
  dried, see above (1½ lbs)
Chicken or veal bouillon (about
  1 qt)
Parsley (a small handful)
Whole cloves (6)

Black pepper, freshly ground,
  to taste
Salt, coarse crystal, to taste
Heavy cream (¾ to 1 cup)
Parmesan cheese (¼ lb)
French Calvados apple brandy
  (1 Tbs)

Active Preparation About 15 Minutes, Plus About 45 Minutes of Unsupervised Simmering
Put the chestnuts (assuming that they have already been previously shelled and/or soaked) into a heavy iron pot (in thin pots, they sometimes tend to burn) and just cover them with bouillon – you will usually need about a quart. Heat it up to gentle simmering, throwing in the small handful of parsley, the 6 whole cloves and a few grinds of pepper. Continue the simmering, covered until the chestnuts are soft enough for puréeing – usually in about 25 to 35 minutes. When the chestnuts are done, pick out the 8 well-shaped whole nuts and hold them for later garnishing. Now purée the chestnuts, with their liquor, in batches in the Cuisinart work bowl. Each batch should be about 1½ cups of chestnuts with about ½ a cup of the liquid. They will achieve a smooth purée in about 10 to 15 seconds of churning.

Transfer all the batches of purée to a saucepan and gently heat it up, at first stirring all the time, to avoid any danger of burning. The soup should be quite hot, but it must not be allowed to boil. Adjust the flavor and thickness to your taste by stirring in salt and pepper, ¼ cup of heavy cream and as much more bouillon as is needed. Meanwhile, grate the ¼ pound of Parmesan cheese in the Cuisinart work bowl and hold it until serving time. Add more cream and bouillon to the soup until it is dead right. Serve the chestnut soup in very hot bowls and stir into each at the table 1 more tablespoon of cream and 1 tablespoon of French Calvados apple brandy, which seems to bring out the chestnut flavor marvelously. Finally, place one whole chestnut in the center of each bowl and liberally sprinkle on the Parmesan. You will hardly be able to resist seconds and thirds!

CREAM OF CORN

(for 4)

We don't care how many times you have had cream of corn soup before and how carefully you have rubbed it laboriously through a fine-mesh sieve. You have probably never achieved quite the creamy smoothness or eliminated the husks so completely as you will when you purée it in the Cuisinart.

Corn, freshly scraped, or canned
   niblets (2 cups or about 1 lb)
Salt, coarse crystal, to taste
Black pepper, freshly ground,
   to taste

Whole milk (about 1 pint)
Chicken bouillon (up to 1 pint)
Heavy cream (up to ½ cup)
Unsalted butter (2 Tbs)
Sweet paprika (about 1 tsp)

Active Preparation About 10 Minutes, Plus About 30 Minutes of Unsupervised Simmering

Put the corn into a 3-quart saucepan, season it fairly heavily with salt, lightly with pepper, add enough of the milk to cover it, then gently simmer everything, covered, until the corn is quite soft – usually in about 30 minutes. Check the saucepan once or twice, stirring its contents and adding a bit more milk, if necessary, to keep the corn just covered. When it is soft enough, lift it out with a slotted spoon and put it, in batches of not more than 1½ cups each, into the Cuisinart bowl. Run the steel blades until the corn is a perfectly smooth, thick purée which does not taste grainy in the mouth – usually in about 7 to 12 seconds. Stir each batch of purée back into the hot milk in the saucepan and now begin adjusting both the flavor and the consistency to your taste, adding salt and pepper, plus, ¼ cup by ¼ cup, up to a pint of the chicken bouillon and up to the ½ cup of cream. You do not have to add the full amount. Finally, still stirring, melt in, sliver by sliver, the 2 tablespoons of butter. Serve in very hot bowls with a few pinches of sweet paprika sprinkled on top, for color.

THE GREAT PEASANT SOUP OF FRANCE – LEEK, POTATO AND TOMATO

(for 4)

With the machine to do the hard work, this soup is smoothly-rich, yet inexpensive and easy to prepare, with an elegant amalgamation of flavors.

Leeks, white parts only, washed, desanded & chunked (4 medium)	Chicken bouillon (4 cups)
	Sugar, white granulated (2 tsps)
	Salt, coarse crystal, to taste
Yellow onions, peeled (2, medium)	Black pepper, freshly-ground, to taste
Potatoes, starchy, boiling, peeled (6, medium)	
	Parsley, leaf only (about 10 sprigs)
Tomatoes, coarsely chunked (3, medium)	
	Light cream (about 1¼ cups)
Butter (4 Tbs)	Milk (up to 1 cup for thinning)

Active Work of Preparation About 10 Minutes – Plus About 40 Minutes of Unsupervised Simmering

Slice the onions with the Cuisinart medium slicing disk and hold them. Cut the 6 potatoes with the Cuisinart French-cutting disk and hold them in water. There is no need to peel or seed the tomato chunks.

In a 3-quart soup kettle set on medium frying heat, melt 3 tablespoons of the butter and then, before it starts frothing, add the leeks and onions, stirring them around to cover them with the butter. The essential trick is to adjust the heat so that they do not fry or brown, but gently simmer and melt. When they are nicely soft – usually in about 5 minutes – add the tomatoes, stir again and continue the gentle bubbling. Meanwhile, in a separate saucepan, heat the 4 cups of chicken bouillon to the boiling point. When the tomatoes are just beginning to mash, add the French-cut potatoes and the boiling bouillon. Stir in the 2 teaspoons of sugar, with salt and pepper to taste. Adjust the heat to the gentlest of simmering and continue it, covered until the potatoes are meltingly soft – usually in about 30 to 40 minutes. When the timer rings, strain out all the solids and put them, in batches of not more than 2 cups each, into the Cuisinart work bowl. Run the machine until they are puréed to a thick cream –

71

usually in about 8 seconds. If it becomes too thick, add a few table-spoons of the liquid. Transfer each completed batch back to the liquid in the soup kettle, thoroughly stirring it in. Gently reheat the soup, remembering that the potato puree can burn if you go too fast.

Meanwhile, rinse and dry the Cuisinart bowl and finely mince in it the 10 sprigs of parsley – usually in about 6 to 8 seconds.

Just before serving the soup, blend into it the 1 cup of light cream. Now taste again and adjust the seasonings, if necessary. Also judge the texture of the soup. For more velvet, add more cream. To thin it, add milk a few tablespoons at a time. When it is exactly right, serve it in very hot bowls with bright green parsley sprinkled on top and a pat of butter melting in the center.

ICE-COLD CREAM SOUPS FOR SPRING AND SUMMER

The puréeing techniques for cold soups are exactly the same as for hot. Only the ingredients are different – lighter and less assertive, more subtly seasoned, aiming at cooling refreshment rather than warming sustenance. The next recipe is designed to demonstrate the basic principles . . .

COLD GREEN CREAM OF SPRING VEGETABLES

(for 4)

Asparagus, young (1 small bunch)
Green beans, small, chunked
  (½ lb)
Broccoli tops, chunked (from
  1 small bunch)
Green celery, chunked (small)
  bunch)
Cucumber, sliced (1 small)
Zucchini, sliced (2 medium)
Parsley (small bunch)
Shallots (10 cloves)

Garlic (1 clove)
Escarole, washed (1 small head)
Whole young peas, shelled (1 cup)
Chicken bouillon, very clear and
  light-colored (up to 7 cups)
Salt, coarse crystal, to taste
Black pepper, freshly ground,
  to taste
Eggs, hard boiled (2)
Cherry tomatoes, well-shaped
  (4 small)

Active Preparation About 40 Minutes, Plus Chilling for Several Hours or Overnight

First, prepare the spring vegetables in the Cuisinart machine. Coarsely chop in separate batches using the steel blades, transferring each batch to a combined assemblage in a large storage bowl, 1 cup each of the following: the asparagus tips chopped for about 2 seconds, the green beans for about 3 seconds, the broccoli tops for about 3 seconds, the green celery for about 3 seconds, the cucumber for about 2 seconds, the zucchini for about 2 seconds, plus a small handful of the parsley leaves for about 4 seconds and the 10 chunked cloves of shallot with the 1 of garlic for about 3 seconds. Then change to the slicing disk and shred the head of escarole by pushing it down the chimney with the motor running. Add the shreds to the other chopped vegetables. Finally add directly to the assemblage the cup of peas.

In a 5-quart soup kettle heat up to boiling 6 cups of the bouillon. As soon as bubbling begins, add the assemblage of raw vegetables and let them gently simmer, uncovered, until they are soft enough to purée – usually in about 12 to 18 minutes. Strain out all the solids and purée them in the Cuisinart, in batches of not more than 2 cups each, until they are a completely smooth cream – usually in about 4 to 8 seconds. Put each finished batch back into the bouillon in the soup kettle. Stir everything completely together, taste the soup and add salt and pepper, as pleases you. Then put everything in a covered storage pot into the refrigerator to chill for at least 3 or 4 hours, or, much better, overnight.

An hour or so before serving, prepare the garnishes. Separate the yolks from the whites of the 2 hard boiled eggs and dice each, separately, in the Cuisinart, just by turning the steel blades quickly on and off. Hold the yellow and white dice separately. Mince not too finely in the Cuisinart about 6 more sprigs of parsley leaf, usually in 2 or 3 1-second bursts. Hold. Neatly skin the 4 cherry tomatoes. Serve the ice-cold soup thinned to taste with a little extra iced bouillon in open bowls, each decorated at its center with a cherry tomato that is ringed first by a circle of yellow eggs, second, by a circle of white eggs, third, by a circle of bright green parsley. This makes a handsome and excellent first course for a spring or summer party.

ICED CREAM OF AVOCADO AND CLAMS

(for 4)

In some mysterious way, avocado seems to magnify the flavor of garlic — so be careful.

Avocadoes (1½ lbs or 2 large or 3 small)
Garlic, unpeeled (1 clove)
Light cream (up to 1 cup)
Lemon (1)
Clam juice (2 cups)
Minced clams, drained (1 cup)
Chicken bouillon, clear, light (up to 1 cup)

Dry sherry (up to 2 Tbs)
Salt, coarse crystal, to taste
Black pepper, freshly ground, to taste
Scallion, finely minced (for garnish)

Active Preparation 15 Minutes, Plus Chilling for Several Hours or Overnight
Cut one of the avocadoes in half, remove the stone and, with a small melon scoop, dig out and hold 8 balls for later garnishing. Put the clove of garlic into the Cuisinart bowl and mash it completely by running the steel blades for about 3 to 5 seconds. Now add the remaining flesh of all the avocadoes, spooned out of the shells, with ½ cup of the cream, 1 tablespoon of juice squeezed from the lemon and 1 cup of the clam juice. Run the steel blades until all this is just smoothly creamed (if avocado is overemulsified, it begins to lose its flavor) — usually in no more than 2 to 3 seconds. Transfer the cream to a large mixing bowl.

Without rinsing the Cuisinart bowl, put in the second cup of clam juice and the cup of clams, running the steel blades until the mixture is perfectly smooth — usually in about 5 seconds. Add this to the avocado cream and blend together thoroughly. Now put this combined mixture back into the Cuisinart bowl in batches of not more than two cups at a time, gradually working in ¼ cup of the cream and ¾ cups of the bouillon. Churn each batch for about 12 seconds until the mixture is completely smooth — almost fluffy. Now combine everything in a covered storage bowl, taste and adjust the flavor and texture by blending in, tablespoon by tablespoon, as your judgment dictates, up to the 2 tablespoons of sherry, up to another ¼ cup each of the cream and bouillon, more lemon juice, plus salt and pepper. The final consistency should be that of heavy cream. Completely chill the soup, covered, in the refrigerator before serving in chilled bowls, each garnished with 2 avocado balls and some bits of the scallion.

ICED CREAM OF WATERCRESS

(for 4)

Chicken bouillon (up to 2¼ cups)   Salt, coarse crystal, to taste
Clam juice (2 cups)   Egg yolks (2)
Potatoes, peeled (3 or 4 medium)   Light cream (up to ½ cup)
Watercress (4 bunches)   Chives, snipped (about 1 tsp)
Scallion bulbs, trimmed (8)   Parsley, chopped (about 1 tsp)

**Active Preparation About 25 Minutes, Plus 15 Minutes
of Unsupervised Simmering**
Put into a 2½-quart saucepan 2 cups each of the chicken bouillon and the clam juice, then heat them up, not too quickly, just to the boiling point. While waiting, slice 3 of the potatoes with the Cuisinart medium slicing disk. This should give you about 2 cups of slices. If not, use the fourth potato. Rinse and dry the Cuisinart work bowl and put in the first 2 large bunches of watercress, including all but the toughest of the stalks, then run the steel blades until the cress is coarsely chopped, starting and stopping in 1-second bursts and, if necessary, scraping the sides of the bowl down with a spatula – usually in about four or five bursts. Transfer the chopped cress to a covered storage dish and hold it. Without rinsing the Cuisinart bowl, put in the 8 scallion bulbs, then start and stop the steel blades in 1-second bursts until the bulbs are fairly finely minced – usually in about 3 to 4 bursts. The moment the liquid in the saucepan begins to bubble, add the potatoes, the chopped watercress and scallions, with salt, to taste, then keep simmering, covered, until the potatoes are quite soft – usually in about 15 minutes.

Meanwhile, entirely cut off the tough stalks from the 2 last bunches of watercress (the leaves will be used as the crisp green filling of the soup.) The leaves must be handled as little as possible until the last moment before serving if they are to hold their bright color and freshness. Put the leaves in a plastic bag in the crisper of the refrigerator and hold them there. In a small bowl, quickly beat the 2 egg yolks

75

with ¼ cup of the cream and hold the mixture, covered. As soon as the potatoes are soft, purée the soup in the Cuisinart work bowl, in batches of not more than 2 cups each, running the steel blades until it is all a smooth cream – usually in about 4 to 7 seconds. Transfer each puréed batch back into the saucepan. When the last batch is in the Cuisinart bowl, while the motor is still running, pour in through the cover chimney the egg yolks and cream, churning them in for a final 2 seconds. When this last batch is safely back in the saucepan, turn on a fairly gentle heat under it and, stirring continuously, but never letting the saucepan boil, keep everything turning until the eggs have given body and richness to the soup. Taste and adjust the seasonings. If the soup becomes too thick, add, tablespoon by tablespoon, up to another ¼ cup of the cream and if necessary, more bouillon. When it is dead right, transfer it to a covered storage pot and chill it in the refrigerator for at least 3 or 4 hours, or, much better, overnight.

A few minutes before serving, pull out 4 neat garnishing sprigs from the stored bunches of watercress and hold them. Put the bunches into the Cuisinart bowl and chop them fairly coarsely, exactly as with the first 2 bunches. Finally check the ice-cold soup and adjust its flavor and texture. Then stir in the freshly chopped watercress. Garnish each chilled bowl with a sprig of watercress and a few snippets of chives and parsley leaves.

SMOOTH SAUCES ALMOST WITHOUT STIRRING

The ubiquitous French-style béchamel white sauce is perhaps the perfect example of how the machine has revolutionized this department of the kitchen. All of us amateur cooks, in the course of our years in the kitchen, must have spent literally hundreds of hours working at our béchamels. First, there is the slow stirring and incorporation of the flour, bit by bit, into the melted butter. Then, more slow stirring as the milk is added, dash by dash, for many minutes, until it all thickens. Finally, there is more intermittent stirring while the sauce cooks for anything between 30 minutes and an hour. What a waste of effort and time, now that there is a far, far better way. The next recipe shows how it can all be done in only a tenth of the time. Later recipes, in this section, are designed to demonstrate the basic principles of cold and hot sauces with the Cuisinart unit. Once you have mastered these principles, you can adapt any sauce to the new techniques. Or you can invent your own.

THE NEW-STYLE BÉCHAMEL WHITE SAUCE

(1 cup)

Flour (2 Tbs) all-purpose   **Whole milk (1 cup)**
Butter (2 Tbs)

Active Preparation 5 Minutes
Sprinkle around the bottom of the Cuisinart bowl the 2 tablespoons of flour. Drop down onto the flour the 2 tablespoons of butter in small chunks. Run the steel blades for 2 seconds, just to amalgamate these two ingredients. Add the cup of milk and again run the steel blades for 5 seconds. The butter and flour will be evenly incorporated throughout the milk in tiny little balls and there will probably be a lumpy foam on top of the liquid. All this will quickly melt away. Transfer the mixture to a 1-pint saucepan and now, because of the complete amalgamation, you can use fairly high heat with very little preliminary stirring. As the liquid begins to approach the boiling point and shows the first signs of thickening, start stirring continuously until the sauce has reached the required thickness – usually in a matter of 10 seconds. Remove the saucepan at once from the heat, give it about 5 seconds more of steady stirring and you will have the quickest and smoothest béchamel you have ever made – ready to be seasoned and garnished according to the recipe or in any way that pleases you.

QUICK HOME-MADE GREEN OR ROSY MAYONNAISE

(about 2 cups – keeps, refrigerated, about 1 week)

We always think, frankly, that the standard yellow mayonnaise looks just a bit sickly. We prefer to color ours, either green with spinach, or rosy red with tomato, either one smoothly puréed in the Cuisinart after the mayonnaise is made. You can make mayonnaise in three colors and then create decorative designs worthy of Picasso!

Egg yolks, large (3)   **Black pepper, freshly ground,**
Salt, fine grind, to taste   **to taste**

Mustard, English dry powdered
(about 2 tsps)
Lemon juice (½ lemon)
Vinegar, Spanish Sherry wine
(about 2 tsps)
Oil, for bland flavor use peanut,
for strong, best quality olive
(up to 1½ cups)

For the green color:
Spinach, fresh leaves, no stalks
(¼ lb) or frozen spinach
(½ standard 10 oz package)

Assortment of dried or fresh
herbs: basil, chives, dill, parsley,
tarragon (½ tsp dried or 2 tsps
fresh leaf)

For the rosy red coloring:
Tomato paste (3 Tbs)
Same assortment of herbs

Active Preparation About 10 Minutes

Place 3 egg yolks in the Cuisinart bowl without breaking them and add ½ teaspoon of fine-grind salt, a few grinds of pepper, 1 teaspoon each of the English mustard and French Dijon mustard, and 1 teaspoon each of the freshly squeezed lemon juice and Spanish Sherry wine vinegar. Turn the blades on and off almost instantly just to break the egg yolks. Even 2 seconds is too much – if the yolks are beaten too long at this point, they may disintegrate. Fill a 1-cup measuring pitcher with the oil. Remove the pusher from the chimney, start the motor, and immediately begin pouring in the oil in a thin steady stream. Stop the motor the moment it is all in. Add, as you please, more or all of the aromatic ingredients: salt, pepper, English or French mustard, lemon juice, or vinegar. Blend in each addition with a one-second burst of the blades, and taste again. Then, adjust the texture of the mayonnaise by pouring down the chimney while the blades are whirling as much more of the oil as you need, and finally blend in 1 tablespoon of hot water to smooth and bind it.

To Color the Mayonnaise Green: Spoon the mayonnaise from the work bowl into a suitably sized mixing bowl. Rinse and dry the work bowl. Bring a pint of water up to boiling in a 1-quart saucepan. As soon as it starts bubbling, put in ¼ lb of fresh, young spinach leaves plus an assortment of a sprig or two each of aromatic herbs, such as basil, chives, dill, parsley, or tarragon. Let them boil for exactly 1 minute, then at once drain off the water. As soon as the leaves are cool enough to handle, squeeze out the remaining water with your clean fingers and drop the leaves into the Cuisinart bowl. Whirl until they are absolutely smoothly puréed, almost the texture of a cream – usually in 5 to 7 seconds. Gently blend this cream, ¼ cup by ¼ cup, into the mayonnaise with a wooden spoon. Never beat the mayonnaise or stir it violently. Continue until you have exactly the color you want. Then spoon the green mayonnaise into a tightly-lidded refrigerator storage jar. You do not, of course, have to color all the original mayonnaise. You can store some of it in its bright-yellow state.

To Color the Mayonnaise Rosy Red: Use 3 tablespoons of tomato paste in place of the spinach, but include the same five aromatic herbs. This time, no boiling is necessary. Drop the tomato paste into the Cuisinart bowl together with the five herbs. Whirl until everything is puréed to a smooth cream – usually in 5 to 8 seconds. Blend this rosy cream, ¼ cup by ¼ cup, into the yellow mayonnaise until it has just the degree of pinkness you like.

JOE'S SUPER-RICH TEXAS RANCH-STYLE BARBECUE SAUCE

(about 5 cups)

Our friend, Joe, is very fussy about the sauce with which he bastes his beef at his big grill on the terrace of his ranch outside Forth Worth. He insists that, after it is made, it must mature for at least a week before being used.

Onions, peeled and chunked
  (2, large)
Garlic, unpeeled (3 cloves)
Butter (1¾ cups or 3½ sticks)
Italian plum tomatoes (one 1-lb
  can)
Chile sauce (1 cup)
Lemon juice, freshly squeezed
  (2 Tbs)
Vinegar, preferably Spanish
  Sherry, or tarragon wine (2 Tbs)

Worcestershire sauce, preferably
  Lea & Perrins (¼ cup)
Honey (3 Tbs)
Chile powder (2 Tbs)
Oregano, dried (2 tsp)
Allspice seeds, whole (2 tsp)
Salt, coarse crystal, to taste
Black pepper, freshly ground,
  to taste
Tabasco, to taste

Active Preparation About 15 Minutes, Plus About 45 Minutes of Unsupervised Boiling, Then Seven Days of Ripening

Put the onion chunks into the Cuisinart bowl, starting and stopping the steel blades until they are fairly coarsely chopped – usually in about 3 to 5 seconds. Transfer them to a covered storage dish and hold. Now mince fairly finely in the Cuisinart bowl the 3 cloves of garlic – usually in about 2 to 3 one-second bursts. Set a large, deep iron frypan on medium-high frying heat and melt in it the 1¾ cups of butter (using butter in place of oil is, according to Joe, "one of my secret tricks") and, as soon as the butter is "good 'n' hot," but certainly not browning, burning, or smoking, put in all at once the chopped onions and minced garlic, stirring them around "plenty," until they are nicely golden – usually in about 4 or 5 minutes. At that moment, add to the frypan and stir in, ingredient by ingredient: the pound of tomatoes, the cup of chile sauce, 2 tablespoons of the lemon juice, the 2 tablespoons of vinegar, the ¼ cup of Worcestershire Sauce, the 3 tablespoons of honey, the 2 tablespoons of chile powder, the 2 teaspoons of oregano, the 2 teaspoons of allspice, plus salt, pepper, and Tabasco to taste. Let it all bubble merrily (uncovered, of course) to reduce and thicken, blending and sharpening the flavors, for about 45 minutes. Stir it occasionally. Then, allow it to cool slightly and pass it through the Cuisinart machine, batch by batch, not more than 2 cups at a time, until it is a "still-slightly-bitty but nicely-smooth" sauce – usually in about 2 to 4 seconds per batch. Joe's final secret is to transfer it to a covered pot in the refrigerator and hold it for about 7 days before using it to baste barbecued, roasted or rotissed meats. JOE'S VARIATIONS: For chicken, Joe uses only half of a large onion and 1 clove of garlic. For charcoal-broiled steaks, he sautées 2½ cups of whole button mushrooms in butter and adds them to the sauce just before grilling, along with 2 ounces of dark rum or brandy.

5

Easy, Fast, Simple Casseroles and Everyday Family Dishes

We sometimes think that too many families have too small a repertoire of regular, everyday meals. When we visit them on Sunday, they are always having roast beef – always fried fish on Friday – always leg of lamb with rice on Wednesday. When our children were still at home, we were all so keen on trying new things that we kept a card index of rating scores for new recipes tried that showed which dishes we grew to like the best and which were most often demanded to be repeated. We have chosen the following recipes from our master list of five-star family menus. Each, of course, has been completely revised to the efficiency and speed of the Cuisinart preparation. Each of these dishes, when accompanied by a salad, some crusty bread, cheese and fruit, makes a whole and wholesome meal.

OUR BEST AND QUICKEST CORNED BEEF HASH

(for 4)

We like our hash neither too dry nor too wet. Our Southern friends give it to us as firm and solid as a fried omelette. In California, it comes so runny with juice that it has to be served in a soup bowl. This is our favorite compromise between these two extremes – a moist and flavorful kind of meat and potato pudding, made interesting and unusual by the subtle fruitiness of the added wine.

This is one of the simplest of all recipes. You need only the Cuisinart machine to do the chopping and mashing, a large mixing bowl for the assembly of all the ingredients and an open baking dish to go into the oven.

81

Yellow onions, peeled and
  quartered (2 medium)
Green pepper, quartered, cored,
  and seeded (1 medium)
Potatoes, boiled, peeled and
  chunked (4 medium)
Milk (1 cup)
White wine, dry (¼ cup)
Eggs (2)

Butter (3 Tbs)
Salt, coarse crystal, to taste
Black pepper, freshly ground,
  to taste
Corned beef, fresh or canned,
  broken or cut into bite-sized
  pieces (1 lb)
Thyme (1 tsp dried or 1 Tbs fresh)

Preparation in Just About 15 Minutes, Plus About 1 Hour of Unsupervised Baking

Preheat the oven to 350°F. Into the Cuisinart bowl put the quartered onions and green pepper, then whirl the steel blades until they are fairly finely chopped – usually in about three 1-second starts and stops. Transfer these choppings to the mixing bowl. Next, without rinsing the bowl, put in the 4 chunked potatoes, ¾ cup of the milk, the ¼ cup of wine, the 2 whole eggs, lightly beaten together, 2 table-spoons of the butter, plus salt and pepper, to taste. Whirl the blades until you have a wettish mash, but be very careful not to overrun, or you will get a sticky paste – usually 4 or 5 seconds is all that is needed. Transfer the mash to the mixing bowl. Add to it the pound of chunked corned beef. If you are using fresh thyme, coarsely chop the leaves by running them through the rinsed and dried Cuisinart bowl for just about 1 second, then add them to the mixing bowl. Dried thyme, obviously, does not need to be chopped. Mix everything thoroughly with a wooden spoon and taste once more, adjusting the seasonings, if necessary. It should all be rather sloppy-wet. If it does not seem to be quite wet enough, add a dash or two more of the milk. Liberally butter your baking dish, pour the hash into it and bake until everything has the consistency of a nicely moist pudding – usually in about an hour. Serve at once on very hot plates, preferably accom-panied by a refreshing green salad.

OUR JUICIEST AND TENDEREST POT ROAST OF CHICKEN

(for 4)

For the ideal result, the chicken must be tightly enclosed within its hot steam bath by a casserole with a very well-fitting lid. The best, for this particular purpose, are the French enameled cast-iron, which can be used both on top of the stove and in the oven and are handsome enough to be brought directly to the dining table. We usually accompany this lovely chicken with a purée of briefly cooked vegetables – say, green beans, carrots, onions, white turnips, etc., all whipped together in the Cuisinart a few seconds before serving.

Lemon (1)

Chicken, capon, roaster, whole (about 3½ lbs)

Butter, unsalted (6 ozs or 1½ sticks)

Parsley, fresh, leaves only (enough to make ⅓ cup, chopped)

Tarragon (2 tsp dried, or 2 Tbs fresh)

Breadcrumbs, white (¼ cup)

Egg (1)

Salt, coarse crystal, to taste

Black pepper, freshly ground, to taste

Olive oil, best quality (about 1 Tbs)

Preparation in About 20 Minutes, Plus up to 1½ Hours of Entirely Unsupervised Baking

Cut the lemon in half and use it to clean and refresh the chicken by firmly rubbing the cut side all over the outside skin and around the inside of the cavity. Then let the chicken rest at room temperature while you prepare the aromatic herb flavoring paste in the Cuisinart work bowl. Put into its bowl: the 4-ounce stick of butter, sliced, enough parsley leaves to fill ¼ cup, the 2 tablespoons of fresh tarragon leaves (or 1 tablespoon of dried), the ¼ cup of breadcrumbs, the whole egg, plus salt and pepper, to taste. Whirl the steel blades until they are all blended to a smooth paste – usually in 4 or 5 seconds. Now gently lift the breast skin of the chicken, being careful not to tear it, and then slide underneath several spoonfuls of the herb butter. Rub more of the butter all over the skin of the bird. Then the remaining butter can be rubbed around the walls of the inside cavity. Put the two halves of the lemon inside the chicken as well. Let it rest while you heat up the casserole.

Set the casserole over fairly gentle frying heat and put in the remaining ½ stick of butter and the tablespoon of olive oil. Bear in mind that the secret of this recipe is that all the cooking should be done extremely slowly. Truss the chicken with string or by pinning back its wings and legs with small trussing skewers. As soon as the casserole is reasonably hot, put in the chicken on its side and gently gild that side by pressing down on it here and there and rocking the chicken, so that the hot fats reach every possible nook and cranny. The gilding is usually completed within about 4 or 5 minutes. Turn the chicken over and repeat the operation on the other side. Then turn over the chicken once more and put on the tight lid, lowering the heat to the equivalent of the gentlest simmering. You are not so much poaching the chicken as steaming it in its own juices. Turn the bird over every 30 minutes and keep it going at its gentlest temperature until the flesh is perfectly done, the leg joints loose, the skin crisp and beautifully browned. This usually takes from 1¼ to 1½ hours. You will find the flesh so juicy and tender that you may never want to cook a chicken in any other way. No extra sauce is needed beyond the juices from the casserole. Snip the remaining parsley over the chicken for decorative color.

A CHICKEN LIVER AND MUSHROOM *QUICHE*

(for 4)

Once upon a time, a *quiche* was simply an appetizer tart of bacon or ham, with cheese and an egg custard – virtually unknown outside the French region of Alsace-Lorraine. Today the *quiche* idea has "caught on" around the world, so that it is now OK to fill it with virtually anything imaginable and to serve it as any part of the meal, from the appetizer to the main dish. This is an attractive and simple main-course supper *quiche*. At least 3 or 4 hours before you start preparing it, you should whirl together in your Cuisinart work bowl a batch of the butter dough for the crust of the tart (see recipe on page 86).

Pie pastry, prepared in advanced
and refrigerated, see above
(1 batch)
Mushrooms, wiped clean, left
whole (½ lb)
Shallots, whole and unpeeled
(5 cloves)
Butter, unsalted (8 Tbs)

Safflower oil or vegetable
alternative (2 Tbs)
Salt, coarse crystal, to taste
Black pepper, freshly ground,
to taste
Chicken livers, trimmed and cut
into bite-size pieces (½ lb)
Eggs (4)
Light cream (1½ cups)

84

Active Work of Preparation About 1¼ Hours, Plus About Another 2 Hours for Resting the Pastry and Baking the *Quiche*

For our *quiches,* we use the outstanding Belgian 10-inch, blue steel pans with fluted sides and removable bottoms. Take the previously made, chilled pastry out of the refrigerator and, on a floured board in the usual way, roll it out into a circle just about ¼ inch thick and line the *quiche* pan. Wrap it and refrigerate it for an hour.

Meanwhile, start the preparations for the filling. Chunk the mushrooms and put half of them into the Cuisinart bowl, chopping them fairly coarsely by whirling the steel blades for about 1 or 2 seconds. Transfer them to a covered storage dish while you repeat the operation with the other half of the mushrooms. Combine both batches. Without rinsing out the Cuisinart bowl, put into it the 5 cloves of shallot (no need to peel them, the cooking will disintegrate the skins), then chop them finely – usually in about 3 to 5 seconds. Add the shallots to the mushrooms. Set an 11-inch sauté pan over fairly high frying heat and lubricate its bottom with 3 tablespoons of the butter and 1 tablespoon of the safflower oil. When quite hot, but certainly not browning or smoking, spread in the mushroom mixture and sauté it over high heat. After the water in the mushrooms has been evaporated off, the hissing will stop and the mushroom bits will become quite dry. At once turn off the heat, sprinkle on salt and pepper to your taste, then transfer the contents of the sauté pan to a covered storage dish and hold. Add 3 more tablespoons of the butter and the remaining tablespoon of safflower oil to the sauté pan and, again when it is quite hot, quickly sauté the chicken livers until they are prettily browned outside, but still nicely pink and soft inside – usually in 4 to 5 minutes. Add salt and pepper, to your taste. Transfer the livers to a second covered storage dish and hold them while you complete the baking of the pie shell.

About 10 minutes before bringing the *quiche* pan out of the refrigerator, preheat your oven to 400°F. Lightly prick the pastry bottom of the tart shell all over with a fork to release expanding air from underneath, so that the bottom will remain flat in the heat of the oven. Also, to weight it down, we line our tart shell with aluminum foil and place on top of it a layer of dry haricot beans or small glass marbles (or even raw rice). Bake at once until the pastry is set – usually in about 10 minutes. Next, remove the weighty filling and the foil and return the now uncovered pastry shell to the oven for just long enough to produce a crust which prevents the shell from absorbing moisture and becoming soggy — usually in just about 5 minutes more. Then let the pie shell cool for about 10 minutes. Reduce the oven temperature to 375°F.

During this short waiting period, mix the custard in the Cuisinart work bowl. Put in the 4 eggs and the 1½ cups of cream, with salt and pepper to your taste, but do not yet switch on the machine.

As soon as the tart shell is cool enough to touch, spread the chicken livers across its bottom and then fill in the spaces around and between the livers with the mushroom mixture. Press it all down to make a nicely level layer. Now whirl the steel blades for just about 3 seconds to churn and mix the custard, then remove the blades from the Cuisinart bowl and pour the custard directly over the livers and mushrooms in the *quiche*. Finally, dot the top surface with the remaining 2 tablespoons of butter. Slide the *quiche* into the center of the oven and bake it until the top is nicely browned and puffy and the shiny knife test shows that the custard is thoroughly set — usually in about 30 to 45 minutes. After bringing it out of the oven, you should allow it to cool for about 10 minutes before serving it, to give both the custard and the pastry the chance to set.

LIGHTNING ALL-PURPOSE CUISINART PASTRY DOUGH FOR PIE, *QUICHE*, AND TART SHELLS

(one 9 or 10-inch shell)

We have a deep and devious plan in making this the first pastry recipe of our book. It is simple and straightforward. It will show you precisely how pastry-making works in the Cuisinart machine If you have never done it before, you will hardly be able to believe your eyes. Remembering all the hand-kneading, pinching, rubbing, and mixing that you have done in the past, you will watch with amazement the almost-instant formation of the "niblet corn" and the almost-magical appearance of the single ball of dough riding up under its own momentum on to the top of the whirling blades. It is nothing less than the production of a live rabbit out of an empty hat!

Flour, all-purpose white, unsifted
  (1¾ level cups)
Salt, fine-grind (1 tsp)
Butter, unsalted, cold, thinly sliced
  (6 oz, or 1½ sticks)

Solid vegetable shortening,
  preferably natural soybean
  margarine, cold, coarsely
  chunked (1 oz or 2 Tbs)
Ice water (about ¼ cup)

Preparation in Just About 2 Minutes, Plus at least 2 Hours of Chilling

First, place a small pitcher for the ice water, (a creamer will do nicely) in the freezer to chill. Measure the flour by dipping the measuring cup directly into the bag or crock and then leveling the cup off with the back of a knife. The sifting is done by the whirling blades. Spread the 1¾ cups of flour and the teaspoon of salt across the bottom of the Cuisinart work bowl with the steel blades in place and whirl for a single one-second burst just to sift the ingredients. Then neatly spread or sprinkle around on the floury bed, the sliced butter and the chunked margarine (or alternative). Start the machine, run it for exactly 1 second, then stop it, take off the lid and inspect the mixture. You are shooting for the complete and even incorporation of the fats into the powders, resulting in the formation of little balls rather like niblet corn. The speed at which they are formed depends on the precise temperature of the fat and flour, so the timing may be different by an odd second or so each time. This is why you must continuously inspect the mixture. If 1 second has not done it put back the lid and run the machine for exactly 1 more second. Inspect again. In our machine at our refrigerator and kitchen temperature, we usually reach the niblet stage in three 1-second bursts. Beyond this, be very careful indeed. If you overrun the machine, you will have a sticky mess and you would be wise to start over.

When you have good niblets, carefully measure ¼ cup of ice water into the ice-cold pitcher. Remove the pusher from the chimney of the Cuisinart cover, restart the motor and at once begin pouring the ice water in a steady trickle down the chimney. Watch closely for the almost-magical transformation when the dough suddenly unites into a single ball that rides up onto the top of the blades. If this happens before you have finished pouring the ice water, stop pouring instantly. Too much water will make the dough soggy and unmanageable.

Usually, however, the single ball forms about 5 seconds after all the ¼ cup of ice water is in. Stop the machine at once. Its job is done.

Transfer the ball of dough to a lightly floured marble, wooden or plastic pastry board. Knead the dough lightly with the heel of your hand for not much more than 1 minute. Dust your hands with a minimum of flour to prevent the dough from sticking to you. However, if too much extra flour gets worked into the dough, both from the board and your hands, the pastry will toughen. Press your fingers into the center of the dough and push down with the heel of your hand moving the dough away from you as if you were smearing it. Keep turning the disk of dough a quarter circle at a time as you knead, folding it over every few seconds, to be sure you are pressing and smearing every part of it. The objective, of course, is to work the fat more thoroughly into the flour. After about 1 minute of quick and continuous movements, the dough will begin to feel elastic and satiny smooth. Shape it at once into a thick, round slab, very lightly sprinkle it with a bit more flour, wrap it with plastic or wax paper and set it in the coldest part of your refrigerator for at least 2 hours, or, even better, overnight. Then the dough is ready to be rolled out as described in the previous recipe.

A FAMILY CASSEROLE FROM INDIA–
PAN-ROASTED LAMB WITH GARLIC AND GINGER

(for 4 to 6)

When we go to an Indian restaurant in New York, Washington, Chicago, or San Francisco, the menus are always full of Moglai dishes, so-called because they were part of the menus of the Mogul emperors. But what about a Sunday dinner of an average working family in, say, Bombay, Calcutta, or New Delhi? Restaurants generally deny us the people-to-people gastronomic contact with other cultures. Here is an everyday Indian family recipe brought to me by a Bengali friend who is an excellent amateur cook. This spicy way of pan-roasting lamb is so good and so simple that it has become a regular favorite in our family. It uses one extraordinary and rather rare herb: the fresh leaves of the coriander plant from which the well-known coriander seeds come. Fresh leaf coriander can often be found in Chinese, Indian, or Spanish grocery stores. If you cannot find it, you can replace it in the recipe by fresh leaves of better known herbs, such as basil, tarragon, or thyme.

Lamb, lean, cut by butcher into
  1-inch cubes, best from leg
  (2 lbs)
Ginger (¾-inch piece of fresh root,
  or ¾ tsp dried, ground)
Garlic, unpeeled (2 cloves)
Coriander leaves, fresh, if available
  (about 7 leaves) (if coriander
  not available, replace by the
  same amount of fresh leaves,
  in season, of basil, tarragon,
  or thyme, see above)

Lemon (½)
Oil, corn, peanut, or safflower
  (2 tsps)
Salt, coarse crystal, to taste
Black pepper, freshly ground,
  to taste

Active Work of Preparation About 10 Minutes, Plus 2 Hours of Marination and About 1¼ Hours of Unsupervised Roasting

Put the lamb cubes into a mixing bowl with a fair amount of room to spare. Put into the Cuisinart bowl the piece of fresh ginger, chunked, the 2 garlic cloves, unpeeled, the coriander leaves (or alternative), the squeezed juice of the ½ lemon, the 2 teaspoons of oil, with salt and pepper to taste. An Indian cook would make it fairly peppery. Whirl the steel blades until all this is churned into a finely chopped blend – usually in 3 to 5 seconds. (If the mixture sticks to the sides of the bowl, stop the machine and scrape it back down). Using a spatula and a wooden spoon, thoroughly amalgamate this aromatic mixture with the lamb cubes. (If you are using dry, ground ginger, sprinkle it, at this point, directly onto the meat.) Make sure that each piece of lamb is covered by the aromatic mix. Cover the bowl and let its contents marinate at room temperature for about 2 hours.

About 10 minutes before you are ready to go ahead, preheat your oven to 350°F. Choose an open, shallow roasting pan large enough to hold all the meat in a single layer – ours is 12 x 8 x 2 inches deep. Spoon the lamb cubes into it, taking care to transfer all the spice mix as well, and spread everything evenly across the pan. Cover the pan with foil and set it in the center of the oven, leaving it to roast without stirring it even once for 1 hour. Then remove the foil and roast for ½ hour more. By this time, the lamb should be very tender and there should be excellent liquid juices. If the lamb is not quite tender enough, leave it in the oven for another 10 minutes. Serve it on a bed of rice, which will nicely absorb the aromatic juices.

PICK-'EM YOURSELF GRILLED SHRIMP IN AROMATIC BUTTER

(for 4)

For years and years, this has been our family's favorite way of preparing shrimp. Besides the simplicity and speed of preparation, its attraction, especially for our children, has always been the picnic atmosphere at the table with everyone picking up the shrimp by their tails. In those days, we did not have the Cuisinart. Now the making of the aromatic sauce is a matter of a few seconds.

Jumbo shrimps, in their shells (1½ lbs)
Flour, all-purpose (6 Tbs)
Salt, coarse crystal, to taste
Butter, salted (8 Tbs)
Olive oil, fine quality (¼ cup)
Garlic, unpeeled, whole (3 cloves)

Parsley, fresh leaf (enough for ¼ cup, chopped)
Madeira, dry Sercial (¼ cup)
Clam juice (8-oz bottle)
Lemon (1)
Black pepper, freshly ground, to taste

Preparation in About 25 Minutes from Start to Serving

Preheat your broiler to medium-high temperature and set the shelf so that the top surface of the shrimp in their pan will be about 3 inches below the heat. Wash the shrimp, pull off their legs and peel off the main parts of the shells, but leave the tails firmly attached. Devein the shrimp under running cold water, then dry them and hold them. Spread 4 tablespoons of the flour evenly across a large dinner plate, then lightly sprinkle it all over with a teaspoon of the salt. For our broiling, we use an enameled cast-iron *au gratin* dish 10 inches across, but a pie pan or plate will do. Put into it 4 tablespoons of the butter and the ¼ cup of oil, then set it under the broiler to get hot, but watch it carefully to make sure that the butter does not brown or burn. Meanwhile, lightly dip the shrimp in the flour and, as soon as the grilling pan is good and hot, arrange them neatly in the hot fat, making sure that each is well coated all around. Put the pan back under the broiler and broil until the shrimp are beautifully pink and their flesh is just opaque. Under our broiler, it takes about 8 minutes, but the first time you try it, it would be wise to taste a bit of one of the shrimp.

In the old days, before the Cuisinart machine, it would sometimes be a bit of a struggle to have the sauce done within those 8 minutes. Now, there is time to spare. Put into the Cuisinart bowl the 3 cloves of garlic, whole and unpeeled, plus the parsley with its tough stalks removed, then run the machine until they are finely chopped – usually in 3 or 4 seconds. Now add to the bowl the ¼ cup of Madeira, the remaining 2 tablespoons of flour and 2 more tablespoons of the butter. Whirl the steel blades until this is a smooth and completely blended paste – usually in 3 to 5 seconds. Transfer this paste to a 1-quart saucepan and gently heat it, stirring it continuously, over medium-low temperature. In a second saucepan, of 1-pint capacity, heat up the clam juice to just below boiling point. As soon as the garlic paste in the larger saucepan has melted and is thickening, begin working into it the hot clam juice, tablespoon by tablespoon, using only enough to produce a smooth, satiny sauce, slightly thicker than heavy cream. Adjust the heat so that it gently simmers. Add, squeeze by squeeze, enough lemon juice to give the sauce a nicely acid flavor – usually, to our taste, about a tablespoon. Also add salt and pepper. Keep the sauce gently simmering, stirring it now and then, until the broiling of the shrimp is almost completed. At the last moment before pouring it over the shrimp, stir into the sauce the remaining 2 tablespoons of butter, at the same time tasting it and, if needed, adjusting the lemon juice and the seasonings. Take the pan out from under the broiler, turn up the broiler to its highest temperature and raise the grill shelf so that the shrimp, when they go back under, will now be about 2 inches below the heat. Give the sauce a final stir and pour it over the shrimp, making sure that it covers every one of them. Put the pan back under the broiler for a final 2 or 3 minutes, until the sauce is bubbling and the shrimp are just lightly flecked with brown. Watch carefully that they do not overcook. Lay them at once on a bed of rice on very hot plates. Eat the shrimp by picking them up by their tails. (Incidentally, don't worry about the amount of garlic in this recipe – a good part of its flavoring oil evaporates during the cooking. In fact, as you get to know this marvelous dish, you may even want to add more garlic at the start.)

EMERGENCY SCRATCH-MEAL SALMON LOAF WITH CUCUMBER OLIVE WINE SAUCE

(for 4)

This is for the emergency – when you are faced with preparing a meal at the last moment. You were going out to dinner with friends. They call to say that there has been an accident and the dinner has to be cancelled. You don't feel like going out to the corner restaurant. For just such an emergency, we always keep a large can of salmon on the shelf. But, then, we don't just turn it out boringly into a salad. We make something sparkling of it with, for example, this casserole trick with refrigerator staples and this uplifting sauce.

Yellow onions, peeled and
   chunked (2 medium)
Celery, green Pascal, destringed,
   chunked, with leaves (4 sound
   stalks)
Saltine crackers (12)
Eggs, whole (2)
Milk (1 cup)
Salmon, best sockeye, Chinook,
   or Coho (1 lb can)
Salt, coarse crystal, to taste

Black pepper, freshly ground,
   to taste
Butter (2½ Tbs)
Cucumber, peeled (1 medium)
Black olives, pitted, drained
   (about 20, according to size)
Lemon juice and rind (1)
Flour, all-purpose (1 Tbs)
White wine, very light and dry
   (1 cup)
Egg yolks (2)

Preparation in Just About 50 Minutes from Start to Serving
Preheat your oven to 350°F. This recipe is simplicity itself. Simply let the Cuisinart machine do the chopping and assemble all the ingredients for the loaf in a large mixing bowl. Put into the Cuisinart bowl the 2 chunked onions with the 4 chunked celery stalks and their leaves, then start and stop the steel blades in one-second bursts until they are not-too-finely chopped – usually in 2 or 3 bursts. Transfer the vegetables to the mixing bowl. Rinse and dry the Cuisinart work bowl and put in the 12 saltines, whirling the blades until they are a fairly fine powder – usually in 2 to 3 seconds. Transfer them to the mixing bowl. Without rinsing the Cuisinart work bowl, put in the 2 whole eggs and the cup of milk, whirling the blades for not more than 2 seconds, just to blend and churn them. Transfer the liquid to the mixing bowl. Now coarsely flake the drained salmon into the mixing bowl and, according to the saltiness of the fish, add salt and pepper, to taste. Mix everything thoroughly and put it all into a buttered loaf pan, then set it, uncovered, of course, in the center of the oven and leave it to bake until it is firm enough to unmold and cut in slices – usually in 35 to 45 minutes.

Meanwhile, prepare the sauce. Fit the shredding disk into the Cuisinart bowl and, with the motor running, feed the cucumber and the 20 black olives down the cover chimney to shred them. Transfer them to a lidded storage dish and hold them. Rinse and dry the Cuisinart work bowl, now fitting it with the steel blades. Using a sharp potato peeler or a French zest scraper, thinly peel the yellow outer rind from the lemon into the work bowl and whirl the blades until the lemon is finely minced – usually in 3 or 4 seconds. Put the rind into a small container and hold. Then put in the Cuisinart work bowl the remaining 2 tablespoons of butter, coarsely chunked, the tablespoon of flour, and ¼ cup of the wine, whirling the blades for no more than 2 seconds or so to mix them lightly. Transfer the mixture to a 1½-pint saucepan, but hold it for the moment without heating it. Put the remaining ¾ cup of wine into a small saucepan and heat it up almost to boiling. Set the larger saucepan with the butter-flour mixture over medium heat and, stirring it continuously, warm it until it first softens then thickens. At this point, begin working into it, tablespoon by tablespoon, the remaining hot wine, until you have a satiny smooth sauce with about the consistency of heavy cream. You will almost certainly not use all the wine. Now salt the sauce to your taste. No pepper. Work in the minced lemon peel and enough lemon juice to give it a nice tangy flavor – usually from about half the lemon. Now work in the shredded cucumber and olives, then turn off the heat. In a small separate bowl, beat the 2 egg yolks until they show the first signs of frothing and become lemon colored. While continuing to beat, ladle into them a few tablespoons of the still-hot sauce. When the eggs have been slightly warmed up and diluted, beat them strongly into the sauce and return it to gentle heat, stirring it continuously, until the eggs thicken and give the sauce a richly solid base. If it becomes too thick, beat in a little more of the hot wine. Finally, taste it and, if needed, adjust its flavor with a few more spritzes from the other half of the lemon, plus possibly more salt.

Serve the salmon loaf in solid ½-inch slices, with the sauce poured over them.

6

Easy Basic Breads, Brawny Breakfast Elegance

We have already demonstrated how easily, efficiently, and swiftly the Cuisinart's blades amalgamate pastry doughs (the recipe on page 86). Now we enlarge the range of the machine's accomplishments to include basic bread doughs and elegant bran muffins for breakfast. Again, the following recipes are designed to establish basic principles. After you have mastered them, you will be able to adapt almost any normal recipe to the machine technique or, you will be able to invent your own.

60-MINUTE NATURAL HOT ROLLS

(a dozen rolls)

Before starting, you should reread the detailed and general instructions for mixing doughs (page 21) and for kneading and working doughs on the pastry board (page 88). You can, in fact, serve these rolls, all crispy and hot from the oven exactly 1 hour after you put the first cup of flour into the Cuisinart machine. Since the yeast temperature is quite crucial to the fast rising, you really should have a thermometer with a range of up to 125°F.

Milk (½ cup)
Flour, natural, unbleached,
   unsifted (2 level cups)
Sugar, natural, raw, or alternative
   (4 tsps)

Salt (½ tsp)
Yeast, granulated dry (1 envelope
   or 1 Tbs)
Butter, chilled (4 Tbs)

Total Mixing and Baking Time 1 Hour

In a 1-pint saucepan mix the ½ cup of milk with ¼ cup of water and set it over quite gentle heat, using the thermometer to bring the liquid to precisely 120°F. This control is absolutely essential. If the liquid is too cool, it will not bring the yeast to life. If it is too hot, it will kill the yeast stone dead and you will have to start over. With one eye on the thermometer, focus your other eye on the Cuisinart work bowl. Pour evenly around its bottom the 2 level cups of flour, sprinkle on top the 4 teaspoons sugar, the ½ teaspoon of salt and the yeast. Just start and stop the steel blades to mix and sift these dry ingredients. Now drop down on top of them, in small chunks or thin slices, 2 tablespoons of the butter. Whirl the steel blades until the butter is completely amalgamated with the flour in tiny little balls – usually in about 2 or 3 seconds. By this time, if you have been watching carefully with your other eye, the milk mixture should be precisely at 120°F. With the blades whirling, pour the warm milk in a steady stream through the chimney of the cover. Watch for the magic moment when the dough forms a ball which rides up on top of the blades – usually in 4 to 6 seconds. Transfer this neat ball of dough to the middle of your floured pastry board and knead it (as described on page 88) for not more than 2 minutes.

Grease a mixing bowl with about 1½ tablespoons of the remaining butter, roll the dough back into a ball and put it into the bowl, gently rolling it around so as to butter the entire surface. This prevents it from drying out and cracking. Cover the bowl with a towel. Now fill a larger bowl or pan with warm water, again measured with the thermometer at exactly 98°F. Set the bowl with the dough to rest in the bowl of warm water. This is the fast-rising trick. The dough should roughly double its volume in about 15 minutes. Then, we usually divide the dough, cutting and rolling it into our favorite shapes . . .

Butterflies: For a half-dozen, roll out a quarter of the dough on your floured board to a rectangle about 9 x 5 inches and about ¼ inch thick. Brush the top surface lightly with melted butter and cut the rectangle into 5 strips, each about 9 inches long and about 1 inch wide. Stack them on top of each other. Cut the stack every 1½ inches, butter six muffin tins and set one stack sideways in each. Again, lightly butter each stack and set it to rise before baking (see below).

Twists: Roll out another batch of the dough into a rectangle exactly

96

the same size as above. Again cut strips 9 inches long, but this time a shade less than ¾ inch wide. Tie each strip into loose bow knots and set them on a buttered cookie sheet. Let them rise before baking (see below).

Palm Leaves: Roll out another batch of the dough into a rectangle about 18 x 6 inches and ¼ inch thick. Fold each of the short sides over so that they almost (but not quite) meet in the center of the rectangle. Fold a second time in the same way so that you now have four thick-nesses on each side of the central division. Now fold at the center so that the 2 halves are on top of each other. Now treat this 6-inch length of folded dough as if it were a jelly roll, cutting it from its end into slices about ¾ inch thick. Each of these will expand into a "palm leaf." Set them on an ungreased baking sheet and let them rise before baking (see below).

Clovers: Roll another batch of the dough into separate balls, each just large enough to fit comfortably into a greased muffin pan, then, when it is nicely nested in the pan, arm yourself with a pair of kitchen scis-sors and make two criss-crossing cuts in the tops of the balls which will make them open out into 4-leaf clovers in the oven. Set them to rise before baking (see below).

Our own trick for encouraging the rolls to rise quickly is to turn on our oven to 500°F for exactly 1 minute, then turn off the heat, set all the rolls in it to rise and shut the oven door for about 15 minutes. (The oven will not, of course, have reached anywhere near 500°F in the short time it was on. But it will be at about the right temperature to make the rolls rise.) After the 15 minutes, take out all the rolls, pre-heat the oven to 425°F and put in the rolls to bake. (If you happen to have 2 ovens, you can leave the rolls to continue rising in the first one, while the second heats up.) Watch the different shapes of rolls. They will take slightly different times to reach a beautiful golden brown – on the average from about 12 to 15 minutes. Let the rolls cool slightly on racks while you wait to serve them.

NATURAL ITALIAN-STYLE BREAD

(2 standard loaves)

The method here is nearly the same as in the previous recipe, except that the finished dough must be chilled overnight in the refrigerator.

This excellent bread is not crispy-fluffy in the French style, but chewy-nutty as the Italians like it. Again, you will need a thermometer with a range of up to 125°F.

Flour, unbleached white (5 cups)
Salt (1 Tbs)
Sugar, natural, raw, or
   alternative (1 Tbs)
Yeast, granulated dry (2 packages
   or 2 Tbs)

Butter, chilled (1 Tbs)
Water, warm (2 cups)
Yellow cornmeal (1 Tbs)
Egg yolk (1)
Milk (2 Tbs)

Active Work of Preparation About 30 Minutes on the First Day, Overnight Chilling and About 40 Minutes for Baking on the Second Day

Spread around the bottom of the Cuisinart bowl, in turn: 2½ cups of the flour, unsifted, ½ tablespoon of the salt, ½ tablespoon of the sugar, and 1 package of the yeast. Whirl the steel blades for exactly 2 seconds to mix and sift these dry ingredients. Now drop in around the bowl, in small bits, ½ tablespoon of the butter. Start and stop the steel blades in one-second bursts until the butter is thoroughly amalgamated, usually in about 3 bursts. Warm 1 cup of the water, tested by the thermometer, to exactly 120°F, to bring the yeast to life. Start the machine and pour the water through the cover chimney in a small, steady stream. When the flour and water balance is exactly right, the usual large ball of dough will suddenly ride up on top of the blades. Complete the kneading by allowing this ball to spin around the bowl 50 times, usually in about 45 seconds. Your dough job is done.

Set the ball of dough at the center of your lightly floured board. Cover it with a sheet of plastic wrap and a towel, then let the wet dough rest and rise on the board for just about 20 minutes.

Meanwhile repeat the entire operation for the second ball of dough and let it rise alongside the first one.

Now, lightly flouring both your hands, take each ball of dough separately and roll it into a long loaf of about 15 inches. Taper the ends by giving them a little extra gentle back-and-forth rolling at an angle. Place both the loaves on a greased baking sheet (or, better still, one of those curved double-loaf pans which prevents the loaves from spreading out) that is generously sprinkled with fine yellow cornmeal. Cover the whole contraption with plastic wrap and set it in the refrigerator to chill and rise overnight, or for a full 24 hours.

On the next day, preheat your oven to 425°F. About 20 minutes before baking bring the loaves out of the refrigerator and unwrap them. Cut 4 diagonal slits, preferably with a razor, about ¼ inch deep in the top of each loaf. Set the loaves on their pan in the center of the oven and bake them for 10 minutes, just until they are set. Remove them from the pan and let them rest directly on the bars of the oven shelf, continuing to bake them until they are just beginning to brown – usually in about 10 minutes more. Meanwhile, in a small mixing bowl, beat together 1 egg yolk and 2 tablespoons of cold milk. As soon as the loaves are beginning to brown brush the top of each loaf with the egg mixture and put them back in the oven until they are browned and glazed – usually in about 5 to 10 minutes longer. Cool the loaves on racks to allow air to circulate all around them. A spare loaf can always be frozen for future use.

JOHN'S BRAWNY BREAKFAST BRAN MUFFINS

(for 12 large or 24 small muffins)

Our friend, John, a brilliant and highly experimental amateur cook, has taught us that with the help of the Cuisinart it is possible to enjoy the ultimate breakfast luxury – bran muffins hot from the oven, even on a day when you have to be in the office by 9:00. He has all the ingredients measured and ready the night before. He preheats his oven and whips up the dough in 10 minutes while sipping his first, wake-up cup of black coffee. The muffins bake for 25 minutes while he shaves and showers. Then he bites into their hot, natural flavors and strengthening, chewy textures to "get ready for it all," with more coffee and a glance at the morning paper. All his ingredients are planned for health and nutrition, while eliminating cholesterol-loaded butter and processed sugar. They include nutty bran for bulk, whole wheat flour, honey, nonfat milk, molasses, natural raisins and yoghurt.

Yoghurt, low-fat (½ cup)
Bran flakes, coarse, raw, natural (1½ cups)
Flour, whole wheat pastry, unsifted (¾ cup)

Flour, unbleached all-purpose, unsifted (¾ cup)
Milk powder, non-fat (½ cup)
Baking powder, double-acting (3 tsp)

Salt (1 tsp)	Honey (⅓ cup)
Oil, corn or safflower (6 Tbs)	Egg, whole, lightly beaten (1)
Molasses, dark sorghum (¼ cup)	Raisins, dark seedless (⅔ cup)

Active Preparation 10 Minutes, Plus 25 Minutes of Unsupervised Baking

In a small mixing bowl, beat together with a wire whisk ½ cup each of low-fat yoghurt and cold water. Measure 1½ cups of coarse, raw, natural bran flakes into a larger mixing bowl and thoroughly soak it with the yoghurt and water, stirring it around until it is a mush. Fit the plastic blades into the Cuisinart bowl and spread around its bottom: ¾ of a cup each of whole wheat pastry flour and unbleached all-purpose flour, both unsifted, ½ cup of nonfat dry skimmed milk powder, 3 teaspoons of double-acting baking powder and 1 teaspoon of salt. Whirl the plastic blades for just about 1 second to mix and sift these dry ingredients. Preheat the oven to 400°F. Now add the following ingredients, one by one, whirling the plastic blades for 2 seconds after each addition to mix it in: 4 tablespoons of the oil, ¼ cup of dark sorghum molasses, ⅓ cup of honey and 1 lightly beaten whole egg. Now whirl the blades for 10 seconds, until the batter is glutinous and smooth. Then add the bran mush all at once, and whirl the blades for about 10 more seconds. The batter will now be somewhat more liquid. Finally, add to the bowl ⅔ cup of dark seedless raisins, then turn the blades on and off just to distribute the raisins without cutting them up. Lightly oil 12- or 24-muffin pans (whichever you prefer) and fill each one about ¾ full with batter. Bake the muffins until they are bronze brown – usually in about 20 to 25 minutes. The moment the muffins are cool enough to handle, turn them out onto the serving dish. We find these so marvelously good that it would be a crime to put either butter or jam on them. As for the leftovers, they keep for at least 2 weeks in tightly lidded tins and make memorable midnight snacks. It seems to us that, although we are strictly from the city, we can taste the sunlight in the grain of these muffins as if we were prairie farmers a century ago.

7

Juicy, Flavorful Chopped (Not Ground) Beef – Ideas from Around the World

The Cuisinart chopper-churner is surely one of the most efficient of machines for the chopping – as against grinding, which tends to squeeze out the juice – of all kinds of meat. It is the automated equivalent of a skilled professional chef in your home chopping away with a super-sharp knife in each hand. So it follows naturally that, when you cut-and-chop your own beef, every dish you prepare with it is upgraded and uplifted to something better than you have had before. Chopped beef becomes one of the most important staples – most economical, most convenient, most time-saving, most appreciated as a simple everyday meal – of the repertoire of your cuisine. Here are some new ways – and some very old ones adapted to the new techniques, all dramatic and unusual – of bringing custom-chopped beef to your table. For some of these recipes you can buy the cheaper cuts, because the razor-sharp, scythe-shaped Cuisinart knives cut through the tough fibers, softening and tenderizing the lean flesh while chopping it. The result is a new experience in simple, everyday gastronomy.

THE RAW ELEGANCE OF CLASSIC STEAK TARTARE

(for 4)

When the Emperor Genghis Khan led his Tartar tribes on their 3,500-mile victorious march from Mongolia across Asia and into Europe, the irresistible power of his armies was said to be due to the fact that each man ate at least one meal per day of raw beef. Ever since, a dish of

101

well-spiced uncooked beef has always been called, on classic French menus, a Steak à la Tartare. Perfectly prepared, it is a great meal – solid protein, very healthy and strengthening – and it is our "secret weapon" for weight control. It is probably the most elegant dish with the fewest calories you could possibly find. *Esquire* recently published "The Perfect Recipe" but we have modified it slightly on the basis of a visit to Schellhase's, the famous German restaurant in Baltimore, where the great humorous American writer H. L. Mencken dined every Saturday night on a huge dish of what he called "cannibalia." If Mencken had owned a Cuisinart machine, I am sure he would have prepared it this way . . .

Parsley, fresh leaf (small handful)
Purple onion, peeled and chunked
  (1 medium)
Capers, drained (2 tsp)
Chives, fresh (enough for 2 tsp
  after chopping)
Dill, use only fresh fronds, in
  season, never dried (enough for
  1 tsp after chopping)
Mustard, French Dijon (2 tsp)
Olive oil, best quality virgin (2 tsp)
Anchovy fillets (2)

Beef, absolutely lean, cut by
  butcher into 1½-inch cubes, top
  round, rump, or sirloin (2 lbs)
Lemon juice, freshly squeezed
  (from ½ lemon)
Salt, coarse crystal, to taste
Black pepper, freshly ground,
  to taste
Cognac, fine quality (2 Tbs)
Paprika, Hungarian,
  medium-sweet (1 tsp)
Egg yolks, very fresh (4)

Prepared in About 15 Minutes from Start to Serving

Set the 4 serving plates in the freezer to get thoroughly cold. Leave the beef in the refrigerator while you prepare the aromatic garnishes. Put the parsley into the Cuisinart bowl and chop it, not too finely – usually in one second. Transfer it to a covered storage dish and hold it. Without rinsing out the Cuisinart bowl, put in the chunked onion and whirl the blades for one second, then add the two teaspoons of capers, the chives, and the fresh dill (if available; otherwise omit it) and whirl for one second more. Transfer the mixture to a covered storage dish and hold it. Again without rinsing out the Cuisinart bowl put in the 2 teaspoons each of mustard and olive oil, plus the two anchovy fillets, then whirl them for 2 seconds. Transfer to a covered storage dish and hold.

Now rinse and dry the Cuisinart bowl for the chopping of the beef.

On a largish wooden board, divide the beef cubes into four equal parts. Put the first into the Cuisinart bowl and run the steel blades for not an instant more than 4 seconds. The meat will have been chopped to exactly the right slightly coarse texture. Repeat the operation with the second, third and fourth parts of the beef. Combine the four parts of the meat into one. Spread it out on the board into a flat, circular disk, about ½ inch thick.

For the next operation – the even blending in of the garnishes – there is really no adequate alternative to the use of your clean and sensitive fingers. But you *must* treat the meat gently and lightly – no pressing or squeezing. You should end up with a loose, almost fluffy mixture, never a solid and soggy paste. Work fast, so that the meat remains cold. All of the mixing should take no more than a couple of minutes. Spread evenly across it, first, the mustard-anchovy-paste, second, the chopped herb and onion mixture, third, about half the parsley. Lightly spritz everything with lemon juice and sprinkle with salt, remembering that some saltiness has already been provided by the anchovies. Grind on a little pepper. Sprinkle on the 2 tablespoons of Cognac and the teaspoon of paprika. Now fold the disk of meat over from the edges towards the center, lightly working everything together, so that the flavoring garnishes are evenly distributed.

Divide the beef into four parts, shape each into an oval or round smooth patty, then, with the back of a soup spoon, make an indentation in the top and slip into it a raw egg yolk. Decorate the top of the egg and meat by sprinkling with more bright green parsley, then serve at once on the ice-cold plates. Each diner breaks the egg yolk with a fork and blends it into the meat. This, of course, is a main dish, ideally accompanied by a separate salad of raw greens, or crisply cooked (preferably steamed) vegetables, slices of black bread and a fine bottle of red wine – a Château-bottled from Bordeaux or a Cabernet Sauvignon from California – or a mug of very cold beer. After the meal, you will feel like Hercules!

BEEF-FILLED RUSSIAN-STYLE PIROSHKI

(for 4)

These savory pastry turnovers are more or less a national specialty of the Russian cuisine. They are extremely flexible, as they can be filled with all kinds of fresh or leftover meats, fish or vegetables; and they can be baked in miniature sizes as hors d'oeuvres or in larger versions as main supper dishes, either in individual portions, or as a single, double-crusted savory pie to be cut and divided at table. They are as simple to prepare as any pastry turnover and, with a Cuisinart to do the chopping of the ingredients for the filling and to whip up the raised-dough pastry in a matter of seconds, the process of making piroshki is now speeded up. Once you have mastered the basic technique from this recipe, you can adapt it to any kind of savory or sweet filling.

Parsley, fresh leaf only (small handful)
Dill, fresh, in season, do not use dried (small handful)
Yellow onion, peeled and chunked (1, fairly large)
Sour cream (¼ cup)
Worcestershire sauce (2 tsps)
Anchovy flat fillets (4)
Beef, lean, chuck or bottom round, cut by butcher into 1½ inch cubes (1 lb)

Butter (5 Tbs)
Salt, coarse crystal, to taste
Black pepper, freshly ground, to taste
Flour, all-purpose (about 2 Tbs)
Eggs, hard-cooked, shelled and diced (2)
Vermouth, dry white (about 2 Tbs)
Pastry dough for piroshki, quick (see next recipe), have ready in refrigerator (1 batch)

Prepared in 45 Minutes from Start to Serving, Including 15 Minutes of Unsupervised Baking

We assume, of course, that you have previously prepared a batch of the quick piroshki pastry dough (according to the recipe on page 106) and that you have it, safely wrapped and refrigerated, ready to roll out as soon as this filling is prepared. Now, first, chop the ingredients with the Cuisinart steel blades. Put into its work bowl the parsley and (if you have it) the dill, then chop them – not too finely – in about one second. Transfer to a covered storage dish and hold. Next, without rinsing the bowl, put into it the chunked onion and chop it, again not too finely, in about 2 seconds. Transfer to a second covered storage dish and hold it. Next, again without rinsing out the bowl, put in the ¼ cup of sour cream, the 2 teaspoons of Worcestershire sauce and the 4 anchovy fillets, then whirl the blades until they are all perfectly blended and the anchovies have been finely minced – usually in 4 or 5 seconds. Transfer the mixture to a third covered dish and hold it. Now rinse and dry the Cuisinart bowl and chop the beef in it. Put in half the meat chunks and chop them fairly coarsely – in no more than 4 or 5 seconds. Transfer to a fairly large mixing bowl and hold it while you repeat the operation with the remaining meat chunks. Combine the two batches. All is now ready for the brief cooking and assembly of the piroshki filling.

Set a roughly 11-inch sauté pan over medium frying heat, melt in it 4 tablespoons of the butter and as soon as it is hot, but not yet beginning to brown, put in the chopped onions, stir them around for a few seconds to coat them with the butter, then add all the meat. Keep it moving around until it has just lost its red color – usually in 2 to 3 minutes. At the same time, salt and pepper it, to your taste. The instant the meat is done, sprinkle over it and work into it just enough of the flour to absorb any remaining liquid butter. As soon as this is accomplished, lightly and quickly work in the sour cream sauce. When it shows the slightest signs of bubbling, turn off the heat and finally work in three tablespoons of the parsley-dill mixture (or parsley alone) plus the 2 diced eggs. Mix gently without crushing anything, preferably using a wooden fork. If the mixture becomes too thick, work in, a tablespoon at a time, some of the wine. Let this filling cool while you roll out the pastry.

Preheat your oven to 375°F. Bring the pastry ball out of the refrigerator and pinch off a piece about the size of a small egg. On a lightly floured board, roll it out to an oval about 3 to 3½ inches long, about 2½ inches wide and about ¼ inch thick. At its center, make an elongated heap of about 1½ tablespoons of the beef filling, then bring the edges of the pastry oval up and over the filling, exactly like a folded envelope, with about ¾ inch of overlap at the center. The ends of each piroshki should be pointed as if they were French bread rolls. Turn the whole thing over so that the overlap is now underneath, and pinch the sides gently to plump up and round the envelope. It is now ready to wait for its companions to be filled and shaped. When they are all done, lightly grease and flour a cookie sheet, place the piroshki on it about ½ inch apart and bake them in the center of the oven until they are golden – usually in about 15 minutes. They may be served immediately, hot, or later at room temperature.

QUICK PIROSHKI PASTRY

(for 8 to 10 piroshki)

This is our fifth lesson in the almost-magical techniques of making doughs and pastries in the Cuisinart chopper-churner. (See the earlier general instructions for the *quiche* pastry on page 86 and the various bread and muffin doughs in Chapter 6. Some other extraordinary and unusual pastry recipes will be found in Chapter 14. This *piroshki* pastry is perhaps the most generally useful of all of them. It can line a dessert or savory pie, cover a deep-dish pie, or enclose a terrine or a whole chicken. It is, so to speak, the foundation recipe, which can be adapted to different fillings by varying the amount of eggs, butter, baking powder, etc., or by adding sugar for dessert pastries. Once you have fully mastered this recipe, you will be able to use your Cuisinart machine for virtually any kind of dough (except for flaky pastry, which always has to be buttered and turned by hand).

Flour, no sifting necessary, scooped up with the measure and leveled off with the back of a knife (1¾ cups, almost exactly 8 oz, plus extra for flouring)
Baking powder, double-acting (1½ tsp)

Salt, fine grind (1 tsp)
Butter, unsalted, chilled (¼ lb stick)
Lard, or vegetable shortening, chilled (3 Tbs)
Egg, whole (1 small)
Ice water

About 2 Minutes To Make, Plus About 2 Hours in the Refrigerator
Pour the flour around the bottom of the Cuisinart bowl, then sprinkle on top of it the 1½ teaspoons of baking powder and the teaspoon of salt. Whirl the steel blades for one second to sift these dry ingredients together. Quickly cut the chilled butter into thin slices and drop them on top of the flour. Do the same with the chilled lard. Whirl the steel blades for exactly one second, then stop them, take off the cover and inspect the mixture. You are shooting for the complete, even incorporation of the fats into the powders, resulting in the formation of little balls rather like niblet corn. The speed at which they are formed depends on the precise temperature of the fat and

106

flour, so the timing may be different by an odd second or so each time. This is why you must continuously inspect the mixture. If one second has not done it, put back the lid and whirl the blades for exactly one more second. Inspect again. In our Cuisinart machine, at our refrigerator and kitchen temperature, we usually reach the niblet stage in 3 or 4 one-second bursts. Beyond this, be very careful indeed. If you overrun the blades, you will have a sticky mess and you would be wise to start over.

Now beat the egg with a fork just enough to mix it, and put it into a ½-cup measure. Fill up the measure with ice water, then remove 2 tablespoons of the water. Pour the eggs and its water, all at once, into the Cuisinart bowl, then start up the machine and watch carefully for the dramatic transformation. At the end of 5 or 6 seconds the dough will ride up onto the top of the blades, massing into a single ball. Instantly turn off the machine.

Place the ball of dough in the center of your floured marble or wood pastry board and give it a few light and rapid kneadings to achieve the final blending, pressing the heel of your hand into the dough with a forward motion, then folding the dough, turning it on the board, and pressing it forward again. The dough should be light and satiny soft. If it seems dry, sprinkle on and work in a few extra droplets of ice water as you knead. Keep it malleable. Do not let it become damp and sticky. Form it into a ball, sprinkle it lightly with flour, put it into a plastic bag and refrigerate it for at least two hours.

For its final use, see the previous recipe.

FRENCH-STYLE "HAMBURGER À CHEVAL" FROM A THREE-STAR CHEF

(for 4)

Chef Jean Troisgros is perhaps the greatest of French cooks. The restaurant he runs with his brother Pierre in central France has the highest rating of three stars. One evening, recently, after we had spent a day in Burgundy with Jean tasting wine and returning to his place for dinner, we all decided that we were not very hungry. Jean said: "I make you a *Hamburger à la française*. I will serve it *à cheval*, on horseback, which means with an egg riding on top of it. Come with me to the kitchen. I show you how." It was certainly different from a Big Mac!

Green scallions, trimmed (4)	Butter, unsalted (about 1½ Tbs)
Beef, entirely lean, bottom round or chuck, cut by butcher into 1½-inch cubes (1½ lbs)	Olive oil, first quality virgin (about 1½ Tbs)
Salt, coarse crystal, to taste	Eggs, perfectly poached just before serving (4, large)
White pepper, freshly ground, to taste	Anchovy fillets, flat (8)
	Cognac, fine quality (⅓ cup)

Prepared in About 15 Minutes from Start to Serving
Cut the scallions into 1½ inch pieces (including the bulb) and put them into the Cuisinart bowl. Chop them not too finely by starting and stopping the steel blades twice for one second each time. Transfer the scallions to a covered storage dish and hold them. Now, without rinsing the work bowl, put in ⅓ of the cubes of meat and chop them fairly coarsely in no more than 4 or 5 seconds. Transfer the meat to a mixing bowl and repeat the operation twice more with another half pound of the beef for each batch – adding each in turn to the mixing bowl. Working lightly with your clean fingers, blend into the meat the chopped scallions, plus salt and pepper to your taste. Lightly shape the meat into 4 patties, each large enough to hold an egg. Note that Jean Troisgros does not include the usually recommended 20% of fat in his hamburgers. He likes them firm and solid, fat-free, in tune with the new light cooking of France.

Set your frypan on high heat and put into it a mixture of 1½ table-spoons each of the butter and the olive oil. Let them get quite hot and then sizzle in the hamburger patties. Sear them quickly on both sides, then lower the heat to medium frying temperature and continue the cooking, turning each patty once or twice, until they are precisely as rare or as well-done as you like them. During this operation, poach the 4 eggs, keeping the yolks just runny so that when they are eventually cut open they will spread over and mingle with the hamburgers. Finally, on each hot dinner plate, place a hamburger patty with an egg on top and cross 2 anchovy fillets on the egg. The moment the frypan is empty, deglaze it by pouring in the ⅓ cup of Cognac. As it comes up towards the boiling point, set it on fire. Pour it, still flaming, over the eggs and hamburgers.

ANOTHER FRENCH-STYLE HAMBURGER – WITH GARLIC AS THEY DO IT IN PROVENCE

(for 4)

Our American hamburger is now universal all over France, but in each different region the cooks add their own special local twist to it. Our friends in Provence always include garlic and tomato, because those are two of the principal products of the sunny Mediterranean coast. The cooking techniques here are the same as in the previous recipe – only the ingredients are slightly different. The amount of garlic, of course, is to your personal taste.

Fresh herb leaves, in season, possibly basil, or rosemary, or tarragon, or thyme, do not use dried (enough for 2 Tbs after chopping)

Garlic, whole, unpeeled (4 cloves)

Tomatoes, halved, peeling unnecessary, but juice and pits squeezed out (2, medium)

Beef, entirely lean, bottom round or chuck, cut by butcher into 1½-inch cubes (1½ lbs)

Salt, coarse crystal, to taste

Black pepper, freshly ground, to taste

Olive oil, preferably Provençal green virgin (3 Tbs)

Prepared in About 15 Minutes from Start to Serving

First, do the speed chopping. Put into the Cuisinart work bowl the fresh herb leaves, if available, either one kind or a mixture of 2 or more. Chop them not too finely by starting and stopping the steel blades for a one-second burst – then (only if necessary) for a second similar burst. Transfer the chopped leaves to a covered storage dish and hold them. Without rinsing the bowl, put in the 4 cloves of garlic – no need to peel them, the skin will disintegrate in the cooking – and chop them fairly finely in 2 one-second bursts. Transfer the chopped garlic to a second covered storage dish. Chunk the tomato halves (there is never any need to peel them, since their skins will be disintegrated by the blades) and put them into the unrinsed Cuisinart work bowl, then whirl the steel blades to dice them with 1 or 2 one-second bursts. Transfer them to a third covered storage dish.

Now rinse and dry the bowl. Put in half the beef and coarsely chop it, exactly as in the previous recipe, by whirling the blades steadily for 4 or 5 seconds. Put the chopped beef into a mixing bowl, do the

109

second batch and combine the two. With the light touch of your fingers, work the tomato dice and fresh herb leaves into the beef, plus salt and pepper, to your taste. As soon as the patties have been formed, cover them all around with the chopped garlic by lightly pressing it into the surface. The trick is that, by leaving the garlic on the surface in this way, a good part of its bite is burned off by the hot olive oil during the frying. What remains is an extraordinary nuttiness that is one of the glories of the Provençal cuisine. Sear the hamburgers in the very hot olive oil in a frypan, exactly as in the previous recipe, then cook them, turning them occasionally, at medium heat until they are done just as well as you want them to be. Serve at once on very hot plates. After this experience, you may understand why the people of the South of France are so devoted to their garlic.

CHINESE-STYLE HAMBURGER WITH WHOLE-GRAIN SZECHUAN PEPPER

(for 4)

If you have never tried Chinese Szechuan pepper, you should certainly get some from your local Chinese grocery store. It is a remarkable spice in many ways. The tiny berries of various shades of brown are about the same size as standard whole black pepper and are picked from a mountain bush that grows wild in the Chinese interior of Szechuan, near the headwaters of the Yangtze River. You can put these tiny buds into your pepper mill and grind them in the normal way, but one of the especially felicitous ways to use them is to press and pound them with the heel of your hand into the surfaces of hamburgers and steaks as an unusual variation of *Steak au Poivre*. Under the heat of the broiler, the Szechuan peppers burn into a marvelously crackly crispy crust, with much of their peppery bite eliminated leaving an aromatic flavor – unlike anything you have ever tasted before. Here is a simple way of trying them first on a hamburger.

Beef, entirely lean, bottom round
  or chuck, cut by butcher into
  1½-inch cubes (1½ lbs)
Chinese five-flavor spice powder,
  or see recipe for substitutions
  on page 43 (1 tsp)

Salt, coarse crystal, to taste
Chinese whole Szechuan pepper,
  see above (¼ cup)

110

Prepared in About 15 Minutes from Start to Serving
Preheat your broiler to its highest temperature, adjusting the height
of the grill pan so that the top surface of the hamburger patties will
be about 4 to 5 inches below the heat. Chop the beef coarsely in two
equal batches in the Cuisinart bowl, as described in detail for our
perfect hamburger recipe on page 55, never whirling the blades
longer than about 4 to 5 seconds. Combine the two batches in a
large mixing bowl. Sprinkle over it the 1 teaspoon of Chinese spice
powder and salt to your taste. Lightly and quickly work these aro-
matics into the beef, then form the patties and set them out on the
board. Press into them, on both sides, the whole-grain Szechuan
pepper, using about 1 tablespoon per patty. Grill them under the
broiler to the exact degree of doneness you prefer. Serve them at once
on very hot plates.

ANCIENT FRENCH BEEF-STUFFED CABBAGE IN A MODERN STREAMLINED ADAPTATION

(for 4 to 6)

All across southern France, in hundreds upon hundreds of farmhouse
kitchens, this is still the traditional dish for Sunday dinner – gently
glub-glubbing in its huge tin-lined copper pot on the stove – filling
the kitchen with the sound of a tiny brook bubbling over rocks. No
one ever grows tired of eating stuffed cabbage, because it has such an
infinity of variations. Once you have learned the basic trick, you can
vary the flavors and the stuffing in dozens of different ways. The
ancient recipe involved a great deal of chopping and cutting, but with
the Cuisinart appliance, all that is now out of date. What remains
always the same is long, slow, completely unsupervised cooking to
develop the rich aromas and wonderful balance of contrasting textures. You start it going earlier in the day and then, when it is time
to eat, there is nothing more to be done than to lift the lid and serve.
This is ideal for the new type of slow crock cooker that is filled and
forgotten until mealtime – and the final bonus is that all the ingredients are relatively inexpensive.

Green cabbage, leaves firmly
   packed (about 2½ to 3 lbs)
Gruyère cheese, 1 piece (¼ lb)

Carrots, scraped (5 medium)
Watercress (small bunch)
Garlic, unpeeled, whole (2 cloves)

111

Shallots, whole, unpeeled (about
a dozen cloves)
Smoked pork, lean, cut into 1-inch
cubes by butcher (½ lb)
Beef, lean, bottom round or chuck,
cut into 1-inch cubes by butcher
(1½ lbs)
Bacon, lean and smoky (½ lb)
Eggs, whole (2, large)
Rice, boiled in advance (1 cup)
Salt, coarse crystal, to taste
Black pepper, freshly ground, to
taste
Olive oil, preferably best quality
Provençal (about 4 Tbs)
Yellow onions, peeled (6 medium)
Thyme, preferably fresh, but dried
if not possible (3 to 4 springs
fresh, 2 tsps dried)

Bay leaves, whole (2)
Cloves, ground (¼ tsp)
Mace, ground (½ tsp)
Orange peel, outer rind only
(3 or 4 1-inch slivers)
Vinegar, tarragon white wine
(¼ cup)
Beef bouillon, clear, fatless (1 cup)
Dry white wine (1 cup)
Red wine (1 cup)
Apples, tart cooking (3 large)
Lemon juice, freshly squeezed
Sausages, small, smoky flavor,
perhaps Bratwurst (8)

**Preparation in About 1 Hour, Then Forget It for About
3 to 4 Hours of Slow Cooking**

First, blanch the cabbage by covering it with cold water in a large
pot, bringing it just to the boil, and then draining it at once. Meanwhile, prepare the stuffing ingredients in the Cuisinart machine. Fit
the shredding disk into the bowl and grate the ¼-pound piece of
cheese, then transfer it to a large mixing bowl in which the meat
stuffing will be assembled. Next, fit the slicing disk to the Cuisinart
and slice the 5 carrots and 6 onions, transferring both to a covered
storage dish and holding them. Now fit the steel blades back into
the Cuisinart bowl and put in the bunch of watercress, first cutting
off the thicker and harder stalks, then whirling the blades until the
leaves are not too finely chopped – usually in 1- to 3-second bursts.
Add it to the cheese in the mixing bowl. Without rinsing the Cuisinart bowl, put in the 2 garlic cloves and the 12 shallots (no need to
peel them, the skins will be completely disintegrated in the cooking),
then coarsely chop them in about 1 or 2 seconds. Transfer them to
a covered storage dish and hold them. Without rinsing the bowl, put

in together ⅓ of the pork cubes and ⅓ of the beef, then whirl the blades until the meat is fairly coarsely chopped – usually in about 4 to 6 seconds. Add it to the cheese and watercress in the large mixing bowl. Repeat the operation with the second and third batches of mixed pork and beef. Add each to the large mixing bowl. Without rinsing out the Cuisinart bowl, put in the ½ pound of bacon slices and whirl the blades until they are converted into a quite-coarse mash – usually in about 4 to 5 seconds. Add it to the large mixing bowl.

All is now ready for the final mixing of the stuffing and the filling of the blanched cabbage. Tear off and throw away any damaged or very tough outer leaves and cut off horizontally as much as you can of the hard bottom stalk, leaving enough so that all the remaining leaves are still firmly attached and the cabbage has a kind of base on which to stand. Now set it on your work surface and carefully open up the leaves one-by-one all the way to their base, as if you were unfolding the petals of a flower. When you reach the center, neatly cut out the central core, leaving a hole about 1½ inches in diameter. Chop the tender core you have removed in the Cuisinart for about 2 or 3 seconds, then add it to the waiting meat. Leave the cabbage to dry while you complete the mixing of the stuffing.

Preferably using your clean and sensitive fingers – working gently and lightly, lifting and folding rather than pressing and squeezing – blend together the bacon, cheese, meats and watercress, while adding to them the 2 eggs, lightly beaten together, the chopped garlic and shallots, the cup of cooked rice, and salt and pepper, to taste. Set a 12-inch sauté pan over medium heat and lubricate its bottom with the 4 tablespoons of olive oil. When it is hot, but certainly not smoking, spread in the stuffing mix. Work it around gently with a wooden spoon until the beef has just lost its redness – usually in about 2 to 3 minutes – then turn off the heat at once. Overcooking blurs the flavors. Now stuff the cabbage. First, firmly fill the central cavity with the meat mixture. Then, working in neat circles from the center to the outside, layer the meat mixture about ¼ inch thick in between every one of the leaves, packing slightly more of it at the strong base of the leaves and thinning it a bit towards the top. Tightly close up each leaf as it is filled, leaving the last layer or two unstuffed to serve as a wrapping. At the end of the job, the cabbage will be completely closed up, but considerably fatter than it was at the beginning. Tie up the cabbage with string and, if there is any leftover stuffing, push it down into the remaining crevices from the top.

Now choose a tightly lidded casserole, Dutch oven, soup kettle, or any other fairly heavy cooking pot large enough to fit the cabbage neatly with about an inch or 2 of space all around it and about 2 inches between its top and the lid. If the pot is too large, the cooking is less efficient because the hot steam becomes diffused. Although the cooking will be started on top of the stove, you may, if you wish, complete it in the oven. If so, preheat your oven to 275°F. Stand the cabbage in the center of the pot and spread around it, in turn, the sliced onions and carrots, the fresh (or dried) thyme, the 2 bay leaves, the ground cloves and mace, the slivers of orange peel, with more salt and pepper to taste. Pour over the cabbage, in turn, the ¼ cup of vinegar and the cup each of bouillon, white wine, and red wine. Bring the liquid up to a gentle but steady bubbling, so as to provide a reasonable (but certainly not too strong) supply of steam. Then cover the pot and let it simmer for a few minutes, listening occasionally without opening the lid to make sure that the glub-glubbing remains steady, but never too fierce. Under no circumstances should steam start hissing out from under the lid. When the bubbling is well established, you can either transfer the pot to the oven or leave it on the burner for 3 to 4 hours.

As soon as everything is under control, peel and core the 3 apples, cut each into 8 wedges, spritz them with lemon juice to prevent them from discoloring, and hold them in a covered storage dish. At the end of the first hour of cooking, drop the apple wedges into the pot around the cabbage. At the same time, ladle up plenty of the juice from the bottom and baste the top of the cabbage with it. Re-cover the pot and continue the very gentle cooking.

About 20 or 30 minutes (according to the size of the sausages) before you plan to serve the cabbage, put in the sausages around it, pushing them down into the aromatic vegetables. When you serve the dish, bring the entire pot to the table. When you first lift the lid, the aromas that burst out of the pot will overwhelm the diners with their irresistible flavors and will magnify the appetites to an almost uncontrollable hunger. Cut the cabbage into wedges and set them on very hot plates surrounded by the sausages and the aromatic conglomeration from the bottom of the pot, with the wonderful juices spooned over everything. A memorable dish!

8

Super Sandwiches and Their Fancy Fillings

For our family, the Cuisinart chopper-churner has opened up a whole new range of informal, picnic-style preparations. It can churn all types of nuts into butters. We shall show you how it encourages us to launch into bold experiments. Hardly a day passes without our trying out some new combination of meats, fruit, nuts and vegetables. It can make sausage fillings that don't have to be stuffed into sausage casings but can be sliced from a terrine pan. The following recipes are planned to offer you some new ideas and teach you some new tricks. After that, we shall leave you to do your own inventing.

HOME-MADE NATURAL PEANUT BUTTER

(about 2 cups of butter)

It takes just about 3 minutes to make the finest peanut butter we have ever tasted – crunchy or smooth, dry or oily, solid or fluffy, all precisely controllable according to the way we handle the machine.

Peanuts, salted (2 cups)   **Peanut oil, optional (3 Tbs)**
Salt, coarse crystal, to taste

Preparation in 3 Minutes from Start to Serving
Put the 2 cups peanuts (this is the maximum for one batch) into the Cuisinart work bowl. Run the steel blades, at first starting and stopping them in one-second bursts, then, as the nuts become finely minced, running the blades continuously until the paste begins to form – usually in about 30 to 45 seconds. At this point, there will often be plenty of nut paste sticking to the sides of the bowl. Scrape it down with a spatula to get it back into the action. Run the blades

115

again and keep on running, stopping and scraping, now watching carefully for a strange little display that happens inside the bowl. Quite suddenly, the peanut paste will form a ball which will ride up and spin around on top of the blades. Just as suddenly, the ball will disappear and the blades will again take over the churning. The ball usually appears after about 90 seconds of running time. Scrape again and keep on running until the smooth, oily butter begins to form – usually in a total time of 2 to 2½ minutes. You can control the degree of oiliness and smoothness by running the blades for a longer or a shorter time. The longer you run, the more oil is extracted. At last, taste it and, if there was not quite enough salt on the peanuts, add more now and blend it in with a single, one-second burst of the blades.

If you want very crunchy peanut butter, follow a different technique right at the start. Have ready the 3 tablespoons of peanut oil. After putting in the 2 cups of peanuts, start and stop the steel blades in one-second bursts, to crack and grind the peanuts rather than churn them, until they are as coarsely or finely ground as you want and are beginning to coat the sides of the bowl – usually after about 12 or 15 one-second bursts. Now remove the pusher from the chimney of the cover and, with the motor running, quickly spoon in the 3 tablespoons of peanut oil. It will amalgamate at once with the chopped nuts and form a very crunchy butter. Taste it, and add salt, to your taste, blending it in with a one-second burst. If the butter, at this point, is too crunchy, simply run the blades for a few seconds longer, being careful to stop every couple of seconds to check. Otherwise, your nicely coarse grind will become a superfine grind before you can say "peanut."

An Interesting Variation – Chocolate Peanut Butter: Instead of the original 2 cups of peanuts in the above recipes, put in only 1⅓ cups of the salted peanuts, together with ⅔ cup of Nestlè's semi-sweet chocolate bits. Whether you then make it a butter that is dry or oily, crunchy or smooth, you will have a pleasant chocolate flavor.

Another Variation – Banana Peanut Butter: Whether you are making the plain peanut butter, or the chocolate flavored, you can produce an entirely different texture by coarsely slicing a ripe banana and dropping it in, bit by bit, through the cover chimney while the blades are whirling. It will make the butter very light – almost fluffy –

116

as well as adding a distinct banana flavor. It can either be banana-plain-peanut, or banana-chocolate-peanut. Take your pick.

NEW ORLEANS POOR BOY OYSTER SANDWICH WITH HOT SAUCE

(4 sandwiches)

The Italian Hero sandwich – that marvelous assemblage of cold cuts and cheese inside a long loaf – is not exclusively Italian. The same idea has been a staple of New Orleans since the time when it was owned and run by the French. A quartered French-style long loaf filled with a variety of good things has always been called a Poor Boy sandwich because it used to be sold in the bistros around the French Quarter market for ten cents a sandwich. No more! But it is easy and relatively inexpensive to reproduce at home. If you want to add an authentic Hot Sauce, you will have to find Mexican-style hot peppers in Latin American or Spanish groceries.

Hot Sauce, see page 118 (about
  2 cups)
Garlic, unpeeled (1 clove, or more,
  to your taste)
Butter (6 Tbs)
Bread, French or Italian loaves
  (2 fairly long)
Oysters, freshly shucked (2 doz)
Cornmeal, white (½ cup)
Flour, all-purpose, (½ cup)

Salt, coarse crystal, to taste
Black pepper, freshly-ground, to
  taste
Peanut oil (to fill a deep fryer)

For garnishing:
Torn lettuce leaves, sliced
  tomatoes, dill pickles, sliced
  cucumber, etc.

Preparation in About 20 Minutes from Start to Serving
First, make a batch of the Hot Sauce, according to the recipe on page 118. Next, whirl the garlic butter in the Cuisinart – put into its bowl 1 whole unpeeled clove of garlic (or more, if you like it that much) then start and stop the steel blades in one-second bursts until the garlic is minced almost to a purée – usually in 5 to 8 bursts. Add the 6 tablespoons of butter, in smallish pieces, then whirl continuously until both ingredients are completely amalgamated to a smooth paste – usually in another 5 to 10 seconds. Transfer the butter to a covered storage dish and hold it. Cut the 2 loaves in halves, and then

slit each half horizontally to make 4 sandwiches. Hold them. Drain and dry the 2 dozen oysters, and hold them. Thoroughly mix together in an open bowl or dish the ½ cup of cornmeal, the ½ cup of flour, with a little salt and pepper, to taste. Have ready your deep fryer, filled with the peanut oil. Now preheat your oven to 425°F and the oil in your deep fryer to 375°F. Divide your garlic butter into 8 parts and dot it onto the cut sides of the 8 pieces of bread. Coat each oyster all around with the cornmeal-flour mixture and lower each carefully into the frying fat. Get in as many as you can, but do not let them touch each other. Lift each out as soon as it is nicely browned – usually in 2 to 3 minutes – and drain it on absorbent towels. While the frying is in progress, put all the pieces of bread, cut side up, into the oven, and bake them until the butter has melted and the bread is slightly crisp, but do not let it brown and dry out. In our oven the bread is perfect in 2 to 3 minutes.

Now construct the sandwiches. Put 6 oysters on each of 4 bread pieces and garnish them, as you please, with torn lettuce leaves, sliced tomatoes, pickles, cucumber, etc. Dribble over as much of the Hot Sauce as pleases you and close the sandwiches with the remaining pieces of bread.

NEW ORLEANS-STYLE HOT SAUCE

(about 2 cups)

Jalapeño peppers, red or yellow, Mexican, chunked (4 or 5 according to size)

Serrano peppers, green, Mexican, chunked (3 or 4 according to size)

Onion, peeled and chunked (1 medium)

Garlic, unpeeled (2 cloves)

Shallots, unpeeled (10 cloves)

Vinegar, white wine (¼ cup)

Lime juice, freshly squeezed (3 Tbs)

Chives, coarsely snipped (¼ cup)

Turmeric, ground (½ tsp)

Salt, coarse crystal (1 tsp)

Dry white wine (1 or 2 Tbs)

Preparation in About 10 Minutes from Start to Serving
Simply put everything (except the wine) into the Cuisinart work bowl and whirl the steel blades until the mix is a smooth purée – usually in about 10 to 15 seconds. Transfer the mixture into a 1½-pint saucepan and heat it up to gentle bubbling while stirring to bring out and blend

the flavor oils. Finally, taste it and adjust the flavor and thickness. It can be thinned with a tablespoon or two of the wine. Thicken it by continuing the bubbling for a couple of minutes longer. Let it cool while you prepare the Poor Boy sandwiches. This sauce can also be used with many other meat or fish dishes. If you make it in larger quantities, it will keep for weeks in a covered jar in the refrigerator and is a useful basic stand-by.

ARAB-ARMENIAN-GREEK-SYRIAN-MEDITERRANEAN PITA POCKETS

(6 pockets)

This is a savory meat filling for the pita bread rounds which you cut open across the top to find an ample pocket inside. Pita is now widely available in supermarkets and specialty stores.

Onions, peeled and chunked
  (2 medium)
Green celery, with leaves,
  destringed and chunked
  (1 stalk)
Green pepper, cored and chunked
  (1 small)
Garlic, unpeeled (1 clove)
Basil, tarragon and thyme, fresh
  leaves, if available (1 Tbs each,
  or 1 teaspoon each, dried)

Beef, lean top round in 1-inch
  cubes (1 lb)
Butter (3 Tbs)
Tomato sauce, canned (1 lb)
Lemon juice, freshly squeezed
  (1 Tbs)
Salt, coarse crystal, to taste
Black pepper, freshly-ground, to
  taste
Pita bread (6 rounds)

Preparation From Start to Serving in About 10 Minutes
Put into the Cuisinart bowl: the 2 onions, the stalk of celery with leaves, the green pepper, the clove of garlic, and the tablespoon each of basil, tarragon and thyme. Start and stop the steel blades in one-second bursts until everything is not too finely chopped – usually in about 4 to 8 bursts. Transfer the choppings to a covered storage dish and hold them. Put half the beef cubes into the unrinsed Cuisinart bowl, and whirl the steel blades until the meat is chopped – again not too finely, usually in about 4 seconds. Put the first batch into a mixing bowl and repeat the operation with the second batch, then combine it with the first. Thoroughly mix the chopped vegetables into

119

the meat. Set an 11-inch sauté pan over medium frying heat and lubricate its bottom by melting in the 3 tablespoons of butter. As soon as it is hot, spread in the meat mixture, adding and working in the 1 pound of tomato sauce, the 1 tablespoon of lemon juice, with salt and pepper to taste. Just bring it up to the boil, stirring all the time, then let it gently bubble for about 2 minutes. Turn off the heat, taste it and adjust the seasonings if necessary, then let it slightly cool before spooning it into the pockets of the pita bread.

A FRENCH SALAD SANDWICH FROM PROVENCE

(1 loaf for 4)

This is, in essence, a long French loaf filled with a marvelously refreshing, cold mixed salad. It can be prepared in about 10 minutes, but you should always make it the day before, so that it can be chilled overnight in the refrigerator, where its flavors blend and gradually impregnate the bread.

Bread, long, French loaf (1)	Garlic, peeled and sliced (2 cloves)
Tomatoes, ripe, chunked (4 medium)	Green beans, trimmed and chunked, raw (a handful)
Yellow onions, peeled and chunked (2 medium)	Olive oil, fine virgin (up to 2 Tbs)
Green pepper, cured and chunked (2 small or 1 large)	Wine vinegar (up to 2 tsps)
Black olives, pitted (1 doz)	Sweet paprika (1 or 2 tsps)
Green olives, pitted (1 doz)	Salt, coarse crystal, to taste
Capers (3 Tbs)	Black pepper, freshly-ground, to taste
Dill pickles, chunked (1 medium)	

Active Preparation About 10 Minutes, Plus Overnight Chilling in the Refrigerator

Put into the Cuisinart bowl: the 4 tomatoes, the 2 onions, the green pepper, the dozen each of black and green olives, the 3 tablespoons of capers, dill pickle, the 2 cloves of garlic, plus the handful of green beans. Start and stop the steel blades in 1-second bursts until everything is quite coarsely chopped, more or less in small, crisp dice — usually in about 5 to 8 bursts. Transfer the salad to a large mixing bowl. Cut the loaf in half lengthwise. With your fingers, pull out all the central crumb of the loaf, leaving a fair thickness of crust, adding the crumb to the bowl. Now, with a wooden spoon, thoroughly work the crumb into the mixture. The crumb will absorb some of the juices which have been exuded, but you should expect it all to remain reasonably soggy. Now flavor it to your salad taste by blending in a tablespoon or two of the oil, a teaspoon or two of the wine vinegar, a teaspoon or two of the paprika, with salt and pepper. When you have it dead right, pile the mixture into the hollow loaf, mounding it up on the bottom half so as completely to fill the top half when it is put on as the lid. Wrap the loaf tightly in aluminum foil, squeezing the two halves together as you roll the foil around them. Chill it in the refrigerator overnight. If you can find a way of doing it, put a weight on top of it to press it together. The next day, serve it cut in 1-inch thick slices. Wonderfully refreshing at a picnic on a hot summer day. (This salad sandwich is quite flexible – it can also, or alternatively, include anchovies, cooked artichoke bottoms or hearts, or any kind of crisp lettuce, etc.)

HOME-MADE NATURAL LIVERWURST WITHOUT THE WURST

(a supply of about 4 pounds – keeps well)

With our Cuisinart chopper-churner, we often make (in a matter of seconds) all kinds of spiced meat fillings which could be stuffed into sausage casings and suspended from the kitchen ceiling to drip fat onto our heads. But why bother with all the folderols of sausage stuffing? For example, we prepare this liverwurst and bake it in a loaf pan. It can then be sliced into sandwiches. It tastes exactly the same as if it were sliced from a sausage.

Pork livers, fresh, cut into 1″ cubes (2½ lbs)

Fresh bacon, lean and unsmoked, cut into 1-inch cubes, rind removed (2½ lbs)

Onions, peeled and chunked (3, medium)

Marjoram, fresh leaves (1 Tbs, or 1 tsp, dried)

Sage, fresh leaves (1 Tbs, or 1 tsp dried)

Thyme, fresh leaves (1 Tbs or 1 tsp dried)

Cardamon seeds (1 tsp)

Ginger, ground (½ tsp)

Mace, ground (¾ tsp)

Corn syrup, white (2 Tbs)

Salt, coarse crystal (2 Tbs)

Black pepper, freshly-ground (about a dozen grinds)

Butter (about 2 Tbs)

Active Preparation in About 40 Minutes, Plus About 1 Hour of Unsupervised Baking:
Put the liver and bacon cubes into the Cuisinart work bowl in 5 batches, each batch consisting of 1 cup of liver and 1 cup of bacon, then whirl the steel blades until it is all a very smooth, completely amalgamated purée – usually in about 10 to 15 seconds per batch. If the purée begins to climb the walls of the bowl, stop the blades and scrape the walls down with a spatula. Transfer each puréed batch to your largest mixing bowl. When all the batches have been assembled, rinse and dry the Cuisinart work bowl, and put into it the 3 onions, starting and stopping the blades in 1-second bursts until the onions are finely minced – usually in 2 to 4 bursts. Add the onions to the meat. If you have the fresh leaves of marjoram, sage and thyme, put about 1 tablespoon of each into the rinsed and dried Cuisinart bowl, then start and stop the steel blades in 1-second bursts, until the leaves are finely minced – usually in about 2 or 3 bursts. Add these herbs to the meat. (Alternatively, use 1 teaspoon each of dried herbs.) Now also add and completely work in: the teaspoon of cardamom seeds, the ½ teaspoon of ginger, the ¾ teaspoon of mace, the 2 tablespoons of corn syrup, plus the 2 tablespoons of salt and the dozen grinds of black pepper. (More salt and pepper may have to be added after the mixing is completed and you do your final tasting.) Now preheat your oven to 325°F. When the liverwurst mixture is dead right, butter as many loaf or terrine pans as you will need and fill them fairly tightly (but not jammed down) with the liverwurst, smoothing the top and covering the pans either with their lids or with aluminum foil. Bake the liverwurst until a meat thermometer shows that the center of each loaf has reached 160°F – usually in about 45 to 75 minutes. When the loaves are done, chill them, still covered, in the refrigerator overnight. Then they will slice easily for any sandwich combination at any time. Keep them, always refrigerated and tightly covered so that they will not dry out.

KATHERINE'S 30-SECOND ANCHOVY SANDWICH SPREAD

(about 1 cup)

Anchovy fillets, flat, chunked (8 fillets)	Carrots, baked in foil and chunked (4 medium)

Celery or fresh fennel heart,
   chunked, with some leaves (1)
Green pepper, cored and chunked
   (1 small)

Cottage cheese or pot cheese
   (2 Tbs)
Black pepper, freshly-ground
   (a few grinds)

Active Preparation About 5 Minutes, Plus About 40 Minutes for Baking the Carrots

She first bakes the carrots, wrapped in foil, in a 350°F oven for about 40 minutes, then chunks them. Next, she simply puts all the ingredients into the Cuisinart work bowl and whirls the steel blades, at first, starting and stopping them in 1-second bursts, then, after 3 or 4 bursts, whirling continuously until she has a smooth, completely blended, spreading paste – usually in a total running time of 5 to 10 seconds. She tastes and adjusts the seasoning, if necessary. The anchovies usually provide all needed salt. If the paste gets too thin, she adds a tablespoon or two more cheese.

THE GREAT OLIVE SPREAD OF PROVENCE – TAPENADO

(about 2 cups)

This is the famous Mediterranean "Black Pâté," which is often served as an appetizer but can equally well be an aromatic and habit-forming sandwich filling. We consider it one of the great mixtures of the world. But, to achieve the supreme result, you must search for top-quality, preferably fresh anchovies and Greek, Moroccan, or Spanish black olives. Try Greek, Italian, or Spanish groceries. If you fail, use canned flat anchovy fillets and the best canned black olives you can find.

Anchovy fillets, flat, chunked
   (8 fillets)
Fine virgin olive oil (up to
   ¾ cup)
Cognac (up to 5 Tbs)
Mustard, English dry (1½ tsp)

Black olives, pitted (½ lb)
Tunafish, flaked (2-oz can)
Capers, drained (up to 7 Tbs)
Black pepper, freshly-ground, to
   taste

Preparation in About 15 Minutes From Start to Serving

Put into the Cuisinart bowl: the 8 anchovy fillets, ¼ cup of the olive oil, 1 tablespoon of the Cognac, 1 teaspoon of the mustard, the ½ pound of olives, the 2 ounces of tuna, 6 tablespoons of the capers, plus a few grinds of black pepper, to your taste. Salt is, of course, provided by the anchovies. Now start and stop the steel blades in 1-second bursts until everything is chopped and churned to the texture of a still-coarse, yet thoroughly spreadable paste. After the second burst, begin adding alternate tablespoons of more olive oil and more Cognac. Your limit should be an extra 4 tablespoons of olive oil and 3 tablespoons of Cognac, but one seldom needs this much, unless the olives are unusually dry.) If the mixture begins to climb the sides of the bowl, scrape it down with a spatula. Watch carefully. The moment you achieve the bitty, chewy texture of the tapenado, stop the blades. Taste it and adjust the flavor and texture. If it is too thick, work in a dash more olive oil with a single one-second burst. The flavor should be aggressively tangy. If not, work in more Cognac, mustard, capers and/or pepper.

A basic supply of tapenado in your refrigerator is useful in many different ways. You can serve individual small portions of the black pâté on plates or in tiny individual crocks as a first course hors d'oeuvre, garnished with the contrasting colors of red caviar and green baked eggplant. It is usually eaten with dry, thin, whole wheat toast. Or it can be an outstanding sandwich filling, with, for example, thin slivers of crisp apple, thin rounds of baby carrots, slices of cherry tomatoes, shelled walnut halves, sprigs of watercress, thin slices of celery or cucumber, etc. Tapenado, somehow, seems to radiate the luxurious life and warm sunshine of Mediterranean Provence.

9

Salads at Speed and Vegetables with Vitamins

No one is suggesting for a moment that you should change your normal way of preparing a green salad – tearing the crisp leaves by hand and tossing the dressing into them with a wooden fork and spoon. No machine can help you with that ancient, delightful and formal exercise. But there are salads and salads. Some are made up of an almost infinite variety of chopped, shredded, or sliced cooked or raw vegetables, and for these the shredding and slicing disks of the Cuisinart, as well as its chopping blade, can be of considerable help in terms of efficiency and speed. You can produce by machine an immense variety of marvelously refreshing and tasty mousses and purées of raw or slightly cooked vegetables with none of their minerals or vitamins boiled away. Also, the ingredients of salad dressings are amalgamated more completely and finely in the machine than by any amount of hand beating. The following recipes will teach you the basic principles. Once you have mastered them, you will be able to invent dozens of your own variations.

ALMOST-INSTANT RICH SALAD DRESSING

(makes 3 cups)

This is a luxurious, general-purpose dressing, which can be stored in the refrigerator for many days. It is particularly good over cold or hot cooked asparagus. We have adapted the recipe that came to us, originally, from Chef Jean Vergnes at the Restaurant Le Cirque in New York.

Mustard, imported French (¼ cup)

Salt, coarse crystal (1¼ tsp)

Black pepper, freshly ground
(about 10 grinds of the pepper
mill)

Worcestershire sauce, preferably
Lea & Perrins (½ tsp)

Tabasco (2 drops)

Vinegar, tarragon white wine
(½ cup)

Salad oil, blended vegetable and
peanut (1½ cups)

Water (¼ cup)

Olive oil, best quality virgin
(½ cup)

Prepared in About 10 Seconds
Simply put everything into the Cuisinart bowl and churn it until it is
perfectly amalgamated – usually in 10 seconds. Transfer to a covered
jar and store in the refrigerator.

SHREDDED SALAD OF YOUNG GREEN BEANS AND ESCAROLE

(for 4)

This is one of the simplest and most refreshing of green salads. We
have adapted the recipe given to us originally by the brilliant young
Chef Georges Blanc at his country auberge in the French village of
Vonnas in southern Burgundy. He served this salad to us as the first
course of a memorable lunch. It would also shine as one of the accom-
paniments at any meal, simply family or luxurious party.

Green beans, small and young,
boiled in salt water until just
crispy-soft (1 lb)

Escarole, whole heads, washed and
thoroughly dried, not torn apart
(2 heads)

Vinaigrette salad dressing, see
previous recipe (4 Tbs)

**Active Work of Preparation About 15 Minutes, Plus About an
Hour of Refrigerator Chilling**
It is best to boil the beans a few hours ahead – they are usually dead
right in about 10 minutes – so that they can be drained, dried and
thoroughly chilled in the refrigerator. The whole escarole heads, too,
should be washed, thoroughly dried and completely chilled. Also, put
your salad serving bowl in the freezer to chill. When you are ready to
start preparing the salad, fit the slicing disk into the Cuisinart bowl.

Remove the pusher from the cover chimney and fill the chimney with the beans, cut in lengths so that.they will fit exactly, sideways, in the chimney. Start the motor and push down gently with the pusher. Almost faster than you can see it, the beans will be "French cut" into long thin slices. Refill the chimney as many times as may be necessary to slice all the beans. If the bowl becomes too full, empty it into the salad serving bowl.

Next, deal with the escarole in more or less the same way. Push each head, upsidedown, into the chimney. If one head is too fat, cut it in half vertically. The chimney should be full, but not jammed tight. Start the motor and push down gently with the pusher. The escarole will be thinly shredded into the bowl. If the bowl again becomes too full, empty it into the salad serving bowl.

Finally, lightly toss the salad with the dressing and serve, nicely chilled, on chilled plates.

INDIAN SALAD OF CUCUMBER, MINT, ONION AND YOGHURT

(for 4)

An Indian family would call this *Dahi Raita,* meaning a "yoghurt refresher." Certainly, served ice cold, it is one of the most refreshing side-dish salads in the world and goes wonderfully with almost any main dish. When a colorful bowl of it is in front of you on the table, you will find it positively habit forming. The chopping of the ingredients used to be quite troublesome – now the machine does the work.

Naturally, we prefer our cucumber unpeeled, but if it is the waxed kind that usually comes from supermarkets this artificial covering will have to be removed.

Cucumber, washed, preferably
   unskinned, see above
   (1 medium)
Purple onion, peeled and sliced
   (1 medium)
Yoghurt (2 cups)
Caraway seeds, whole (¾ tsp)

Mint leaves, fresh or frozen
   (enough to fill 1½ Tbs)
Salt, fine-grind (¾ tsp)
Paprika, preferably Hungarian
   medium sweet, for decoration
   (about ½ tsp)

Active Work of Preparation About 10 Minutes, Plus About 2 Hours of Refrigerator Chilling

Choose a pretty, preferably ceramic open serving bowl with a capacity of about 1 quart. Put it in the freezer to chill. Or you could use 4 individual bowls. Slice the cucumber by first cutting it with the medium slicing disk. Then remove the slices from the work bowl and put the steel blades in position. Put back the cucumber slices into the bowl and whirl the blades in one-second bursts until the cucumber is not too finely diced – usually in about 2 bursts. Drain and transfer it to a covered storage dish and hold it in the refrigerator. Now repeat this operation with the onion. Transfer the onion to a covered storage dish and hold in the refrigerator. Without rinsing the Cuisinart bowl, put in the 2 cups of yoghurt, the ¾ teaspoon of caraway, the 1½ tablespoons of mint and the ¾ teaspoon of salt. Run the machine until these are all perfectly mixed and the mint leaves have been not too finely chopped – usually in about 4 to 6 seconds. Transfer to a mixing bowl and quickly work in with a wooden spoon the diced onion and the shredded cucumber. Taste as you work and add more salt, if necessary. The whole thing should be crisp and tangy. Now cover the bowl with aluminum foil and set it in the refrigerator to chill for at least 2 hours. Do not stir any more. Just before serving, lightly sprinkle the top surface with some of the paprika – just enough to give it a bright red glow. Serve ice cold in small chilled bowls.

JAPANESE SALAD OF CHICKEN WITH EXOTIC VEGETABLES

(for 4)

This is a most delightful and unusual salad with, we are assured by our Japanese friends, the authentic delicacy and subtlety of the gastronomy of Japan. If you are lucky enough to have a Japanese grocery within range of your shopping excursions, you will have no difficulty in finding all the proper Japanese ingredients. In case that is not possible for you, we propose Western alternatives, which will still give you a very fair idea of the dish. It will certainly be a focus of attention on any party menu – both because of its lovely coloring and its unusual and memorable balance of flavors.

Japanese dried wild mushrooms, or
Chinese, or Italian (2-oz pkg)
(or can be replaced by ¼ lb of
standard fresh mushrooms,
sliced)
Chicken breasts, skin discarded
(about 6 oz)
Sake ("Japanese rice wine") or
Spanish dry Sherry (2 Tbs)
Carrots, scraped and julienned
(3 small)
Bamboo shoots, cooked fresh or
canned, julienned (about ¼ cup)
Burdock root (*Gobo*) from a
Japanese grocery, peeled. If
unavailable, can be replaced by
raw parsnip, peeled and
julienned (about ½ cup)

Japanese cellophane noodles, or
Chinese (about 6 oz)
Watercress, leaves only (small
handful)
Salad oil (3 Tbs)
Clam juice (¾ cup)
Sugar, white granulated (3 Tbs)
Salt, coarse crystal, to taste
Japanese light soy sauce (2 Tbs)

Active Work of Preparation About 25 Minutes, Plus About 2 Hours of Unsupervised Chilling in the Refrigerator

If you are using dried mushrooms, soak them in a small mixing bowl with warm water until they begin to soften – usually in about 20 minutes. A Japanese traditional cook would laboriously scrape the chicken breasts with a knife to produce fine little shavings of the meat. It might take him half an hour. We can do it in the Cuisinart machine in about 4 seconds. Chunk the raw chicken meat into the work bowl, then whirl the steel blades until the flesh is quite finely minced – usually in about 3 to 6 seconds. Transfer the choppings to a covered storage dish and pour over them the 2 tablespoons of Sake or Sherry, stirring thoroughly to make sure that all the meat is well soaked. Leave it until you need it later. When the dried mushrooms are soft, drain them and squeeze them out, then cut them into julienned strips about 1 inch long with the fine or medium serrated slicing disk (see pages 23 and 25), to match the carrots and bamboo shoots. (If you are using fresh mushrooms, they should be wiped clean, trimmed and very thinly sliced.) Slice the burdock root as thinly as you can by shaving the pointed end diagonally with a knife, turning the root as you go, as if you were sharpening a large pencil. The cellophane noodles are so light and thin that they are perfectly cooked simply by having boiling water poured over them and then being drained immediately. After draining, put them into the Cuisinart bowl and chop them coarsely by whirling the steel blades for usually no more than 1 second. Transfer the noodles to a covered storage dish and hold them. Rinse and dry the Cuisinart bowl and put into it the small handful of watercress leaves, then whirl the blades until the leaves are quite coarsely chopped – usually in no more than 1 second. Transfer the leaves to a covered storage dish and hold them.

Now heat the 3 tablespoons of oil to quite high frying temperature in a wok or a sauté pan, then plunge-fry, for hardly more than a second or two, the burdock, carrots and mushrooms. Turn down the heat and at once hiss in the ¾ cup of clam juice, 3 tablespoons of sugar, 2 tablespoons of soy sauce, and salt, to taste – for us, usually, ½ teaspoon of salt is about right. Stir in thoroughly and let it gently bubble for about 5 minutes. Put the minced chicken and its Sake marinade into a 1-quart saucepan and simmer it until the tiny bits of chicken are just firm – usually in no more than a couple of minutes – then, with a slotted spoon, remove all the vegetables from their boiling bouillon and add them to the chicken. Hold the bouillon to use as a dressing. Turn off the heat at once, then transfer the chicken mixture and the bouillon to two covered refrigerator containers and chill them for about 2 hours. Last of all, a few moments before serving, toss the salad with a couple of tablespoons of the chilled bouillon and incorporate the crisp and fresh watercress.

A VARIETY OF MOUSSES AND PURÉES – VEGETABLES WITH VITAMINS

Certainly the puréeing of vegetables is nothing new. Which of us does not remember the pounding in a mortar and the slow, slow rubbing of fibrous mixtures repeatedly through fine sieves. Sometimes it seemed as if the hard, arm-aching work went on for hours. Now it is all a matter of a few seconds.

The work rules are quite simple. Different vegetables, prepared in different ways, serve two distinct and carefully balanced purposes in the finished mousse or purée. Some of the vegetables are soft to begin with, or are baked or boiled until they are soft, so that they will provide the smooth base of the mixture. Other vegetables are hard and are very finely grated, so that they add a lightly crispy texture to the soft mix. The result, when there is exactly the right balance between crispness and softness, can be a memorable side dish – an irresistible balance between crackle and velvet on the tongue. The pieces of whatever vegetable goes into the Cuisinart bowl should be no more than an inch square. Normally, do not put in more than a total of 2 cups at a time. But, of course, you can do as many batches as you need. Soft vegetables should be run for about 4 seconds. Then check and continue puréeing, if necessary, for a few seconds more. With experience, you will soon learn the precise timing of every combination you use regularly. If some of the vegetables stick to the side of the bowl, stop the machine and scrape them down with a spatula. Then continue running the machine until the mixture is as smooth as velvet.

As a starter, try this one: Preheat the oven to 375°F. Lightly rub the skins of 2 medium yellow onions with butter or oil and set them, uncovered, in an open baking pan in the center of the oven. Wash 2 medium zucchini, rub their skins with butter or oil, wrap them in foil, including inside the wrapping a few sprigs of fresh dill or other fresh herbs, then set the package in the baking pan in the oven alongside the onions. With no further supervision whatsoever, both vegetables will be about perfectly done in 45 to 50 minutes. Meanwhile, to supply the texture, open a 3-ounce can of Chinese water chestnuts, drain and dry them, chunk 3 or 4 of them and put them into the Cuisinart bowl. Run the machine in one-second bursts until they are very finely minced – almost a crispy-crunchy grain – usually in about 2 to 4 bursts. Transfer them to a storage dish and hold them. As soon as the onions and zucchini are done, peel the onions and chunk them into the Cuisinart bowl. Chunk the zucchini and add to the onions, with a ¼ teaspoon of English mustard, a teaspoon of mayonnaise, with salt and pepper, to taste. Run the machine until you have a velvet purée – usually in about 3 to 4 seconds. Transfer to a mixing bowl and stir in with a wooden spoon tablespoon by tablespoon of the grated water chestnuts until you have the near-perfect balance of crispness and velvet. Put this mousse into a covered serving dish and keep it warm in the oven at about 200°F until serving time. Please note, with satisfaction, that no butter or cream is added to this mousse, so that it is quite low calorie!

Now that you know the basic principles, you can start experimenting with other vegetables, both hard and soft, cooked and raw. Among the soft vegetables: lightly boiled green beans or broccoli tops, brussels sprouts, an eggplant baked with garlic slivers, a baked sweet potato or yam, young spinach leaves, baked acorn squash . . . Among the aromatic and garnishing ingredients to be added to the purées, try almost any of the fresh leaf herbs, fresh ginger root, Chinese Szechuan pepper, a tablespoon or two of yoghurt . . . Among the hard vegetables to be ground in advance in the Cuisinart for texture, an excellent mixture includes finely chopped salted peanuts, scraped raw carrots, or chunked raw white turnips, or, during their short season, raw Jerusalem artichokes. The possible combinations are almost endless. Here are two more examples from famous young chefs in France . . .

BUTTERED AND CREAMED MOUSSE OF ROMAINE LETTUCE

(for 4)

We have adapted this recipe from the original which came to us from the young, imaginative Chef Gérard Vié at his restaurant in Versailles, outside Paris.

Romaine lettuce (2 small, or 1 large head)	Heavy cream (up to 6 Tbs)
Gruyère cheese (up to 6 ounces)	Salt, coarse crystal, to taste
Butter (¼-pound stick)	Black pepper, fresh ground, to taste

Active Preparation 20 Minutes, Unsupervised Draining 2 Hours, and Chilling Overnight

You start the day before. Tear apart 2 small (or one large) heads of romaine, cutting away the tough base and lower stalks. Plunge the leaves into salted water at a rolling boil for 5 minutes. Then they must be completely dried by letting the water drain out of every crevice for several hours. Tear the leaves and put them into the

Cuisinart bowl, batch by batch, running the machine until the lettuce is smoothly puréed, usually in about 3 to 6 seconds. Stop during the process and push the mixture down with a spatula. Again, drain the purée by transferring it to a fine-mesh sieve and leaving it to drip for several more hours. The mousse can now be refrigerated, covered, overnight. Meanwhile, grate ¼ pound of Gruyère cheese in the Cuisinart with the medium grating disk. Then, shortly before serving, put the mousse back in the bowl of the machine with a ¼-pound stick of butter, sliced, 4 tablespoons of heavy cream, and the grated Gruyère cheese. Run the machine until it is all completely mixed – usually in about 2 to 4 seconds. Transfer the mousse to a saucepan and gently heat it up, stirring continuously, until the butter and cheese melts and the mousse solidifies and thickens. Taste and adjust the seasonings. Adjust the texture by adding more cream to thin it, or more grated cheese to thicken it. Serve it quite hot.

PARISIAN PURÉE OF JERUSALEM ARTICHOKES

(for 4)

We have adapted this recipe from the original by one of the most famous of the younger Paris chefs, Alain Senderens.

Jerusalem artichokes, thinly peeled – only in season for a short time each year, (1 lb)	**Heavy cream (6 Tbs)**
	Salt, coarse crystal, to taste
	Black pepper, freshly-ground, to
Butter, sliced (¼ lb)	**taste**

Preparation From Start to Serving About 35 Minutes
Thinly peel and gently boil the artichokes in salted water until they are quite tender. Try them with a fork after the first 15 minutes. Drain and dry them completely, then chunk them into the Cuisinart bowl, with a ¼-pound stick of butter, sliced, 4 tablespoons of heavy cream, with salt and pepper, to taste. Whirl the steel blades until the mixture is smoothly puréed – usually in about 3 to 6 seconds. Transfer the purée to a saucepan and gently heat it up, stirring continuously, adjusting the seasonings and thinning it, if necessary, with a few more teaspoons of cream. Serve it very hot.

133

CONCENTRATED AROMATIC PURÉE OF TOMATOES

(for 4)

We learned this superb trick with tomatoes originally from the "great master" himself, Paul Bocuse, at his superb, three-star restaurant outside Lyon. Our adaptation for the Cuisinart needs, for complete success, tomatoes that are beautifully ripe and sweet. When your local tomatoes are hard and tasteless, as they so often are these days, you can improve matters by preparing this recipe with half fresh tomatoes and half imported Italian canned plum tomatoes, which will add color, flavor, sweetness and texture. Drain off, of course, as much as possible of the liquid from the can.

Shallots, whole, unpeeled
(5 cloves)
Garlic, whole, unpeeled (2 cloves)
Tomatoes, see above (total 1½ lbs)
Butter (3 Tbs)
Salt, coarse crystal, to taste
Black pepper, freshly ground, to taste

Sugar (about 1½ tsp)
Basil (1 tsp dried, or 1 Tbs fresh leaves)
Marjoram (1 tsp dried, or 1 Tbs fresh leaves)
Parsley, leaf only (about 5 good sprigs)

Prepared in About 30 Minutes from Start to Serving
Put the 5 shallots and the 2 cloves of garlic into the Cuisinart bowl and run the machine until they are not too finely minced, starting and stopping in usually about two or three 1-second bursts. Transfer them to a covered storage dish and hold them. Cut each fresh tomato in half and, squeezing each half gently (as if it were a lemon), get rid of the juice and the seeds. With the Cuisinart, there is no need to skin the tomatoes as the skins are disintegrated by the whirling blades. Chunk the tomatoes into the bowl and run the machine until the tomatoes are finely diced, but not quite puréed – usually in about 2 to 4 seconds. Leave the tomato mixture where it is for the moment. Heat up a 10-inch frypan over medium frying heat and melt in it the 3 tablespoons of butter. As soon as it is reasonably hot, put in the minced shallots and garlic, stirring them around for hardly more than a few seconds. At once add the tomato mixture and adjust the heat so that it bubbles merrily, getting rid of its excess water and concentrating its flavors. Encourage this process by stirring it almost con-

stantly. At the same time, blend in salt, pepper and sugar, to your taste. Continue the bubbling until all the water is out and the tomatoes have thickened to a nicely solid purée. This should be achieved in about 20 minutes of steady but not too strong bubbling. Meantime, if you are using fresh basil, marjoram and parsley, rinse and dry the Cuisinart bowl and put the herbs into it, mincing them not too finely in about two or three 1-second bursts. As soon as the tomatoes have thickened and have a beautifully concentrated flavor, stir into them the minced herbs. (Dried herbs, of course, will not need to be chopped.) Finally adjust the seasonings and serve the purée very hot.

MOST LUXURIOUS WAY OF SERVING POTATOES – A FRENCH GRATIN

(for 4)

We learned this superb method with potatoes from the great, three-star French chef-brothers, Jean and Pierre Troisgros, at their marvelous restaurant in central France. A *gratin* involves slicing the potatoes and baking them in ½ pint of heavy cream. If that sounds an awful lot, let us say without hesitation that we would gladly do without cream in our coffee and over our fruits all through the year, just so that we could consume it all at once in this irresistibly lovely dish. It represents the humble potato glorified into a heavenly body!

Potatoes, starchy rather than waxy (1 lb)
Garlic, whole, unpeeled (2 cloves)
Butter (5 Tbs)
Yellow onions, peeled and chunked (2 medium)

Heavy cream (1 cup)
Salt, coarse crystal, to taste
Black pepper, freshly ground, to taste

Active Work of Preparation About 15 Minutes Plus About 1 Hour of Unsupervised Baking

Thinly peel the pound of potatoes and, if necessary, cut them to fit easily down the chimney of the Cuisinart cover. Fit the medium slicing disk into the work bowl and slice all the potatoes, pushing them down quite gently so that the slices will be nice and thin. As the

135

bowl fills up, empty it, batch by batch, into a large mixing bowl filled with cold water. It is essential to immerse the potato slices at once in the water to wash away their starch and to keep them from discoloring in the air. Choose an open baking dish, about 2 inches deep and 9 inches across, preferably of enameled iron or tinned copper, so that it can be used on top of the stove as well as in the oven. Preheat the oven to 275°F. Cut the 2 garlic cloves in half and thoroughly rub each half all over the inside of the baking pan. Then butter it liberally, using at least 2 tablespoons. Rinse and dry the Cuisinart bowl and put into it the chunked onions and the remains of the garlic cloves. Then run the machine until they are mashed to a purée – usually in about 3 to 6 seconds. Add the cup of cream and run the machine for another 2 seconds to amalgamate completely the cream and onions. Hold the mixture where it is. Drain the potato slices and dry them thoroughly with a cloth, then layer them neatly in the baking pan, carefully overlapping each layer so as to leave room for the cream to run between the slices. Lightly season the layers as you build them with salt and pepper. Pour all around and over the top the creamed onion mixture and set the baking pan over gentle heat on top of the stove. Adjust the heat so that the cream comes to a very gentle simmer and keep it going, uncovered, for exactly 10 minutes after the first bubbling begins. Then dot the top with the remaining 3 tablespoons of the butter and set the pan, un-covered, in the center of the oven. The secret for persuading the potatoes to absorb the cream is to cook everything extremely gently for about 2 hours. If, at any time, the cream begins to bubble too hard, turn the oven temperature down 10 degrees. Taste a bit of a potato and, if it is now quite soft, turn up the oven to 425°F to brown the top of the gratin to a gold crust – usually in 5 to 10 minutes. Bring the baking pan to the table and serve the gratin on very hot plates. It can be the accompaniment to the main dish, or, better still, we think, it can be a course on its own after the main entrée.

10

Three International Menus for Prestigious Parties

So far, we have stressed the uses of the Cuisinart chopper-churner as an everyday kitchen helper for family meals – cutting costs, saving time and eliminating many of the most boring of kitchen chores. But – I can hear you ask the question – what about the preparation of a superb party menu for a group of friends who are knowledgeable gastronomes, when the sky is the limit so far as cost and effort are concerned? Isn't hand work still the best? Can any machine do the chopping and mixing as well as sensitive human fingers? What about the so-called "supreme skills" of a great professional chef?

There need not be a shadow of a doubt about the answers to these questions. The Cuisinart, in this respect, is unique among kitchen machines. It does its work better than human fingers. It chops more evenly. It can completely amalgamate and marry certain food ingredients that simply fail to unite under the lesser power of hand beating. In fact, the great professional chefs themselves now use the Cuisinart blades and disks as essential tools, so that they spend less time laboring at the work counter and more time applying their supreme skills to the invention of brilliant new recipes – and imaginative new ways of making the machine work for them.

In this chapter, then, we offer three great menus – for a small dinner party, a cold buffet, and an informal supper for a crowd of 50 friends – in which the chopper-churner can help you to make everything more nearly perfect with no compromise in quality, yet with great saving of effort and time. Some of them can be prepared in advance. In fact, several of these recipes could not have been invented and could not now be prepared without the advent of the Cuisinart machine. We shall explain this as we go along . . .

A MAGNIFICENT AND MEMORABLE SMALL FRENCH DINNER PARTY

Baked Featherlight Gâteau of Foie Gras with Oyster Sauce
Classic Mousse of Fresh Salmon with Champagne Sauce
Green Salad
Sweet Glacéed Chestnuts in Croquette Balls

BAKED FEATHERLIGHT GÂTEAU OF FOIE GRAS WITH OYSTER SAUCE

(for 4)

This is one of the most revolutionary recipes of the current "new wave" of off-beat cooking by the brilliant young chefs of France. It was invented for the Cuisinart machine. Without it, there would be no possibility of completely amalgamating and lightening the extraordinary mixture of goose livers, milk and white Porto wine. We got this recipe from the highly creative young French chef, Gérard Vié, at his restaurant, Les Trois Marches, The Three Steps, in Versailles near Paris. The fantastic combination of ingredients sounds almost shocking, but it is quite marvelous and has quickly become a sensational success among the gastronomes of Paris. The foie gras used in our adaptation of the French recipe does not have to be the supreme quality of a Bloc of pure, Solid Goose Liver. It can be the much-less-expensive mousse, often called "Délice de STRASBOURG" or "Purée de Foie d'Oie Truffé de Perigord."

Foie gras, French goose liver pâté, see above, (7 oz can)	Butter (¼ lb)
Eggs (5)	Oysters, very fresh (12)
Milk (¾ cup)	Shallots, peeled, whole (4 cloves)
White Porto wine (3½ Tbs)	Sweet white wine, or sweet Champagne (7 Tbs)
Salt, coarse crystal, to taste	Heavy cream (¾ cup plus 2 Tbs)
Black pepper, freshly ground, to taste	

Active Work of Preparation About 30 Minutes, Plus About 50 Minutes of Unsupervised Baking and Simmering

Preheat your oven to 325°F and place at its center a *bain marie* – an open baking pan about 12 × 12 × 2 inches, filled about 1 inch deep

138

with boiling water, in which the small baking dishes will stand surrounded by steam. We use 4 individual small soufflé dishes, each
about 4 inches wide and 2 inches deep.

Put into the Cuisinart work bowl: the 7 ounces of foie gras,
chunked, the 5 whole eggs, the ¾ cup of milk, the 3½ tablespoons
of Porto, plus very little salt and pepper. Run the machine until all
these elements are completely amalgamated into a fluffy, smooth
cream – usually in 10 to 15 seconds. Watch carefully. Do not overchurn. Lightly butter the 4 baking dishes and divide the foie gras
mixture equally between them, leaving enough room on top for the
oysters and sauce to be added at serving. Stand the 4 dishes in the
boiling water in the oven. Leave them to bake until the bright knife
test shows that each little gâteau is completely set all the way through
– usually in somewhere between 40 and 50 minutes.

Meanwhile, prepare the oyster sauce. Drain the dozen oysters,
carefully catching their juices, which will probably not amount to
more than about ⅓ cup of liquid. Dry the drained oysters with a light
cloth and hold them at room temperature. Having rinsed and dried
the Cuisinart work bowl, put into it the 4 peeled shallot cloves and
finely mince them in 2 to 4 one-second bursts, carefully checking
after each burst. Add to the shallots the strained oyster juice and the
7 tablespoons of sweet wine or champagne, then run the machine
just to mix them thoroughly – usually in 2 or 3 seconds. Transfer the
liquid mixture to a 1½-quart saucepan, then heat it up to the boiling
point. Leave it uncovered and let it bubble merrily but not fiercely for
about 5 minutes to reduce it, thus concentrating and sharpening its
flavors. Then remove the saucepan from the heat, stir in carefully
all the cream. Reheat it to a merry bubbling, stirring continuously,
to continue the reduction until the level of the liquid in the saucepan
has fallen by about half. This may take between 15 and 20 minutes.
When the reduction is complete, turn down the heat to just below
bubbling and stir in, curl by curl, the remaining 7 tablespoons of
butter. Taste and adjust the seasonings. Turn off the fire and, when
the sauce has cooled to about blood heat, put the oysters into it to get
warm. They must not, under any circumstances, cook and harden.
They are to be served virtually raw.

When the little gâteaux in their dishes are perfectly baked and set,
place 3 oysters on top of each, pour in some of the sauce and serve
immediately, very hot. Bring the rest of the sauce to table in a warm

sauceboat. These gâteaux are best eaten with a fork and a medium-sized spoon.

CLASSIC MOUSSE OF FRESH SALMON WITH CHAMPAGNE SAUCE

(for 4 to 6)

This is one of the greatest of all French dishes, but, before the Cuisinart machine, the perfect, professional preparation of it was virtually beyond any possibility for the average amateur cook. It took too long. It required too much strength in one's arm. Now, since almost every professional chef makes it in the Cuisinart appliance, we amateurs can achieve the same results as they do by simply adopting their methods with the machine. The result is an elegant and superb main dish.

Salmon, fresh, boned and skinned, cut in 1-inch cubes (1 lb)	Black pepper, freshly ground, to taste
Heavy cream (1½ cups)	Butter (about 2 tsp)
Egg, whole (1)	Champagne sauce, see recipe on page 141 (1 batch)
Nutmeg, freshly grated, to taste	
Red cayenne pepper, to taste	Watercress (small bunch)
Salt, coarse crystal, to taste	Cherry tomatoes, halved (about 6)

Active Work of Preparation About 20 Minutes, Plus About 1 Hour of Unsupervised Baking

Preheat your oven to 400°F and place at its center an open baking pan, large enough so that the ring mold will stand in it, then fill the baking pan to a depth of 1 inch with boiling water. For this mousse, we choose a ring mold of a little more than 1-quart capacity.

The entire churning and puréeing job is done all at once in the Cuisinart work bowl. Put the pound of cubed raw salmon into the bowl, with the 1½ cups of cream, the whole egg, a few grinds of nutmeg, 2 or 3 pinches of cayenne, plus salt and pepper, to taste. Run the machine until the salmon is perfectly puréed and everything is completely and smoothly amalgamated – usually in 4 to 7 seconds. Watch carefully – do not overchurn, or the mixture may become pasty. Lightly butter the ring mold and spoon the mousse into it, smoothing the top surface with the back of the spoon. Wipe off the inside top rim of the mold, cut a ring of wax paper exactly to fit the top surface, butter one side of the paper and lightly press this buttered side down onto the top surface of the mousse. Stand the ring mold in the boiling water in the oven and leave it to bake until the bright knife test shows that the mousse is completely set all the way through – usually in 50 to 70 minutes. After the first 10 minutes of baking, reduce the oven heat to 350°F.

Meanwhile, prepare the champagne sauce according to the recipe on page 141. When the mousse is perfectly done, remove the paper ring, unmold the mousse onto a hot serving platter and spoon some of the champagne sauce over it, allowing it to dribble down the sides. Garnish the platter with sprigs of watercress and the top of the mousse, if you like, with halves of cherry tomatoes. Bring the rest of the sauce to the table in a warm sauceboat. Boiled saffron rice makes a fine accompaniment to the dish.

CHAMPAGNE SAUCE FOR SALMON MOUSSE OR OTHER FISH OR SHELLFISH

(for 4 to 6)

Mushrooms, wiped clean, trimmed and quartered (¼ lb)
Shallots, unpeeled whole (6 cloves)
Black peppercorns, whole (2 tsp)
Champagne, dry (½ cup)
Fish bouillon, or bottled clam juice (1¼ cups)

Flour, all-purpose (about 2 Tbs)
Butter (2½ Tbs)
Heavy cream (1 cup)
Salt, coarse crystal, to taste
Black pepper, freshly ground, to taste

Active Work of Preparation About 20 Minutes, Plus About 1 Hour of Unsupervised Simmering

First, put the ¼ pound of mushrooms into the Cuisinart bowl and coarsely dice them in 1 or 2 one-second bursts, carefully checking after each burst. Transfer the mushrooms to a 1½-quart lidded saucepan. Without rinsing out the Cuisinart bowl, put into it the 6 unpeeled shallot cloves and mince them finely by running the machine for between 2 and 4 seconds. Add the shallots to the mushrooms in the saucepan. Again without rinsing the bowl, put in the 2 teaspoons of whole peppercorns and run the machine just long enough to crack them – usually in 1 or 2 seconds. Add the peppercorns to the mushrooms and shallots. Also add the ½ cup of champagne and ¼ cup of the fish bouillon or clam juice, then bring everything up to the boiling point and simmer for about 10 minutes.

Rinse and dry the Cuisinart bowl, then put into it the 2 tablespoons of flour, 1½ tablespoons of the butter and the remaining cup of the fish bouillon or clam juice. Run the machine until these are thoroughly mixed, the amalgamated butter and flour forming tiny balls within the liquid. Transfer this to a second saucepan and heat it up, stirring continuously, until it thickens into a smooth sauce, then simmer it very gently, covered, to cook the flour for about 10 minutes. Now carefully work the mixture into the champagne bouillon. Continue simmering for another 10 minutes. Then work in the cup of cream and continue the simmering, stirring regularly, for 30 minutes longer. Finally, work in, curl by curl, the remaining tablespoon of butter. Taste the sauce and adjust its seasoning, as you please. Bring the sauce almost back to boiling just before you dribble it over the fish and bring it to the table.

SWEET GLACÉED CHESTNUTS IN CROQUETTE BALLS

(for 4)

Another of the unique performances of the Cuisinart is its almost perfect puréeing of chestnuts. In our experience no other kitchen machine – and no human hands – can work the chestnuts finely and firmly enough to bring out all the glutinous oils and meld them with the nutty flesh into such a creamy-smooth, velvety fluff. Chestnuts done in this way – whether as a savory mash to accompany a main dish in place of potatoes, pasta, or rice (see recipe on page 153) or as a dessert whip as in this recipe below – are a memorable gastronomic experience. For supreme results, of course, it is well worth the trouble of shelling and skinning fresh chestnuts in season. Out of season, you can use the Italian dried chestnuts, which are already shelled and skinned in advance, but which lose something in flavor and texture. They must be soaked overnight before using. There are, also, canned versions of puréed chestnuts, but these are a large compromise. This recipe expects you to start with the best.

**Chestnuts, fresh or dried, see
above (about 40, or roughly
2½ lbs fresh, or 2 lbs dried)**

**Milk, scalded (1¼ cups)
Salt, coarse crystal, to taste**

Vanilla, whole bean, or pure
   extract (1 bean, or 1 tsp extract)
Glacéed chestnuts, French
   marrons glacés (10 whole)
Egg, whole (1)

Olive oil (1 tsp)
Breadcrumbs, fine (about 1 cup)
Sugar, fine-grind white (about
   ¾ cup)
Frying oil in deep fryer

If You Use Fresh Chestnuts Allow About 30 Minutes for Shelling and Skinning Them, Then About 45 Minutes for the Active Preparation of the Dish, Plus About 1½ Hours of Unsupervised Boiling

With fresh chestnuts, use a small-bladed, tough oyster knife to make a cross-cut gash in the flat side of each, then drop them into a large pan of cold water, bring them rapidly to the boil, let them bubble hard for 2 minutes and drain them. As soon as they are cool enough to handle, shell and skin them, making sure to get the furry bits out of each crevice. (Since they are going to be puréed, you can break them up as much as you need to get at the inner convolutions of the skin.) Put the chestnuts into a fairly wide bottomed saucepan, with the 1¼ cups of scalded milk, a pinch of salt and the whole vanilla bean, slit in half lengthwise. (If you are using vanilla extract, add it later.) Simmer and steam the chestnuts, covered, until they are quite soft – usually in about 40 minutes.

Meanwhile, break the 10 glacéed chestnuts in half with your fingers – do not use a knife – and hold them aside in a covered dish. Lightly beat the egg with the teaspoon of olive oil and spread it out on a dinner plate. Spread out, on a second dinner plate, a layer of the breadcrumbs and, on a third plate, a layer of the sugar. Heat up the oil in your deep fryer to 375°F.

As soon as the chestnuts are soft, remove the vanilla bean and purée them, with the milk, in the Cuisinart work bowl. Depending on how much the chestnuts have expanded, you may have to divide them into 2 or 3 batches. Run the machine until the chestnuts have been churned into a completely smooth, fluffy purée – usually in about 10 to 15 seconds. Put this chestnut purée back into the saucepan and reheat it to gentle bubbling, stirring it every couple of minutes or so to prevent it from sticking to the bottom, until it becomes stiff and thick – usually in about 5 to 10 minutes. Then turn off the heat and, if you were not using a vanilla bean earlier, stir in thoroughly the teaspoon of vanilla extract. Spoon the purée into an open, fairly wide, china, enamel, or stainless steel pan that is large enough so that the purée will form a layer not more than 1 inch thick. Press wax paper down onto its surface and place it in the refrigerator to set – usually in about 15 to 20 minutes.

When the purée is quite stiff, mold it into 20 balls by wrapping it around each of the 20 halves of glacéed chestnuts. Roll each ball in the egg, then in the breadcrumbs, and lower it gently into the frying basket in the hot oil. You can put as many balls into the basket as it will hold, but they must not touch each other. Bring each ball out as soon as it is a good golden brown, roll it on absorbent paper to dry it, then lightly roll it in the sugar. Serve these chestnut croquette balls very hot. When you taste them, you will agree that the time and trouble were well worth while. They make a memorable party dessert.

A BRILLIANT BUFFET SUPPER

Here are more imaginative recipes which virtually depend for their unusual blend of flavors and balance of textures on the efficiency and power of the Cuisinart machine. We have never been able to prepare them so well or so quickly and easily, by hand or by any other machine, as we can now. You would expand this basic buffet menu, of course, with seasonal vegetables, a salad, some cheese, fruit, coffee, plus, if you choose, wines, brandies and liqueurs.

Aromatic Pâté of Smoked Salmon
Cold Circassian Chicken with Almond, Filbert, and Walnut Cream
Spanish Crema Catalana Custard with Burnt Sugar

AROMATIC PÂTÉ OF SMOKED SALMON

(for 4 to 6)

If you have always thought that a thin slice of smoked salmon is the ultimate in appetizer luxury, read on. When smoked salmon is puréed with the Cuisinart steel blades and delicately blended with subtle aromatic herbs, it can be magnified into something positively celestial. Quite apart from its flavor, it has a creamy, melting smoothness on the tongue that is an extraordinary gastronomic experience. Also, for this recipe, you can start with the cheaper cuts of smoked salmon – or even the "ends of the sides," often offered at a discount by the specialty shops. You must use unsalted butter of the best possible quality and freshly squeezed lemon juice. Then, at the table, have more lemon wedges, a pepper mill and thin slices of crisp whole wheat toast. A dry white wine, or very dry champagne, gives everything a final dazzle and sparkle.

Smoked salmon, thinly sliced, see
   above (¾ lb)
Butter, unsalted, see above (½ lb)
Lemons (2 or 3, according to size)
Black pepper, Indian or Chinese
   Szechuan, freshly ground, to
   taste

Red cayenne pepper, to taste
Salt, coarse crystal, to taste
Brown whole wheat thin toast

Prepared in Less Than 5 Minutes, Followed by a Couple of Hours of Chilling in the Refrigerator
Spread the slices of salmon around the bottom of the Cuisinart bowl. Slice the butter and drop it down evenly on top of the salmon. Add, at first, about 2 teaspoons of the lemon juice, plus a few grinds of the pepper and a pinch or two of the cayenne. All necessary salt may be provided by the salmon. (Incidentally, if you can get the Chinese Szechuan pepper, it adds a mysterious nuttiness to the mixture.) Run the machine until everything is churned and chopped into a creamy-smooth purée. Stop after the first 4 seconds and taste, adding more lemon juice and pepper, if it pleases you. Also, if the salmon was not salty enough, a minimum of salt. Now, if the texture is not yet perfect, start and stop the machine in one-second bursts, checking after each, until you have it dead right. We usually expect to give it 2 to 4 bursts. Spoon the pâté into a single ceramic serving pot, or into tiny individual pots for each guest. Cover with aluminum foil and chill in the refrigerator until serving time, preferably a minimum of an hour or two. Serve with lemon wedges, more pepper and toast.

COLD CIRCASSIAN CHICKEN WITH ALMOND, FILBERT AND WALNUT CREAM
(for 4 to 6)

This is one of the classic dishes of the Middle East and certainly among the great dishes of the world, but, in the old days, it took enormous effort and time to prepare. A Turkish cook might spend half a day pounding the nuts with a large, stone pestle and mortar, repeatedly squeezing the mash as hard as possible by hand to extract the nut oils. Now, we do that part of the job mechanically in under 30 seconds, and Circassian Chicken can be one of the regular party dishes of any family. It makes a magnificently handsome and rich centerpiece for a cold buffet. You must first – a few hours or a day in advance – gently simmer a couple of chickens in an aromatic bouillon, then let them cool in the liquid, and, finally, carve off the meat in the special way for this dish. Or, in a pinch, you could start with whole rotissed chickens from your local delicatessen.

Chicken meat, boiled as above
(from 2 chickens of about 3
lbs each)
Yellow onions, peeled and
quartered (2 medium)
White bread (5 average slices)
Milk (¾ cup)
Butter, lightly salted (2 Tbs)
Almonds, shelled and blanched
(¼ lb)

Filberts, shelled (¼ lb)
Walnuts, shelled (¼ lb)
Salt, coarse crystal, to taste
Red cayenne pepper, to taste
Walnut oil, pure (about ½ cup)
Chicken bouillon, perhaps from
boiling of chickens, or alterna-
tive (about 3 cups)
Paprika, Hungarian sweet
(2 Tbs)

**Apart From the Advance Boiling of the Chickens, Active
Preparation in About 1 Hour From Start to Serving**
Peel away the skin of the chickens (using it up in some other way) and then carve off the meat in strips about 3 inches long and 1 inch wide. Arrange them neatly, overlapping, to form a low mound on the cold serving platter, then hold, covered with aluminum foil, in the refrigerator, while you prepare the creamy-rich nut garnish.

Put the 2 onions into the Cuisinart work bowl and mince them fairly finely – usually in 2 or 3 one-second bursts. Transfer them to a covered storage dish and hold them. Break up the 5 bread slices into a mixing bowl and thoroughly soak them with the ¾ cup of milk. Mash them around with a wooden spoon and then leave them soaking. Set a small sauté pan over medium frying heat and melt in it the 2 tablespoons of butter. When it is hot, add the minced onions and sauté them, stirring vigorously, until they are just transparent – usually in 2 or 3 minutes – then turn off the heat and hold them. You are now ready to use your Cuisinart machine as a modernized, auto-mated, Middle Eastern pestle and mortar.

Without rinsing the bowl, put into it, all at once, the total ¾ pound of almonds, filberts and walnuts. At first, start and stop the machine in one-second bursts, checking carefully after each, until the nuts are fairly coarsely minced. This may take up to 10 bursts. Then, you can run the machine continuously until the nuts are ground and mashed into an oily powder, possibly up to 2 minutes. At this point, you begin using the machine as a super-mixer. Add the entire con-tents of the sauté pan, butter as well as onions, plus salt and cayenne pepper to taste, then run the machine for exactly 2 seconds to mix them in. Tightly squeeze the soaked bread to get out as much milk as possible, then spread about half of it, in chunks, around the Cuisinart bowl. Also add the first 2 tablespoons of walnut oil, then run the machine for another 2 seconds, to mix. You should now begin to have a very thick and oily paste. Measure the first ½ cup of the chicken bouillon, remove the pusher from the chimney on the Cuisinart cover, then, with the machine running, pour the bouillon down the chimney in a steady stream. Now you must use your own judgment, adding and balancing more of the bouillon, bread, and walnut oil in one-second bursts until you achieve a luscious, smooth mixture – half-paste, half-sauce – not quite thin enough to pour, yet not so thick that it cannot be easily spooned and smoothed over the chicken.

When you have it dead right, spread it evenly and fairly thickly over the entire mound of chicken on the platter, smoothing it with the back of the spoon. No chicken meat should be visible. In a small bowl, mix the 2 tablespoons of paprika with ¼ cup of the remaining walnut oil. Dribble this bright red garnish in pretty designs all over the nut-cream-covered mound on the platter. Keep it all refrigerated, lightly covered, until serving time.

SPANISH CREMA CATALANA CUSTARD WITH BURNT SUGAR

(for 4 to 6)

One of the great classic desserts of Spain – a marvelous contrast be-tween the rich, velvety egg custard and the crackly-crisp covering of dark brown sugar. It is by far the best if each diner gets an individual small dish with the sheet of sugar unbroken, but, if you insist, it can also be served in a single dish, say, a 1½-quart heatproof ceramic soufflé dish.

Lemon, for its rind (1)	Sugar, white granulated (1¾ cups)
Milk (2 cups)	Cornstarch (2 Tbs)
Cinnamon stick, whole, 2 to 3 inches (1)	Egg yolks (10)
Vanilla bean, whole, quartered lengthwise, or pure extract (1 bean, or 1 tsp extract)	Anise liqueur, Spanish Anise del Mono or French Pernod or Ricard (3 Tbs)
	Heavy cream (3 cups)

Active Work of Preparation About 45 Minutes, Plus About 3 Hours of Entirely Unsupervised Chilling and Setting

With a sharp potato peeler or a French zest scraper, cut 4 good slivers of the thin, yellow, outer rind of the lemon and put them into the Cuisinart bowl, starting and stopping the machine in one-second bursts until the rind is fairly finely minced – usually in a couple of bursts. Transfer the rind to a 1-quart saucepan and add the 2 cups of milk, the cinnamon stick and the 4 quarters of the vanilla bean. (If you are using the vanilla extract, hold it until later.) Heat up the milk mixture to the gentlest simmering, stirring often, to encourage the aromatic ingredients to release their flavor oils into the milk. Keep it gently simmering, covered, stirring occasionally, until you need it.

Meanwhile, put into the Cuisinart bowl 1 cup of the sugar and the 2 tablespoons of cornstarch. Run the machine for precisely 1 second to sift and completely mix these two dry ingredients. Now add the 10 egg yolks and run the machine until they are completely incorporated into the sugar, making a perfectly smooth yellow cream – usually in from 5 to 8 seconds. Quickly remove the cinnamon stick and the quarters of vanilla bean from the hot milk and set them aside. Then, with the machine again running, pour the milk in a steady stream down the open chimney of the Cuisinart cover. In about 4 to 6 seconds, the milk will be completely amalgamated with the eggs and sugar and the mixture will be just starting to thicken. Transfer the mixture at once to a 1½-quart saucepan and set it over medium heat, stirring it steadily, until all the sugar is dissolved. At the same time, put back into it the cinnamon stick and the quarters of vanilla bean. Keep the mixture just below simmering and stir constantly, steadily scraping every part and corner of the bottom of the pan to make sure that the egg custard does not stick and burn. After about 7 to 10 minutes, the custard will be thick enough to coat the spoon. Then, at once, turn off the heat. If you overcook or overheat it, it may curdle. Strain the custard through a sieve, discarding the cinnamon and vanilla bean. If you are using vanilla extract, now is the moment to stir in 1 teaspoon. Also blend in the 3 tablespoons of anise liqueur and, ½ cup by ½ cup, the 3 cups of heavy cream. Divide the mixture among the 6 heatproof ramekins or individual soufflé dishes, cover them with aluminum foil and refrigerate them for at least 3 hours.

About 10 minutes before serving time, preheat your broiler to its highest temperature and adjust the height of the grill shelf so that the top surface of the custard will be about 2 inches below the heat. Sprinkle the surface of each custard with an even layer of the remaining sugar, about 2 tablespoons to each ramekin, making sure to cover the entire surface of the custard. Now set all the ramekins at once under the broiler and leave them until the sugar is caramelized to a dark brown, crackly-crisp, solid sheet – usually in 8 to 12 minutes. Do not let it go too far. It must not get black. Serve the Crema Catalana at once before the sugar has a chance to soften. Each diner breaks the sheet of sugar with a spoon and eats bits of this almost bitter-sweet garnish as a dramatic contrast to the luxuriously smooth unctuousness of the rich custard. No wonder this is the most famous dessert of Barcelona and the Catalonian region of Spain.

A SAN FRANCISCO FISHERMAN'S WHARF SUPPER FOR A CROWD OF 50

This is an entirely informal array of good things to eat – relatively easy to prepare, not too expensive to buy, and full of hearty and robust flavors that reflect the enthusiasm for good food of the Italian communities of San Francisco. They invented the cioppino, the wonderful, one-dish fish and shellfish stew – a kind of Olympian fisherman's picnic – that is the great specialty of the San Francisco waterfront. A savory purée of chestnuts adds solidity to the main dish and a French cherry batter pie provides the dessert. You could expand this supper menu with a salad, some cheeses and fruit, plus, of course, some Italian chianti or a good California Barbera.

Canapés Spread with a Smooth Pâté of Parmesan and Romano Cheeses
San Francisco One-Dish Cioppino of Fish and Shellfish
Buttery and Savory Purée of Chestnuts
French Clafoutis of Bing Cherries

CANAPÉS SPREAD WITH A SMOOTH PÂTÉ OF PARMESAN AND ROMANO CHEESES

(for about 50)

Well-aged Parmesan and Romano are very hard cheeses, often quite difficult to grate finely, and there seems to be no other way than with the Cuisinart of grinding them to the finest of powders and then completely and smoothly amalgamating them with other soft ingredients. You might say that this is another recipe more or less invented by and for the new machine. Once you have mastered the basic technicalities, you can use this recipe for many kinds of aromatic spreads with all kinds of cheeses.

Parmesan cheese, aged, hard, cut into 1-inch cubes (1¼ lbs)
Romano cheese, aged, hard, cut into 1-inch cubes (1¼ lbs)

Cottage or pot cheese, large curd (3¾ lbs)
Heavy cream (about 1¼ cups)
Canapé toast rounds, or alternative (about 150)

Prepared in 10 Batches at About 8 Minutes per Batch
Put into the Cuisinart bowl ¼ cup each of the Parmesan and Romano, then run the machine until they are ground to a quite fine powder, starting with about 4 or 5 one-second bursts and then, after the cheeses have been chopped up, running the motor continuously – usually for 25 to 40 seconds. When you have achieved a fine grind of the cheeses, remove the pusher from the chimney of the cover, restart the motor and drop in, tablespoon by tablespoon, 12 level tablespoons of the cottage or pot cheese, running the machine until the mixture has become an absolutely smooth and spreadable paste. If it is too thick, thin it slightly by adding, teaspoon by teaspoon, a little of the heavy cream. After each addition, run the motor for one second to mix the cream in. You may need up to 2 tablespoons of cream per batch. Repeat this operation with 9 more batches of the

150

ingredients. Spread the cheese pâté on the canapés and hold them, covered, in the refrigerator. Let them come to room temperature before serving them – or you can grill them briefly under a very hot broiler until the cheese is slightly melted and flecked with brown.

SAN FRANCISCO ONE-DISH CIOPPINO OF FISH AND SHELLFISH

(for 50)

For some inexplicable reason, this great party feast dish of the Italians of San Francisco has been enthusiastically adopted by all the other inhabitants of the Bay City, but has never traveled far out of sight of the Golden Gate. Perhaps this is because nowhere else, in the U.S., is the fish and shellfish as sparklingly fresh as it is on Fisherman's Wharf. However, we have taken this basic San Francisco recipe with us to all parts of the country (and even to Europe) and have given great dinner parties with it everywhere. The tomato sauce must be thick at the beginning – the fish and shellfish will release their juices into it, combining their flavors with garlic, the herbs and the wine. Nothing in the preparation is difficult. It is a magnificent, monster one-dish meal.

Parsley, fresh leaf to be chopped (about 7 bunches, according to size)

Onions, large Bermuda, peeled and chunked (about 4 lbs)

Green celery, destringed (50 stalks, or about 5 heads)

Carrots, scraped (40 medium carrots, or about 5 bunches)

Olive oil, best quality Italian (about 1 quart)

Garlic, whole cloves, unpeeled (10, or about 2 heads)

Tomato sauce, good and thick (3 gallons)

Rosemary (2 Tbs fresh or 2 tsp dried)

Sage (2 Tbs fresh or 2 tsp dried)

Thyme (2 Tbs fresh or 2 tsp dried)

Crabs, whole, washed and cracked (30)

Clams, in shells, well-scrubbed (30 lbs)

Shrimp, medium, raw in shells (10 lbs)

Cod fillets, or other white fish, skinned and boned (20 lbs)

White wine, dry (1 quart)

Salt, coarse crystal, to taste

Black pepper, freshly ground, to taste

Prepared in About 2 Hours from Start to Serving
You will need a huge 12 to 15 gallon 2-handled lidded pot, preferably of copper (or other handsome material) in which the cioppino will be prepared and served. Cut the thick, woody stalks away from the parsley and discard them – put the parsley leaves, bunch by bunch, into the Cuisinart work bowl, then run the machine until the leaves are fairly coarsely chopped – usually in 3 to 5 seconds, but you may have to stop the machine and push down the leaves every couple of seconds or so. Transfer the first 5 bunches to the big cooking pot. Hold the remaining two bunches, chopped, for the final decoration of the cioppino. Now put the onions, divided into about 10 batches, into the bowl and run the machine until they are coarsely minced – usually in 2 to 3 seconds. Transfer each batch to the big cooking pot. Fit the slicing disk into the machine and slice, batch by batch, first the celery and then the carrots. Add each sliced batch to the big pot. Add the quart of olive oil, set the big pot over medium frying heat and sauté the vegetables, stirring them around, until the onions are just transparent – usually, with this large amount, in about 5 to 10 minutes. Meanwhile, chop the 10 unpeeled cloves of garlic moderately finely with the Cuisinart steel blades for about 2 seconds. As soon as the sautéeing is completed, add to the big pot: the minced garlic, the 3 gallons of tomato sauce, 5 quarts of fresh cold water, the rosemary, sage and thyme (if fresh, chop them for a second or two with the steel blades), heat everything up to gentle simmering, then cover the pot and keep the cooking going, stirring occasionally, for 45 minutes.

Layer the 30 crabs across the bottom of the pot, pushing them down into the sauce. Cover them and weight them down with a layer of the 30 pounds of clams. Re-cover the pot and continue the gentle simmering for another 30 minutes. From now on, there must be no more stirring, but you can prod gently here and there with a long wooden spoon to level things off and encourage a slight movement as the clams begin to open.

Then put in the layer of the 10 pounds of shrimp and, as the next layer on top of them, the 20 pounds of cod fillets. Each such addition cools the pot, so you should turn up the heat to bring back the gentle simmering as quickly as possible. Then re-cover the pot and adjust the heat to keep the simmering going for another 10 minutes.

Now sprinkle around all over the top surface the quart of wine.

Spoon out some of the sauce and taste it. It may already be salty enough, but, if it is not, add the requisite amount of salt, plus a fair grinding of pepper, to your taste. Bring everything back to simmering, re-cover the pot and keep it gently bubbling to heat up the wine for a final 10 minutes. Serve the cioppino – preferably in wooden bowls – with parsley sprinkled over and large napkins to be tied around the necks of the guests. They will eat partly with their fingers, partly with large soup spoons, and there should be garbage bowls around in which to put the empty shells.

A BUTTERY AND SAVORY PURÉE OF CHESTNUTS

(for 50)

Since there are no potatoes in the cioppino (previous recipe), we find that our guests are enchanted by the contrast between the peasanty, picnic-style shellfish stew and the elegant smoothness of these chest-nuts, puréed as you have never known them before by the whirling blades of the machine. This recipe can be used (divided by 10) at any time, with almost any main dish, to replace an accompanying serving of pasta, rice, or potatoes. See the recipe for Sweet Glacéed Chestnuts in Croquette Balls on page 143 for the best method of shelling and peeling fresh chestnuts and for a word about Italian dried chestnuts.

Chestnuts, fresh or dried, see
    above (25 lbs fresh, or 20 lbs
    dried)
Chicken bouillon (10 quarts)

Butter (1¼ lbs)
Salt, coarse crystal, to taste
Black pepper, freshly ground,
    to taste

After You Have Shelled the Chestnuts (the Time Depends on How Much Help You Can Muster) Preparation Takes About 30 Minutes, Plus 1 Hour of Unsupervised Simmering
After you (and, we hope, your many helpers) have shelled and skinned the chestnuts as described on page 143, set them to simmer gently in the 10 quarts of chicken bouillon, covered, until they are quite soft – usually in an hour. Then purée them in the Cuisinart in batches of about 2 cups each, running the machine until they are entirely smooth – usually in 10 to 15 seconds. If the purée becomes so stiff that the motor starts to struggle, add a couple of tablespoons or

so of the chicken bouillon. Transfer each batch of purée to a large saucepan for the buttering and reheating. When all the purée is in the saucepan, gently heat it up and stir in, chunk by chunk, the 1¼ pounds of butter, steadily scraping the bottom to avoid any burning or sticking. If the purée is too stiff, work in more chicken bouillon. At the same time taste and season the purée. The amount of extra salt needed will depend on the previous saltiness of the chicken bouillon. When it is all hot, rich and beautifully smooth, serve it at once on hot plates.

FRENCH CLAFOUTIS OF BING CHERRIES – A FRUIT BATTER PIE

(for 50)

This is an excellent and handsome variation from our standard, pastry-crusted fruit pie. The whole cherries are almost completely enclosed in a baked egg batter with a light texture and a richly buttery flavor. For this big party version, you will have to decide whether you bake it in 10 pans of 9 × 9 × 2 inches, or 5 pans of double that size, or any combination you please. Each clafoutis should be between ¾ and 1 inch thick, so that the whole cherries will nest neatly inside it, but with some of them showing through. This recipe was originally given to us by Chef Georges Dumas, of the great three-star Restaurant Lasserre in Paris.

Ginger, crystallized (1¼ lbs)	Eggs, whole (40, large)
Butter, gently melted (1 lb 5 oz)	Milk (10 cups or 2½ qts)
Bing cherries, fresh, whole, unpitted (16½ lbs)	Rum, dark (5 oz)
	Vanilla, pure extract (5 oz)
Flour, all-purpose (17½ cups)	Confectioners sugar for sprinkling
Sugar, white fine-grind (5 cups)	on top (about 2 cups)
Salt, fine-grind (about 3 tsp)	

Active Work of Preparation About 45 Minutes, Plus About 1 Hour of Unsupervised Baking

Preheat as many ovens as you have available (plus, perhaps, a few of your neighbors') to 350°F. Divide the 1¼ lbs of ginger into 3 batches and coarsely chop each batch in the Cuisinart work bowl, starting and stopping the steel blades for usually 3 or 4 one-second bursts, checking the progress after each burst. Assuming that you have large enough pans (18 × 9 × 2 inches) to bake 5 clafoutis simultaneously, divide the chopped ginger into 5 equal parts and hold.

Now load the first baking pan. Liberally butter its bottom and sides and spread it in a single layer of enough unpitted, washed cherries to fill the pan, leaving a good ¾ inch of space all around the sides, so that there will be a solid frame of batter around the outside. Sprinkle ⅕ of the ginger among the cherries. Next, for the first batch of batter, put into the Cuisinart work bowl: 1¾ cups of the flour, unsifted, ½ cup of the fine-grind sugar and a pinch of the salt, then run the machine for 1 second just to sift and mix these dry ingredients. Now add 4 of the eggs, 3½ tablespoons of the melted butter, 1 cup of the milk and 1 tablespoon each of the rum and the vanilla. Run the steel blades until these are completely mixed into a perfectly smooth batter – usually in about 5 to 10 seconds. Pour this batter at once evenly over the layer of cherries in the baking pan. It should about half cover them. At once make a second batch of the batter and pour it over the cherries. If they are just covered, with a few peeping through here and there, set the pan at once in the center of the oven and time it for the first 45 minutes of baking. If there is not quite enough batter, with too many cherries showing too much of themselves, quickly make a third batch and use as much of it as you need to enclose the cherries.

Repeat this entire operation until you have loaded the other 4 baking pans and started them baking in the ovens. They are done when their tops are brown and puffy, and the bright knife test shows that the batter is set all the way through – usually in about 45 minutes to 1 hour.

As soon as each clafoutis is done, turn it out upside down from the pan so that the underside, where more cherries are showing, becomes the top. Sprinkle the cherries with as much of the confectioner's sugar as their relative sweetness or tartness requires and serve the clafoutis piping hot from the oven. Traditionally, in France, it is cut into square or rectangular servings. But no one would object to triangles.

11

The Chopper-Churner Cuts Costs with Lively Encore Entrees

In our earlier book, *Feasts for All Seasons,* we once said that well-prepared "leftovers" ought really to be called "encores," because the food is brought back onto the stage of the dining table to the enthusiastic applause of the diners – just as a great solo performer at a concert is induced to return by the overwhelming demand of the audience for one more taste of his artistry. The artistry of the Cuisinart blades with leftovers is certainly dramatic. It can take any kind of cooked meat, fish, bird, etc., and, in a few seconds, chop and churn it into an aromatic pâté for appetizers, canapés, hors d'oeuvres, sandwiches, stuffings, terrines, or anything else you can dream up. However, we think that, although an extra leftover appetizer can be very fine, we are not really saving money with our leftovers *unless* we can extend them into nutritious, satisfying and sound main dishes. So, apart from a couple of pâté recipes at the beginning, this chapter is devoted to leftovers converted, with flair and imagination, into the principal course of the next meal.

As to low-budget dishes, let us admit right away that, in these inflationary days, the old cliché about "cheaper cuts" is virtually as dead as the dodo. Yet some essential protein ingredients remain considerably less expensive than others, and if your skill with the Cuisinart allows you to buy more of the less expensive ingredients and make them go a longer way, then you have achieved your low-budget objective. We try to show you how to do this in the following recipes. Some of both the leftover and the low-budget dishes are, we think, so good that they can be served even to party guests. Most of them can be prepared ahead. All of them are simple enough to preserve the natural flavors of the ingredients, framed and magnified by the robust qualities of aromatic country cooking.

APPETIZER FRENCH-STYLE PÂTÉS AND OLD-ENGLISH-STYLE POTTED PASTES FROM ALL KINDS OF COOKED MEATS, FISH, OR BIRDS

You really don't need a recipe from us. After we have explained the basic principles, you will want to make up your own recipes. You can use cooked beef (its tongue is especially good), lamb, pork, veal, chicken, duck, goose, turkey, all kinds of game meat and birds, all varieties of fish, cooked in almost any way – the choice is virtually limitless. No bones, of course, and all fat and gristle should be cut away. (Pork is an exception – a bit of white pork fat adds richness to the pâté.)

The method is simplicity itself. You simply put all the ingredients together into the Cuisinart bowl in roughly the following proportions: For each cup (or ½ pound) of coarsely chunked meat, you add exactly half as much unsalted butter (1 stick = ¼ lb), then the aromatic ingredients more or less to your taste, such as 4 or 5 chunked anchovy fillets for saltiness, a chunked quarter of a medium yellow onion, a couple of teaspoons of lemon juice, a pinch or two more salt, if you like, plus a grind or two of black pepper. Whirl the steel blades until everything is a not-too-smooth paste – usually in about 20 to 30 seconds. This gives a slightly chewy coarseness to the pâtés, which we enjoy. Transfer the paste at once to a handsome ceramic serving dish, or a 3-inch white china soufflé dish, and taste it, working in with a wooden spoon more of anything or everything until you have exactly what you want. Refrigerate, tightly wrapped with foil. Serve cold on thin dry toast, or on nonsalty, nonsweet, thin dry crackers, or with thin slices of fresh French bread.

All this may seem very new with the Cuisinart blade, but it is an old trick in English kitchens where, for centuries, they have been making what they call "potted pastes" to preserve and use up cooked meats and fish. We have English cookbooks dated as far back as 1733 which would serve as excellent instruction booklets for the new machine – except that the cooks in those days had to pound the meat in a mortar with a pestle for 30 or 40 minutes to achieve a smooth paste, while we can now do it in less than a minute.

Try this ancient method with cooked beef tongue, either fresh, corned, or smoked: Put into the Cuisinart bowl 1 cup of coarsely chunked boiled tongue, 1 sliced ¼-pound stick of unsalted butter, a teaspoon of ground mace, no salt, but several grinds of black pepper. Proceed exactly as in the first example above. When you taste, you may decide to add some salt, a few drops of lemon juice and anything else you choose. Serve this potted paste cold from the refrigerator.

You can make a marvelously flavorful pâté from cooked venison, or pheasant, or partridge, or rabbit, or hare. Cold corned beef is excellent. Or you can combine the flesh of a boiled or roasted chicken with an equal amount of baked or boiled ham, leaving on some of the white ham fat to add richness. The flavors of many of these English potted pastes are so delicate and subtle that they should never be dominated by any strong personality in the crackers on which they are spread. The best accompaniment is hot, thin, crisp, whole wheat, unbuttered toast. The pastes are also superb in sandwiches.

These are the basic principles – now go ahead and invent your own pâtés and potted pastes with your leftover meats.

AN APPETIZER SHRIMP PASTE

(about 1 ¼ cups)

This most attractive appetizer can be made from almost any other shellfish as well. The principles are exactly the same as for the meats, above.

Shrimp, cooked, shelled (1 cup
   tightly packed)
Olive oil, fine virgin (6 tsps)
Basil, fresh leaf in season
   (1 Tbs, or 1 tsp dried)

Lime (1)
Pepper, red Cayenne, to taste
Salt, coarse crystal, to taste

Active Preparation In About 5 Minutes Plus
Several Hours of Refrigeration
Put the cup of shrimp into the Cuisinart work bowl with the 6 teaspoons of olive oil, the tablespoon of basil (or the equivalent dried), the freshly-squeezed juice of the lime, a pinch or two of the red pepper and salt to taste. Whirl the steel blades until all this has been chopped and churned into a smooth paste – usually in 6 to 10 seconds. Spoon it out lightly into a storage-serving dish (as for the meats, above), then taste it and adjust the seasonings before storing it, covered, in the refrigerator. Serve it cold with thin, dry toast that will not overpower the delicate and subtle flavor of the sea.

LEFTOVER BEEF OR VEAL REHEATED IN AN ONION TOMATO RED-WINE-VINEGAR SAUCE

(for 4)

This is how thousands of average French families serve up the remains of yesterday's beef, whether boiled, fried, grilled, or roasted. It has always seemed surprising to us that, while we import so much in the way of ideas and methods from the French cuisine, this excellent recipe has never become popular on our side of the Atlantic. Yet our family has used it for many years whenever there is a supply of cold cooked beef in the refrigerator. It works equally well with veal.

Yellow onions, peeled and
  chunked (4 medium)
Parsley (8 good sprigs)
Celery leaves, fresh (small
  handful)
Dry breadcrumbs (½ cup)
Butter (6 Tbs)
Vinegar, red wine (2 Tbs)
Flour (2 Tbs)
Thyme (1 tsp dried, or 1 Tbs
  fresh)

Tomato paste (1 Tbs)
Beef bouillon (2 cups)
Bay leaf, whole (1)
Salt, coarse crystal, to taste
Black pepper, freshly ground,
  to taste
Leftover beef, see above, free of
  fat, sliced about ¼ inch thick
  (12 fair-sized slices)

Prepared in About 1 Hour from Start to Serving
Put into the Cuisinart work bowl the 4 chunked onions and chop them not too finely in about 1 or 2 seconds. Transfer them to a covered storage dish and hold them. If you are using fresh thyme, finely chop the leaves with the steel blades in about 1 second. Transfer them to a covered storage dish and hold them. Do the same, separately, with half the parsley combined with the celery leaves, mincing them finely in about 2 seconds. Hold in a covered storage dish. Finely mince the second half of the parsley and hold it, covered, for decoration when the dish is ready to serve. If you have some old crusts of dry bread, you can convert them to fine breadcrumbs in a second or two in the Cuisinart

work bowl, holding the crumbs for the final browning of the dish. You are now ready to prepare the sauce and put everything together.

Choose an oval *au gratin* dish, say about 10 inches long and 1½ inches deep, good looking enough to come directly from the oven to the table. This dish is to be served extremely hot. Set a roughly 10-inch sauté pan over medium frying heat and melt across it 4 table-spoons of the butter. Add the minced onions and stir them around until they become transparent and golden. Then hiss in the 2 table-spoons of vinegar, stir it around, bubble it fairly hard until it is all boiled off, leaving only its tangy taste. Then turn off the heat. Sprinkle over the onions the 2 tablespoons of flour and work it in carefully until it is all absorbed and has virtually disappeared. Now work in the thyme and the tablespoon of tomato paste. Next, begin stirring in, ¼ cup at a time, as much of the bouillon as will be needed to produce a sauce of a nicely solid consistency – neither too thick, nor too thin. As soon as the first ½ cup of bouillon is incorporated, turn on the heat again, so as to bring everything back to the boil. The sauce will get thicker as it heats up, so keep stirring in more of the bouillon. When you have it at about the right consistency, turn down the heat, add the parsley and celery leaf mixture, plus the bay leaf, crumbled, with plenty of salt and pepper. Now cover the pan and let everything gently simmer to blend and develop the flavors for just about 15 minutes. Give it a good stir about every 5 minutes, making sure that it is still gently bubbling. If it becomes too thick, add more boullion. If too thin, bubble hard for a few seconds to boil away the excess water.

About 5 minutes before the sauce is ready, preheat your oven to 450°F. Spoon about half the sauce into your oval *au gratin* dish and spread it evenly across the bottom. On top of this soft bed, neatly lay the 12 slices of cooked beef, letting each piece slightly overlap the next. Cover these slices with the second half of the sauce. Sprinkle over the top the ½ cup of breadcrumbs and dot with little bits of the remaining 2 tablespoons of butter. Set the dish on a shelf at the center of the oven and bake, uncovered, until all of the sauce is bubbling merrily and the breadcrumbs are lightly browned – usually in 10 to 15 minutes. Just before serving, decorate the dish by sprinkling it with the remaining bright green parsley. Serve at once on very hot plates. Boiled or mashed potatoes make the best accompaniment, with a refreshing green salad on the side.

LEFTOVER LAMB WITH EGGPLANT AND TOMATO IN A GREEK-STYLE MOUSSAKA

(for 4)

The marvelous one-dish-meal casserole that is called "moussaka" in many of the countries around the eastern Mediterranean has dozens of different versions – different arrangements of the layers of eggplant, onion, tomato, ground lamb and spiced egg custard – but the most luxurious and memorable moussaka recipes come from the small *tavernas* of Athens where we found this one, many years ago. It is so full of both nutrition and pleasure that we think it should be a staple of the gastronomic repertoire of every American family. Leftover cooked lamb is the authentic and ideal filling, but other meats can also be used.

Eggplant, sliced ½ inch thick, with skin (total about 2 lbs, in any combination of sizes from 1 large to 2 medium to 6 small)
Salt, coarse crystal, to taste
Cheese, Italian Parmesan, or other hard grating, chunked (¼ lb)
Scallions or shallots, scallions trimmed to 2-inch lengths, or shallots, whole unpeeled cloves (6 scallions, or 12 shallot cloves)
Garlic, unpeeled whole cloves (2)
Parsley, without stalks (about 12 good sprigs)
Yellow onions, peeled and chunked (4 medium)
Tomatoes, coarsely chunked, or a can of Italian plum (1½ lbs)
Lamb, leftover cooked, cut into 1-inch cubes, all fat removed (3 cups, fairly tightly packed)

Olive oil, preferably Greek green virgin (about ¾ cup)
Tomato paste, preferably Greek or Italian (about 6 Tbs)
Vinegar, red wine (1 Tbs)
Black pepper, freshly ground, to taste
Eggs (3 large)
Beef or lamb bouillon (about ¾ cup)
Flour (about ½ cup)
Pine nuts (2 Tbs)
Yellow raisins, seedless (½ cup)
Cinnamon, ground (¼ tsp)
Milk (½ cup)
Heavy cream (¼ cup)
Nutmeg, freshly ground (a dash or two)

Preparation in About 2 Hours from Start to Serving

Lightly salt the eggplant slices on both sides and leave them to rest side by side on a board or platter to give up some of their water. Some cooks still believe in pressing down on the slices with an inverted plate and a weight, but with the modern varieties of heavy eggplant this is no longer necessary. While waiting, do the advance preparation with the Cuisinart steel blades.

Coarsely grate the chunks of hard Parmesan cheese in about 6 to 10 seconds. Transfer the cheese to a covered storage dish and hold it. Next, mince in turn, not too finely, the aromatic herbs and vegetables, and hold each in a covered dish. Whirl the blades for the scallions or shallots, 1 or 2 seconds – for the 2 garlic cloves, unpeeled, 1 or 2 seconds – for the parsley, 1 or 2 seconds – for the 4 chunked onions, 2 or 3 seconds – and for the 1½ pounds of tomatoes (no need to peel them), 2 or 3 seconds. Finally, chop the lamb cubes, in three batches of 1 cup each, for 4 or 5 seconds.

Set a 10- to 11-inch sauté pan over medium frying heat, just lightly cover its bottom with some of the olive oil and, as soon as it is hot, sauté the chopped onions until they are just golden. Take them out with a slotted spoon and hold them. Add, if necessary, another tablespoon of olive oil to the pan, heat it up, then quickly sauté the minced scallions or shallots and the garlic, also until lightly golden – usually in 2 or 3 minutes. Transfer them to a large mixing bowl and add to them: all the chopped lamb, the 6 tablespoons of tomato paste, 2 tablespoons of the minced parsley, the tablespoon of vinegar, plus salt and pepper to taste. Work it all together gently and lightly, but thoroughly, folding and lifting rather than pressing and squeezing, preferably using your clean and sensitive fingers. Now moisten the mixture – but not too much – by working in 1 whole egg, lightly beaten, plus some of the beef or lamb bouillon, tablespoon by tablespoon, until you have a moistly soft, but certainly not gloppy mixture. Let it rest to amalgamate and develop its flavors.

Put another ¼ cup of the olive oil in the sauté pan and heat it up fiercely, almost to smoking. Bear in mind that you are now going to fry the eggplant slices not to cook them through, but only to brown and crisp them on the outside. If you fry them for too long at too low a temperature, they will absorb altogether too much oil. Pat each slice dry, lightly flour it, then thoroughly brown and crisp it as quickly as possible. Put in as many slices at a time as your sauté pan will hold. As each slice is done, drain it on paper towels.

We assemble, bake and serve our moussaka in a 3-quart open tinned copper baking dish about 4 or 5 inches deep. Preheat your oven to 350°F. Assemble the layers of the moussaka in the following order: first, spread half the eggplant slices neatly across the bottom, then, all the lamb mixture as a single thick layer, next, half the chopped tomatoes with 1 tablespoon of the pine nuts and ¼ cup of the raisins sprinkled on top, then all the minced sautéed onions, the remaining tomatoes sprinkled with the remaining pine nuts and raisins and, finally, the remaining eggplant slices. Set the baking dish, uncovered, in the oven and leave it to cook for 30 minutes.

Meanwhile, prepare the traditional custard topping. Put into the Cuisinart bowl 1 tablespoon of the remaining parsley, ¼ teaspoon of the ground cinnamon, all but 2 tablespoons of the grated cheese, the remaining 2 eggs, lightly beaten together, the ½ cup of milk, the ¼ cup of heavy cream, a few grinds of nutmeg, plus salt and pepper, to taste. Churn all these together with the whirling steel blades until they are thoroughly blended – usually in about 2 or 3 seconds. Transfer the custard to a saucepan and gently heat it, stirring continuously, until it shows the first signs of thickening. At this point, the casserole should be about ready to come out of the oven. Pour the warm custard evenly across the baking dish, allowing the liquid to seep down into all the crevices, uniting the dish and yet leaving a light, cream-flecked covering about ¼ inch thick over the top. Sprinkle on the remaining Parmesan and parsley. At once put the baking dish back into the oven until the custard is set and the top is a lovely shade of golden brown – usually in another 20 minutes. When you serve the moussaka, make sure that each diner gets a balanced share of each of the layers.

LEFTOVER PORK WITH WATER CHESTNUTS IN THE CHINESE STYLE

(for 4)

This is, of course, a variation of the classic Chinese recipe, which we have adapted for ease and speed of preparation. It is the most-demanded of all our family ways with cooked pork. In fact, whenever we have a pork roast, we always make it larger than we need, just so that there will be plenty left for our Chinese-style "encore."

Garlic, unpeeled, whole (2 cloves)
Ginger, preferably fresh root
(½-inch piece), or dried ground
(½ tsp)
Safflower or peanut oil (about
5 Tbs)
Chicken bouillon (2 cups)
Soy sauce, light (3 Tbs)
Green scallions, trimmed 2-inch
lengths (12)

Parsley, without stalks (6 good
sprigs)
Cornstarch (2 tsp)
Water chestnuts, canned, cut into
¼-inch slices (about 6)
Leftover pork, all fat removed, cut
into 1-inch cubes (2 cups, fairly
tightly packed)
Cabbage, raw, cut into small
wedges (about 2 lbs)

Prepared in About 45 Minutes from Start to Serving

Put into the Cuisinart work bowl the 2 whole cloves of garlic, unpeeled, with the piece of ginger root, sliced (or the dried ginger), then
whirl the steel blades until they are finely minced, starting and stopping them for usually 2 or 3 one-second bursts. Transfer the garlic-
ginger mix to a 10-inch lidded sauté pan and add to it 2 tablespoons of
the oil, 1 cup of the chicken bouillon and the 3 tablespoons of soy
sauce. Heat it all up to gentle simmering and keep it just bubbling,
uncovered, for about 5 minutes. Meanwhile, put into the Cuisinart
work bowl the 12 pieces of scallion and the 6 sprigs of parsley and
mince them not too finely, usually in 2 or 3 one-second bursts of the
steel blades. Hold for garnishing the finished platter.

Next, in a small bowl, moisten the 2 teaspoons of cornstarch with
¼ cup of the chicken bouillon and work them completely together.
After the 5 minutes of simmering in the sauté pan, stir in the cornstarch and keep stirring until it is thoroughly blended and just beginning to thicken – usually in about 2 minutes. Then add the water
chestnut slices and the cubes of pork, making sure that they are thoroughly amalgamated with the sauce and letting them heat up in it for,
say, about 5 minutes. Bear in mind that you are just heating the pork,
not cooking it.

Meanwhile, shred the cabbage in the Cuisinart in 4 batches of about
1 cup each, whirling the blades until you have not-too-fine shreds –
usually in about 3 to 5 seconds per batch. Combine the batches in a
2-quart saucepan and add the remaining 3 tablespoons of oil, plus the
remaining ¾ cup of chicken bouillon. Bring up to the boil, cover,
then cook until the cabbage is, in the Chinese fashion, just edibly soft,
but still quite crisp – usually in no more than 4 to 5 minutes. While it

is cooking, warm up an oval serving platter under running hot water, then dry it. The moment the cabbage is done, drain it thoroughly and spread it evenly as the base layer on the platter. Spread on top of it the entire contents of the sauté pan. Finally, sprinkle on, as decoration, the chopped parsley and scallions. Accompany this attractive dish with boiled rice.

LOW-BUDGET CASSEROLE OF KIDNEYS AND MUSHROOMS WITH FRENCH MUSTARD

(for 4)

This is the recipe to convert kidney-haters into kidney-enjoyers – with advantages to all concerned in terms of minimum expense and maximum protein and vitamin nutrition. Also, this casserole can be prepared in advance, so that, when the time comes to serve it, only about 30 minutes is needed to reheat it – a process which seems to enhance its flavors.

Beef kidney (1 lb)
Buttermilk (1 qt)
Salt, coarse crystal, to taste
Black pepper, freshly ground,
  to taste
Flour (about 4 Tbs)
Butter (6 Tbs)
Basil, fresh leaf (1 Tbs, or 1 tsp
  dried)

Tarragon, fresh leaf (1 Tbs, or
  1 tsp dried)
Porto wine, Portuguese Ruby
  (¾ cup)
Mushrooms, smallish button,
  wiped clean (½ lb)
Mustard, preferably Dijon (2 tsp)

Preparation in About 15 Minutes, After Overnight Marination, Plus About 1½ Hours of Unsupervised Baking
There is a "secret trick" for completely getting rid of all the unpleasant flavor and odor that anti-kidney people are always complaining about. Wash the kidneys, then slice them about ¼ inch thick and marinate them overnight in the refrigerator in the quart of buttermilk, lightly salted, in a covered bowl. Stir them around once, before you go to bed, and again before breakfast in the morning. The acid of the buttermilk is drawn into the tiny tubes of the kidneys, cleaning and sweetening them. Then, before cooking the kidney slices in the casserole, wash them under running hot water and dry them between paper

towels. The heat expels the buttermilk from the kidney tubes, leaving them virgin pure.

Preheat your oven to 275°F. Now lightly salt, pepper and flour the kidney slices. Over gentle frying heat, melt the 6 tablespoons of butter in a casserole, preferably of enameled iron (which can be used on top of the stove as well as in the oven and is handsome enough to be brought to the table). When the butter is hot, lightly sauté the kidney slices until they are just slightly browned on the outside, but still rare and soft on the inside – usually in about 5 minutes. Keep stirring the kidneys and occasionally shaking the pan. Do not, for heaven's sake, overcook them, or they will become leathery. Meanwhile, put the tablespoon each of fresh basil and tarragon (or the dried) into the Cuisinart work bowl and whirl the steel blades until the herbs are finely minced – usually in 2 to 3 seconds. Add to the bowl the ¾ cup of Porto and whirl the blades for another 2 seconds to blend the herb flavors with the wine.

After the kidneys have sautéed for 5 minutes, pour the aromatic Porto over them and heat up the casserole to gentle simmering to evaporate off the alcohol. Then, cover the casserole and set it in the center of the oven, leaving it to bake for 1 hour. Meanwhile, pull the stalks away from the mushroom caps, trim off any dry ends from the stalks and hold both caps and stalks to go into the casserole at the end of the hour. Once they are in, put the casserole, still covered, back into the oven for another 30 minutes. Finally, just before serving, stir into the casserole the 2 teaspoons of Dijon mustard. We usually serve this dish with mashed boiled potatoes flavored with minced lemon rind, both the mashing of the potatoes and the mincing of the rind done separately in the Cuisinart. Alternatively, we have a side bowl of boiled rice.

LEFTOVER MEAT AND TOMATO PIE, ENGLISH-STYLE

(for 4)

Our English friends put almost any kind of leftover cooked meat into this type of pie. The trick is to make sure that it does not dry out, by putting a fair amount of liquid into it and sealing the top tightly with a buttery, firm, golden brown crust. It looks lovely on the table, and when it is cut open, the first whiffs of savory steam make one irresistibly hungry.

Butter (¼ lb stick)

Yellow onions, peeled and sliced
(3 medium)

Mushrooms, smallish button,
wiped clean (½ lb)

Parsley, leaves only (about 12
good sprigs)

Leftover meat, cut into bite-size
cubes (about 3 cups, fairly
tightly packed)

Salt, coarse crystal, to taste

Black pepper, freshly ground,
to taste

Tomato sauce (up to 1½ cups)

Dough for crust, see following
recipe (1 batch)

Active Work About 15 Minutes, with Extra Time for Making the Dough and About 30 Unsupervised Minutes in the Oven

There is really nothing to it. Assuming that you have whipped up the dough in the Cuisinart work bowl at least 2 or 3 hours in advance (see the following recipe), you now preheat your oven to 425°F. and choose an open ovenproof casserole, perhaps 4 or 5 inches deep (the type in which a deep-dish steak and kidney pie would be baked by an English cook.) Set a sauté pan over medium frying heat, melt in 4 tablespoons of the butter and when it is hot, sauté the onion slices until they are just transparent and lightly gilded – usually in 3 to 4 minutes. Remove the onions with a slotted spoon and hold them. Remove the stalks from the mushroom caps and trim off any dried ends. Put the caps and the stalks into the sauté pan, and sauté them gently until they have expelled most of their water and, in its place, sucked in the butter – usually in about 6 to 8 minutes. Add more butter, tablespoon by tablespoon, as it is absorbed. Meanwhile, mince the parsley with the Cuisinart steel blades by whirling the steel blades for about 2 to 3 seconds.

Now begin assembling the pie. Butter the inside of the casserole and put in half the meat, lightly salted and peppered, as the bottom layer. Spread on top of it half the onions, half the mushrooms and half the parsley, salting and peppering as you go. Then repeat the layers in the same order. Pour in enough of the tomato sauce just to cover the top layer of mushrooms. Cover the top of the casserole securely with the rolled-out pastry dough. Set the pie in the center of the oven and bake it exactly 15 minutes. Then at once reduce the temperature to 325°F. and finish off the baking until the crust is golden and the inside of the pie is thoroughly hot – usually in another 15 minutes.

QUICK TOP-CRUST PASTRY FOR DEEP-DISH PIES

(1 batch for 1 pie top)

This recipe should be read in conjunction with the previous pastry instructions on pages 86–88 and 16. Most of the details explained there also apply to this recipe.

Milk (up to ¾ cup)
Parsley, leaves only (9 good sprigs)
Flour, all-purpose, unsifted
  (1¾ cups)

Baking powder, double-acting
  (2¼ tsp)
Salt, fine-grind (1 tsp)
Butter, chilled (5½ Tbs)

Prepared in About 5 Minutes

Put the ¾ cup of milk into a small pitcher and ice it by leaving it in the freezer while you begin preparing the dough. Put the 9 sprigs of parsley into the Cuisinart work bowl and run the machine until they are fairly finely minced – usually in 2 or 3 seconds. Now measure the flour, leveling the cup with the back of a knife, and add it to the parsley in the Cuisinart work bowl. Add the 2¼ teaspoons of baking powder and the teaspoon of salt, and sift these dry ingredients with a one-second burst of the steel blades. Then drop in the 5 tablespoons of chilled butter (cut into thin slices and spread around on top of the flour mixture). Incorporate the butter to the "niblet corn stage" by whirling the blades for just about 3 seconds.

Now take the pitcher of milk from the freezer, remove the pusher from the chimney of the Cuisinart cover, restart the motor, and immediately begin pouring in the iced milk in a thin stream. As soon as enough liquid is in, the dough will ride up as a ball on top of the blades. Instantly stop pouring and switch off the machine. The magical transformation usually takes about 4 to 6 seconds.

Set the ball of dough on a lightly floured board and, flouring your hands as well, knead the dough very quickly, as described on page 88. Now pat it and mold it with your fingers into a disk about half an inch thick and precisely large enough to cover the top of the casserole in the previous recipe. Pinch the crust down all around the edges to seal it securely, cut a couple of small slits in the top to let the steam escape, then bake it as described for the meat pie.

LEFTOVER FISH FILLETS IN A PARTY MAIN-DISH SALAD PLATTER

(for 4)

A French family would call this a *salade composée* – literally a salad composed (rather than tossed) for the handsomest possible display. This is just about the best of all ways of bringing back some leftover fish that would certainly not stand being reheated. Served this way in its cold state, but beautifully dressed up, it can easily be the main dish for a party.

Watercress (small bunch)
Cucumber, peeled (2-inch section)
Scallions, trimmed to 2-inch
   lengths (3)
Parsley, without stalks (6 good
   sprigs)
Tomatoes, quartered (2 medium)
Leftover fish fillets, chilled from
   refrigerator (enough for 4
   people)
Black olives, pitted (12)
Green olives, pitted (12)

For the Mayonnaise:
Egg, coddled by boiling 3
   minutes in shell (1)
Mustard, preferably imported
   French (1 tsp)
Salt, coarse crystal, to taste
Pepper, red cayenne, to taste
Olive oil, best quality (½ cup)
Lemon (½)
Heavy cream (about 1 Tbs)

Prepared in Under 20 Minutes From Start to Serving, with No Cooking at All

Choose a flat, handsome oval serving platter and put it in the freezer to get thoroughly ice cold. Wash the bunch of watercress, dry it and hold it in the refrigerator crisper. Fit the shredding disk to the Cuisinart machine and, with the disk spinning, push the cucumber section with the pusher down the chimney and shred it. Drain away its water and transfer the shreds to a covered storage dish and hold it. Rinse and dry the Cuisinart work bowl, then put into it the 3 chunked scallions and the 6 parsley sprigs, mincing them fairly finely, usually in two or three bursts. Transfer them to a covered storage dish and hold them. Without necessarily rinsing the bowl, put into it the 2 quartered tomatoes (no need to skin them, the whirling blades will disintegrate the skins) and whirl the blades for not more than 1 or 2 seconds to chop the tomatoes as coarsely as possible, but without large lumps. Transfer to a covered storage dish and hold.

Now prepare the mayonnaise in the (rinsed and dried) work bowl by putting in the coddled egg, carefully shelled, with the teaspoon of mustard, with salt and red pepper to taste. Whirl the blades for just about 2 seconds to churn and mix these ingredients thoroughly. Now remove the pusher from the chimney of the cover, start the motor again and at once begin pouring in, in a thin steady stream, the ½ cup of olive oil. When it is all in, you should have a very thick mayonnaise in the bowl. Taste it and begin adjusting its flavor. Add 1 teaspoon of the lemon juice and mix it in by whirling the blades for a one-second burst. Thin the mayonnaise by adding, teaspoon by teaspoon, the heavy cream. Use a one-second burst of the blades to mix in each new addition. Finally, add, as needed, more salt and red pepper. When the mayonnaise meets your taste as to flavor and texture, add and mix in 3 tablespoons of the shredded cucumber, with the minced scallions and parsley. One more burst of the blades to mix everything – and the mayonnaise is ready. (Incidentally, it can be used in many different ways, quite apart from this recipe.)

Take the ice-cold platter out of the freezer and set on it the pieces of thoroughly chilled, leftover cooked fish. Cover and decorate each piece of fish completely by spooning and smoothing over it the mayonnaise. Make the covering thick or thin as you please, to satisfy your personal taste for the balance between the fish and the mayonnaise. Outline and intersperse the pieces of fish with the chopped tomato and dot with whole or half black and green olives. Complete the decorations with bright green sprigs of very crisp watercress. Serve the salad at once on chilled plates.

THE LEAST EXPENSIVE OF ALL DELIGHTFUL AND NOURISHING MEALS – OUR ROMAN BEAN POT

(for 4 to 6)

When our big, brown, earthenware bean pot comes to the table and the lid is lifted and the savory smells come wafting out, there is a lovely sense of the community of the family, joined with all other families all over the world where such pots have been served for thousands of years. This kind of dish, of course, requires almost no attention during the cooking and it can be eaten as is – rich, unctuous, satisfying – or it can be embellished with boiled or braised slices of any kind of meat, sausages, meatballs, grated Parmesan cheese or anything within the range of your imagination. No need to repeat that the dried beans are strong in minerals and proteins. Although we have been making this for many years, it was never so easy and good as it is here.

Dried white beans, preferably
   Italian cannellini, or white
   haricots (1 lb)
Basil (1 tsp dried, or 1 Tbs fresh)
Sage (½ tsp dried, or 2 tsps fresh)
Savory (1 tsp dried, or 1 Tbs
   fresh)
Bay leaves, whole (3)
Olive oil, best quaility Italian
   green virgin (½ cup)

Parsley (medium-sized bunch)
Garlic, unpeeled whole (3 cloves,
   more or less, as you please)
Salt, coarse crystal, to taste
Lemon (1)
Bread, coarse country type
   (8 slices)

Active Work of Preparation About 20 Minutes, Apart from Overnight Soaking of the Beans and About 2½ Hours of Entirely Unsupervised Cooking

The night before, wash the pound of dried white beans, picking them over and discarding any broken or crushed ones, then cover them with fresh cold water and leave them to soak and expand in the refrigerator overnight. In the morning, throw away the soaking water, rinse the beans again and re-cover them with fresh water until they are needed for the cooking.

We find it more efficient and faster to use two pots for this operation: a large soup kettle on top of the stove to bring the water up to the boiling point quickly, and our old earthenware bean pot for the slow simmering in the oven. Preheat your oven to 325°F and put the empty earthenware bean pot into it to get hot. (You don't, of course, have to have a bean pot. We happen to be romantic about ours. The whole job can be done in a soup kettle or Dutch oven, either on top of the stove, or in the oven.) Drain the now much-expanded beans and spread them into the soup kettle. Just cover them with fresh cold water – usually not much more than 3 pints – then at once turn on the heat and bring the kettle up to the boil. Then adjust the heat to the gentlest simmering – what the French call "just smiling" – no bubbles, but the top surface of the water gently and slowly moving around. If you are using fresh leaves of basil, sage and savory, put them into the Cuisinart bowl and coarsely chop them with a one-second burst of the steel blades. Add them to the soup kettle, with the 3 bay leaves and the first 3 tablespoons of the olive oil. (The oil is very important in this dish. If it is of top quality, it adds a delicate and subtle fruitiness to the beans.) Once everything is nicely simmering, we transfer the entire contents of the soup kettle to our now-hot bean pot and set it all in the oven, tightly covered, to cook for at least 2 hours. We check about every half hour and, if the simmering is turning to bubbling, we turn down the oven temperature usually first to 300°F then, towards the end of the time, down to 275°F.

Meanwhile, there are a couple of Cuisinart operations to be completed. Cut away the stiff stalks from the bunch of parsley and put all the leaves into the bowl. Chop them very coarsely with one or possibly two 1-second bursts. Transfer the parsley to a covered storage dish and hold it. Without rinsing the bowl, put into it 2 unpeeled cloves of the garlic and mince them fairly finely – usually with 2 or 3 one-second bursts. Transfer the garlic to a covered storage dish and hold it. Again without rinsing the bowl, put into it the third unpeeled clove of garlic and 1 tablespoon of the olive oil, whirling the steel blades until garlic and oil are completely amalgamated into a sort of syrup – usually 2 or 3 one-second bursts. Transfer the mixture to a covered storage dish and hold it.

At the end of the 2 hours, stir a good tablespoon of salt into the beans, then put the pot back into the oven for about another 30 minutes to allow the salt to be absorbed. At this point, taste a couple of beans. They should be quite soft, but you don't want them to be bursting open. If necessary, continue the simmering for as much extra time as is needed.

Now comes the "secret trick" in which the modern machine converts this ancient, simple pot into something with the feel of creamy-rich, irresistibly smooth luxury. Stand the bean pot on your work surface alongside 2 large bowls. Turn your oven back up to 325°F and arm yourself with your largest long-handled slotted spoon. Divide all the beans into two equal batches by spooning them out, one spoonful into the right-hand bowl, the next spoonful into the left-hand bowl. When they are thus equally divided, put half of them back at once into the bean pot to keep warm. Now purée the second half in the work bowl until the beans are absolutely creamy and smooth. You will have to do this in batches of 2 cups each, possibly adding a few spoonfuls of the liquid from the beanpot to prevent the purée from becoming unmanageably stiff. Each batch is usually beautifully smooth after 7 to 10 seconds of the whirling blades. Stir each batch of purée at once back into the bean pot. The moment the complete job is done, put the bean pot back into the oven to reheat. After about 5 minutes, carefully and thoroughly stir into it, with a wooden spoon, the entire chopped bunch of parsley and the 2 minced cloves of garlic (but not the garlic-oil mix). Leave it in the oven until you are ready to serve.

A moment or two before you bring the pot to the dining table, stir into it the remaining olive oil. It will at once be absorbed and amalgamated into the thirsty beans and will add to them the subtle quality of the scent of Mediterranean olive groves. Finally, squeeze and stir in the juice of the lemon. Warm up your soup bowls and in the bottom of each place 1 thick slice of the coarse bread which has been lightly rubbed with the garlic-oil syrup. Then ladle the beans on top of it. The diners use their soup spoons to break up the bread as it soaks up the bean cream. The Roman Bean Pot virtually demands to be accompanied by a peasanty, strong, Italian red wine.

12

The Chopper-Churner Can Also Cut Calories

The very last thing we intend to do here is to set up a diet regimen with menus and recipes for you to lose five pounds in five days – or whatever! We wouldn't want to add to the traffic jam of diet books. Our objective is simply to show how we use the machine to produce those low-calorie specialties that help us, whenever we need the help, in cutting an odd inch or pound, here and there, now and then. In the first place, it can produce creamy sauces and soups entirely without cream. It does it by simply puréeing the solids – meats, fish, poultry, vegetables, fruits – until they are as smooth as silk. The old system of thickening (and fattening) sauces, soups and stews with a French-style butter-flour *roux* can now be thrown out of the kitchen window. Also, in those old B.C. (Before Cuisinart) days, so many of the recipes for low-calorie dressings required that each of at least a dozen different ingredients be beaten in separately. Those recipes, too, have gone out with the garbage. Now, we simply put everything together into the machine, whirl for 4 or 5 seconds until it is all completely and perfectly amalgamated. Here are a few of the low-calorie techniques we use . . .

200-CALORIE QUICK PARTY CHICKEN SALAD

(for 4)

This is our adaptation of a recipe given us in France recently by one of the great young chefs. It has almost at once become one of our best display dishes for an informal party buffet or sit-down supper. Our best caculation is that one serving of this, including the special salad dressing from page 183, is just about 200 calories.

175

Chicken breasts, boned and
skinned (both sides from one
bird)

Chicken bouillon, clear, entirely
fatless (about 3 cups)

Artichoke hearts, probably canned
or frozen (4)

Mushrooms, wiped clean and
chunked (about 5 medium)

Lemon, for rind only (1)

Tomatoes, chunked (3 medium)

Boston lettuce, washed (small
head)

Escarole, washed (small head)

Whole-kernel corn, cooked and
drained (½ cup)

50-calorie salad dressing, see
page 183 (1 batch)

Prepared in About 30 Minutes from Start to Serving

Choose a lidded saucepan just large enough to hold the chicken
breasts side by side, but do not yet put them into it. First put into this
saucepan the 3 cups of chicken bouillon and heat it up to the boiling
point. Then put in the breasts (which should be just covered by the
hot liquid) and adjust the heat so that they will gently simmer, covered, until they are just cooked through – usually in about 10 to 15
minutes, according to the thickness of the breasts.

Meanwhile, if the artichoke hearts need to be cooked, do so and
then immediately drain, cool and hold them. Set in the freezer to chill
a handsome, oval serving platter on which the salad will be assembled
and brought to table. Next, chop the vegetables with the Cuisinart
steel blades. Put into its bowl the 5 chunked mushrooms with any
dried-out stalk tips removed, then coarsely chop them – usually in 1 or
2 one-second bursts. Transfer them to a covered storage dish and hold
them. Thinly peel the yellow outer rind from the lemon into the
Cuisinart bowl and mince it finely in 1 or 2 one-second bursts. Transfer the rind to a covered storage dish and hold it. Put in the 3 chunked
tomatoes and chop them quite coarsely, whirling the blades for no
more than 1 or 2 seconds. Transfer the tomatoes to a covered storage
dish and hold them. Rinse and dry the Cuisinart bowl and put into it
all the good leaves of the Boston lettuce, running the machine in one-
second bursts until the lettuce is not-too-finely shredded – usually in
about 3 bursts, pushing the lettuce down with a spatula after each
burst. Transfer the shreds to a covered storage dish and hold them.

The moment the chicken breasts are done, lift them out of the bouillon and lay them on a cutting board to cool. Separate the best leaves of
the escarole and keep them cool in the salad crisper of your refrigerator. As soon as the breasts are cool enough to be handled, slice them

thinly into bite-sized pieces. Prepare a batch of the 50-calorie salad dressing according to the recipe on page 183. We are now ready to assemble the salad on its ice-cold platter.

Cover the platter with the best leaves of the escarole. In the center, build a small pyramid with the shredded Boston lettuce. Surround it with a red ring of chopped tomato. Outside this ring place the 4 artichoke hearts as if they were the points of the compass. Distribute the slices of chicken on top of the escarole leaves all across the platter. Then, in turn, sprinkle the platter with the chopped mushrooms, the minced lemon rind and the niblets of corn. The contrasting colors make an attractive display. Finally, dribble the low-calorie dressing over all and serve the salad at once on chilled plates.

40-CALORIE APPETITE-CUTTING CHICKEN AND TOMATO SNACK

(4 servings)

We often drink a small and nourishing ice-cold glass of this at midmorning or midafternoon to dampen our rising hunger pangs. Or it can be a nonalcoholic cocktail before lunch or dinner. Or heated up and served as a first-course soup. To the best of our calculations, an 8-ounce serving has just about 40 calories.

Tomato sauce (2 cups)
Lemon (1)
Celery leaves, fresh (enough to fill
  ¼ cup after chopping)
Parsley, without stalks (also
  enough to fill ¼ cup)
Cucumber, peeled and sliced
  (3-inch section)

Yellow onion, peeled and chunked
  (1 quite small)
Tabasco pepper sauce, to taste
Worcestershire sauce, to taste
Chicken bouillon, clear, entirely
  fatless (2 cups)
Salt, coarse crystal, to taste

Prepared in Under 5 Minutes

Put into the Cuisinart work bowl, all together: 1 cup of the tomato sauce, the juice of the lemon, the ¼ cup each of celery leaves and parsley, the slices of cucumber, the chunked onion, 2 drops of the Tabasco, 2 dashes of the Worcestershire sauce, ½ cup of the chicken bouillon, with salt to taste. Whirl the steel blades until everything is smoothly blended and completely puréed – usually in about 10 to 15 seconds. Transfer the mixture to an ice-cold, 1½-quart serving jug.

Next, churn together in the work bowl the second cup of tomato sauce and the remaining 1½ cups of chicken bouillon. Add this to the serving jug and thoroughly stir it in. Chill the jug completely, then serve 1-cup portions over ice in handsome glasses.

15-CALORIE CLEAR MUSHROOM BOUILLON

(for 4 – if made in larger quantities, it will keep for 2 or 3 weeks in the refrigerator)

Apart from sipping this richly-flavored bouillon from a mug as a snack at our desk, or spooning it from a bowl as a first course at lunch or dinner, it also serves as a first-class basic stock that can replace beef or chicken bouillon in the preparation of all kinds of recipes. It adds up, we calculate, to only 15 calories per 1-cup serving. So it is well worth preparing very carefully, perhaps in double or treble quantities. It will keep for at least 2 or 3 weeks in a covered jar in the coldest part of the refrigerator.

Mushrooms, dried wild (½ cup)
Mushrooms, fresh, wiped clean (1 lb)
Bermuda onion, peeled and chunked (1 large)
Caraway seed, whole (1 Tbs)

Marjoram, dried or fresh (½ tsp dried, or ½ Tbs fresh)
Salt, coarse crystal, to taste
Black pepper, freshly ground, to taste
Chives, or scallions (small bunch)

Best Prepared in Advance, Active Work About 15 Minutes, Plus About 2 Hours of Entirely Unsupervised Simmering
It is best to start this the day before it is needed. We use a 4-quart pressure cooker, which seems to draw out the maximum of the flavor juices and oils from the dried wild mushrooms. (But nearly the same result can be achieved by, roughly, an extra hour of simmering in the soup kettle.) Set the pressure cooker on high heat and put into it 2 quarts of fresh cold water. While it is heating up, put the ½ cup of dried mushrooms into the Cuisinart work bowl and coarsely chop them by starting and stopping the steel blades for 1 or 2 one-second bursts. Add the chopped mushrooms to the pressure cooker. As soon as the water boils, cover the cooker and bring the pressure up to 15 pounds, hold it there for 2 minutes, then bring it down immediately. Pour the entire contents into a soup kettle and heat it back up to gentle simmering.

Meanwhile, cut off any dried stem ends of the pound of mushrooms, then chunk them into roughly uniform pieces and put them into the work bowl in batches of about 2 cups. Coarsely chop each batch in 2 or 3 one-second bursts and add them to the soup kettle. Without rinsing the work bowl, put into it the chunked Bermuda onion and chop it just as you did the mushrooms. Add it to the soup kettle, with the tablespoon of caraway seeds, and keep everything simmering, covered, for about 1 hour. Then cool and rest it to allow the flavors to blend and mature, preferably in the refrigerator, covered, overnight.

When it is eventually reheated, add to it the marjoram (fresh leaves, if you use them, should be chopped for about 1 second with the steel blades), 2 to 3 teaspoons of salt and some black pepper, according to your taste. Simmer everything, covered, for 1 more hour. Then strain out and discard all the solids, squeezing them thoroughly so as not to lose a drop of their juices. When you drink this magnificent bouillon as a soup, garnish each bowl or mug with a sprinkling of chopped chives, or green scallions.

15-CALORIE ASPARAGUS BOUILLON

(for 4 or, made in larger quantities,
keeps for weeks in the refrigerator)

This recipe is not limited to fresh asparagus when it is in season. It demonstrates the extraordinary Cuisinart method for drawing out the flavor juices from all kinds of low-calorie and nutritious green, red, and yellow vegetables. Instead of the asparagus, for example, you could use green beans, bean sprouts, beet greens, Belgian endive, broccoli, cabbage, cauliflower, celery, cucumber, dandelion leaves, escarole, green or red peppers, kale, mustard greens, onions, radishes, spinach, summer squash, Swiss chard, turnip greens, or watercress. Any one or combination of them, we calculate, won't exceed 15 calories per 1-cup serving, and makes a clear bouillon that is nourishing and refreshing as a first course of a meal, as a hunger-reducing snack, or as a cooking bouillon for the preparation of other dishes. This recipe includes one rather unusual herb, borage, which is sometimes hard to find. If you can get it and put it into the bouillon as recommended below, it adds not only its delicately aromatic flavor but also a most handsome, bright green, natural color to this lovely bouillon. (Obviously, borage should be used only with green vegetables.)

Asparagus, fresh, in season (2 lbs)

Bermuda onion, peeled and
   chunked (1 large)

Borage, dried or fresh leaves in
   season – optional (1 tsp dried,
   or 1 Tbs fresh)

Salt, coarse crystal, to taste

Black pepper, freshly ground,
   to taste

Active Work of Preparation About 15 Minutes, Plus About 1¼ Hours of Entirely Unsupervised Simmering

First, deal with the asparagus. Wash it thoroughly under running cold water, cut off about an inch from each tip and put them in a covered storage dish to hold in the refrigerator until just before serving time. Scrape away any rough skin and the scales from the stalks, then break them by hand, so that they come apart naturally at the point where the hard woody part ends and the green, edible stalk begins. Put the hard bottoms as they are into the soup kettle. They will add some flavor. Chunk the edible stalks into the Cuisinart bowl and then coarsely chop them – in usually 5 or 6 one-second bursts. Do not overfill the bowl. You may have to do the job in 3 or 4 batches. Add the chopped stalks to the soup kettle. Then pour 2 quarts of fresh cold water over everything and heat it up to the boiling point. Meanwhile, without rinsing the Cuisinart bowl, put into it the chunked Bermuda onion and coarsely chop it by running the steel blades for about 2 to 3 seconds. Do not churn the onion to a pulp. Add the onion to the soup kettle. When the liquid is bubbling, adjust the heat to gentle simmering and keep it going for about an hour uncovered, so that the liquid gradually boils down, concentrating and sharpening the flavors. Do not worry if about half the water boils away. The resulting broth will be all the better and stronger.

After the first 45 minutes, it is excellent to be able to throw in some borage, either dried, or, best of all, a small handful of fresh leaves first coarsely chopped for 1 second in the Cuisinart. Then, after the final 15 minutes of simmering, strain out and discard all the solids from the bouillon, making sure to squeeze them thoroughly so that they give up every last drop of their juices. Now salt and pepper the bouillon to your taste, and then it is ready to serve at once or to be stored in the refrigerator in a tightly lidded jar. When you serve it as hot soup, garnish the bowl or a mug with the asparagus tips, which should be simmered in the soup for just long enough to bring them to an edible crispness – usually in 4 to 7 minutes of gentle simmering. They add the final, delicate perfection of the asparagus flavor.

70-CALORIE QUICKEST AND SIMPLEST CRABMEAT AND TOMATO ASPIC

(for 4)

This is another recipe to demonstrate the basic technique of the Cuisinart machine for all kinds of cold dishes set in aspic – since the intelligent use of gelatin is one of the principal tools of low-calorie preparation. Aspic provides color, flavor and cool refreshment on the tongue as it encloses and surrounds almost any of the important cold protein elements with minimum calories. You can substitute for the crab other fish or shellfish, or pieces of meat or poultry; you can change the color and the aromatic flavor of the aspic as you please. A wide range of aspic main dishes, first courses, or desserts can be quickly and conveniently prepared in the Cuisinart. We calculate this crab aspic at approximately 70 calories per serving.

Yellow onions, peeled and chunked (2 fairly small)
Bay leaf, whole (1)
White celery, stalks destringed and chunked (1¼ cups), plus leaves (small handful)
Gelatin, granulated, unflavored (2-3 standard 1-tablespoon envelopes)
Chicken bouillon, no fat (1½ cups)

Crabmeat, preferably best quality fresh (¾ lb)
Clam juice (about ¼ cup)
Tomato sauce (2 cups)
Salt, coarse crystal, to taste
Black pepper, freshly ground, to taste
Lemon juice, fresh (2 Tbs)
Escarole leaves (enough to cover serving platter)

Active Work of Preparation About 10 Minutes, Plus About 2 to 3 Hours Setting the Aspic

Choose a 1½ quart aspic mold and set it in the freezer to chill thoroughly. Then, chop the 2 chunked onions, the bay leaf and the celery leaves quite finely in the Cuisinart – usually in 2 to 4 one-second bursts. Transfer the chopped mixture to a 1½-quart saucepan. Rinse and dry the Cuisinart bowl, then put into it the 1¼ cups of chunked celery and finely dice it by starting and stopping the machine as you did before. Check carefully after each one-second burst to make sure that it does not become too fine, since it is to provide a crackly-crunchy texture within the aspic – usually the perfect result comes after 2 or 3 bursts. Now we are ready to prepare the gelatin and assemble the dish.

Soften the 2 envelopes of gelatin in ½ cup of the chicken bouillon, sprinkling the granules on top of the liquid, carefully stirring them in and then leaving them to be absorbed into the bouillon. Strain the crabmeat, breaking it up into bite-size pieces and thoroughly draining it, saving ¼ cup of the juice. At once put the crabmeat into a covered storage dish and set it in the coldest part of your refrigerator until needed. If the drained juice does not have a good crab taste, or if there is only a little of it, substitute or add enough clam juice to make ¼ cup. Add the crab juice and/or the clam juice to the saucepan. If there is more than ¼ cup of crab juice, increase the gelatin by using all or part of the extra envelope – otherwise the aspic will be too soft. Also add to the saucepan: the remaining cup of chicken bouillon, the 2 cups of tomato sauce, plus salt and pepper to taste. Bring it all rapidly up to the boiling point, stir it thoroughly, carefully work in the gelatin paste, making sure that it does not lump, and continue to stir it until it is completely dissolved. Turn off the heat and stir in the 2 table-spoons of lemon juice. Now bring the mold out of the freezer and, as soon as the contents of the saucepan have cooled slightly, pour them all into the mold, cover it with aluminum foil and set it to chill in the coldest part of the refrigerator.

After the first 30 minutes, check every 15 minutes until the point when the aspic is just beginning to thicken, so that it is about as syrupy as thick honey. This usually happens at some point between 45 and 60 minutes, according to the efficiency of your refrigerator.

Precisely at the syrupy stage, carefully fold the crabmeat and the diced celery into the aspic, making sure that they are evenly distributed throughout. Work quickly, because if the aspic returns to the liquid stage, the crab and the celery will sink to the bottom. Re-cover the mold, return it at once to the coldest part of the refrigerator and let it set fully – usually in 1 to 2 hours. Meanwhile, choose your most handsome serving platter and set it in the freezer to chill. Wash and crisp the escarole leaves and, when the aspic is ready to serve, set the leaves on the chilled platter. Unmold the aspic onto this bed and serve it at once on chilled plates.

10-CALORIE QUICK MUSHROOM CASSEROLE

(for 4)

This can be the vegetable accompaniment to a main dish, or itself the main dish of a light lunch or supper. Our calculation is that each serving has just under 10 calories.

Mushrooms, good color and shape (¾ lb, medium size)

Chicken bouillon, clear, concentrated, no fat (¼ cup)

White wine, dry (¼ cup)

Lemon, for juice and rind (1)

Green scallions, trimmed to 2-inch lengths (4)

Marjoram (½ tsp dried, or ½ Tbs fresh leaves)

Thyme (½ tsp dried, or ½ Tbs fresh leaves)

Parsley, without stalks (6 good sprigs)

Salt, coarse crystal, to taste

Black pepper, freshly ground, to taste

Active Work of Preparation About 10 Minutes, Plus About 20 Minutes of Almost Unsupervised Baking

Preheat your oven to 450°F. Choose a low, lidded casserole, say about 2 inches deep, large enough to hold all the mushrooms in a single layer. Wipe the mushrooms clean with a damp cloth or sponge. Do not pull out the stems, but cut them off flush with the backs of the caps. Trim off any dry ends from the stems. Lay the mushrooms, cut sides upwards, across the bottom of the casserole, with the stems sprinkled in between. Put into the Cuisinart bowl the ¼ cup each of chicken bouillon and wine, about 1 tablespoon of the juice of the lemon, about 3 good slivers of its thin yellow rind, the 4 chunked green scallions, the marjoram, thyme and parsley, with salt and pepper to taste. Run the machine until all these are finely chopped and thoroughly blended – usually in 4 to 6 seconds. Spoon this low-calorie sauce over and around the mushrooms, cover the casserole and set it in the oven to bake until the mushrooms are thoroughly hot and crisply soft – usually in about 15 to 20 minutes. Baste the mushrooms with the sauce after 10 minutes and again 5 minutes later.

50-CALORIE REASONABLY LUXURIOUS CREAMY SALAD DRESSING

(for 4)

This dressing is, frankly, a compromise between calories and our love of luxurious dressings. We learned this recipe from the brilliant young

Chef Michel Gúerard, when we visited him in his country hotel in France. Obviously, you can make dressings as low as 15 calories per serving (see next recipe), but we prefer to spend about 50 calories per serving to get that feeling of aromatic richness on the tongue. This dressing, while still being extraordinarily low in calories, can make any salad an important occasion.

Ricotta cheese, low-fat (¾ cup)
Yoghurt, low-fat (2 Tbs)
Vinegar, tarragon white wine (3 Tbs)
Salt, coarse crystal (about ½ tsp or more, to taste)
Black pepper (4 to 6 grinds, to taste)

Mixed fresh herbs, whatever is in season, basil, chives, dill, marjoram, parsley, rosemary, tarragon, thyme, any combination of 2 or 3 (total ½ cup of fresh leaves, loosely packed)

Preparation in 2 Minutes

Simply put everything into the Cuisinart bowl and churn them all together until the herbs are finely chopped and the dressing has been smoothly amalgamated – usually in 4 or 5 seconds. Taste and adjust the seasonings. Spoon the dressing over the salad.

15-CALORIE LESS LUXURIOUS CREAMY SALAD DRESSING

(about 1½ cups, keeps well)

A good deal less rich than the previous one – but then, you can't save your calories and eat them too. Each diner gets about 2 tablespoons over one serving and we calculate that to be about 15 calories.

Tomato sauce (1 cup)
Cottage or pot cheese, low-fat (½ cup)
Lemon juice (2 tsp)
Yellow onion, peeled and chunked (1 quite small)

Salt, coarse crystal (½ tsp or more, to taste)
Mustard, dry English (½ tsp)
Basil, dried or fresh (½ tsp dried, or ½ Tbs fresh leaves)
Black pepper (3 or 4 grinds, to taste)

Preparation in About 2 Minutes

Simply put everything into the Cuisinart bowl, then churn the mixture until the basil is finely chopped and everything is smoothly amalgamated – usually in 4 to 6 seconds. Adjust the seasonings to your taste. Chill and store the mixture in a screw-top jar in the refrigerator.

15-CALORIE QUICK BEET AND HORSERADISH RELISH

(about 2 cups)

We find that each diner seems to consume about ¼ cup, which we estimate to have approximately 15 calories.

Beets, fresh, small, cooked and
  chunked (¾ cup)
Cabbage, young, raw, chunked
  (1½ cups)
Horseradish, preferably fresh root,
  or bottled alternative (1 Tbs)

Lemon juice, freshly squeezed
  (about 4 Tbs)
Salt, coarse crystal, to taste
Black pepper, freshly ground, to
  taste

Prepared in About 4 Minutes
If you are using fresh horseradish root, peel one end of it and cut 2 or 3 ⅛-inch slices (according to your taste) into the Cuisinart work bowl, mincing them finely in 1 to 3 one-second bursts. (If you are using pre-grated or pre-mashed horseradish, simply measure in 1 tablespoon, without running the machine, and then go on to the next step.) Add to the horseradish in the bowl: the ¾ cup of beets, the 1½ cups of cabbage, 3 tablespoons of the lemon juice, about ½ teaspoon of salt and 3 or 4 grinds of the peppermill. Run the steel blades in one-second bursts, checking carefully after each, until all the solid ingredients are not-too-finely chopped – usually in 3 or 4 bursts. Be careful not to make them into a paste. You are aiming for a slightly chewy, crisp, diced texture in the relish. Taste it and adjust the lemon juice and/or the seasonings, if needed. Store it in a tightly lidded jar in the refrigerator.

125-CALORIE LUXURIOUS DESSERT – FRENCH-STYLE LITTLE POTS OF MOCHA CREAM

(for 4)

This may not be exactly a low-low-calorie dessert, but it is, relatively,
a low-calorie version of the classic French *Petits Coeurs à la Crème*

which are, normally revoltingly rich, with whipped cream, full-fat cream cheese and oodles of sugar. We achieve something of the same luxurious effect with low-fat ingredients at approximately 125 calories for each individual "little pot."

Skimmed milk (1¾ cups)
Sugar (4 tsp)
Eggs, separated (3)
Coffee, black, very strong (¼ cup)
Cocoa powder, unsweetened
   (4 Tbs)

Orange rind, minced (1 Tbs)
Mint leaves, fresh, snipped with
   scissors (2 tsps, or dried, ½ tsp)
Vanilla extract, pure (1½ tsps)

Active Work of Preparation About 15 Minutes, Plus About 30 Minutes of Unsupervised Baking and 4 Hours of Chilling

Preheat your oven to 325°F and set up at its center what the French call a *bain-marie*, a pan with hot water in which the little mocha cream pots will stand while they are baking. The pan of water keeps the air inside the oven correctly damp and steamy. You will need a pan about 3 inches deep and large enough to hold the 4 individual pots side by side. Fill this pan two-thirds full of boiling water and set it in the oven to wait for the pots. These can be either the proper French little china pots made especially for this purpose, or individual caramel custard cups, or small individual white soufflé dishes. The water in the pan will, of course, continue boiling and will have to be topped up with more hot water as its level goes down. The hot water should be at least halfway up the pots while they are baking.

In a 1½-pint saucepan, heat the 1¾ cups of skimmed milk until it is just gently bubbling. Dissolve in the 4 teaspoons of sugar. Turn off the heat and let it cool slightly.

Meanwhile, put into the Cuisinart work bowl: the 3 egg yolks, 4 tablespoons of the coffee, the 4 tablespoons of cocoa powder, the tablespoon of orange rind and the mint. Run the steel blades just long enough to amalgamate everything into a smooth paste – usually in about 3 seconds. Now remove the pusher from the chimney of the cover, restart the motor and at once begin pouring the warm milk in a steady, thin stream. Everything will churn together into a smooth cream – usually in about 2 or 3 seconds after all the milk is in. Taste and add, as you please, a dash more coffee, a teaspoon more cocoa, orange, mint. Switch on the motor for one-second burst to blend in any additions. Transfer the mix back to the saucepan and gently reheat it, stirring continuously, to melt the cocoa and allow the egg yolks slightly to thicken the mocha cream. Do not let it boil. As soon as it shows the first sign of thickening, remove the saucepan from the heat.

Beat the egg whites to stiff peaks and then beat the mocha cream into them with the 1½ teaspoons of vanilla. The stiff whites will liquify, but this is part of the plan. Pour the now fluffy cream into the individual pots and bake them, standing in the hot water in the oven, until they are just set – usually in about 25 to 35 minutes. Then, take them out of the oven, cool them slightly and, covering each pot lightly with aluminum foil, chill them in the refrigerator for at least 4 hours before serving them. They are to be eaten with a teaspoon.

13

Fun With Home-Made
Natural Aromatic Herb Salts

There are few ingredients in the world of food which turn us off as instantly and as strongly as commercial packaged garlic salt. If we pick up a cookbook in which it is suggested in the recipes, that cookbook is automatically blacklisted in our subconscious mind. If we dine at a restaurant where we find a garlic salt shaker on the table, we make a mental note never to come back. We have never tasted a garlic salt that is not so full of chemical additives and preservatives that it tastes, at one and the same time, acid, bitter, musty, and putrid. Apparently, the natural flavor of the garlic clove simply cannot be imprisoned in a package, however tightly sealed, to be kept as imperishable hardware on a store shelf for months and years. The oils escape from the processed package and leave behind only a bitter memory.

Yet now, with our Cuisinart steel blades, we make and use our own garlic salt all the time. All natural ingredients. No additives. We cannot guarantee that ours will keep for years, but certainly our supplies last for several weeks, tightly sealed in our refrigerator. We have also learned how to make other aromatic herb salts with the whirling steel blades of our machine, which seems somehow to extract and concentrate the flavor oils from the leaves and roots. No other machine, to our knowledge, can perform these tricks with herb salts. Here are a few of our recipes . . .

HOME-MADE ALL-PURPOSE NATURAL GARLIC SALT

(2 cups, see text below)

We make a substantial quantity of this because we use part of it as the flavor base for the other salts which follow.

Garlic, very fresh and young, unpeeled (12 good-size cloves)   **Salt, coarse crystal (2 cups)**

Active Preparation in About 10 Minutes – Plus About a Week for Drying Out

Put into the Cuisinart work bowl 6 of the garlic cloves, then pour in over them one cup of the salt. Start and stop the steel blades in a series of 1-second bursts until you can see that the garlic is beginning to be fairly finely chopped – usually about 4 to 7 bursts. Then whirl the steel blades continuously until the salt is beginning to be powdered and the garlic has been so finely chopped that it has virtually disappeared – usually in about 15 to 20 seconds. When you open the cover there will be a very strong smell of garlic. Don't worry. Time will reduce it. Transfer the garlic salt to a tightly lidded, 1-pint glass storage jar.

Repeat this operation one more time, until you have 2 cups of garlic salt and the storage jar is full. Keep it in the refrigerator without opening it for 1 week to allow the oils to impregnate the salt crystals.

At the end of that time, you must completely dry out all the remaining moisture, or moldiness will develop. Empty all the salt into a large open oven baking dish – large enough so that the layer of salt will not be much more than half an inch deep. If necessary, use 2 baking pans. Set the salt in the center of the oven at the keep-warm temperature, between 150°F and 200°F. Leave it there until it is completely dry when rubbed between your fingers – perhaps 12 hours, according to the temperature. Finally, whirl the salt again, in 2 batches, with the steel blades until all little lumps have again been broken up and the salt is perfectly smooth. Store tightly capped in an absolutely dry, completely moisture-proof glass jar.

HOME-MADE NATURAL AROMATIC HERB SALT FOR CHICKEN OR VEAL

(about 2 cups)

This recipe is almost exactly the same as the first one above.

Salt, coarse crystal
  (2 cups)
Garlic salt, see previous recipe
  (½ cup)
Chives, fresh, coarsely snipped
  (1 cup)

Parsley, fresh, coarsely snipped
  leaves (1 cup)
Tarragon, fresh, coarsely snipped
  leaves (1 cup)
Lemon rind in small slivers
  (½ cup)

Active Preparation in About 10 Minutes, Plus About 1 Week for Drying Out

Put into the Cuisinart work bowl one cup of the plain crystal salt, the ¼ cup of garlic salt, and the ½ cup each of the chives, parsley, and the tarragon, plus the ¼ cup of the lemon rind. Let the steel blades grind all this to a fine powder, exactly as described in the first recipe, above. Do a second batch, then hold it in the refrigerator, dehydrate it in the oven, regrind it and store it exactly as described above.

HOME-MADE NATURAL AROMATIC HERB SALT FOR FISH

(about 2 cups)

Salt, coarse crystal (2 cups)
Garlic salt – see first recipe
  (½ cup)
Dill, fresh, coarsely snipped fronds
  (1 cup)
Parsley, coarsely snipped leaves
  (1 cup)

Chives, fresh, coarsely snipped
  (2 Tbs)
Lemon rind, in small slivers
  (2 Tbs)

Active Preparation in About 10 Minutes, Plus About 1 Week for Drying Out

Same routine – same time – as before. Put into the Cuisinart bowl: 1 cup of the plain crystal salt, ¼ cup of the garlic salt, ½ cup each of the dill and the parsley, 1 tablespoon of the chives and 1 tablespoon of the lemon rind. Carry on exactly as in the previous recipes.

191

HOME-MADE NATURAL AROMATIC HERB SALT
FOR ALL OTHER MEATS

(about 2 cups)

Same as the others.

Salt, coarse crystal (2 cups)

Garlic salt – see first recipe (1 cup)

Basil, fresh leaves, coarsely
  snipped (½ cup)

Marjoram, fresh leaves, coarsely
  snipped (½ cup)

Chives, fresh leaves, coarsely
  snipped (2 Tbs)

Rosemary, fresh leaves, coarsely
  snipped (2 Tbs)

Thyme, fresh leaves, coarsely
  snipped (2 Tbs)

Hungarian sweet paprika (2 Tbs)

Celery leaves, fresh, coarsely
  snipped (½ cup)

Active Preparation in About 10 Minutes, Plus About 1 Week for Drying Out

Put into the Cuisinart bowl: 1 cup of the plain crystal salt, ½ cup of the garlic salt, ¼ cup each of the basil and marjoram, 1 tablespoon each of the chives, rosemary and thyme, 1 tablespoon of the paprika and ¼ cup of the celery leaves. Carry on exactly as in the previous recipes.

14

More Fun with Off-Beat Pastries

One of the most dramatic skills of the Cuisinart chopper-churner is that it has the power to achieve the complete amalgamation of virtually any ingredient with any other. This can make for some very strange bedfellows, but it also inspires us continually to experiment with all kinds of revolutionary combinations which we dream up in our mental test kitchen and then try out, in the hope that we have made a new and wonderful discovery. In no department of the kitchen is there more scope for experimentation than with savory or sweet pastry crusts or doughs. By changing the character and texture of the shell, you can make pies that vary dramatically in the way they cut and taste. Wednesday's apple pie can be quite different from Monday's, even though the apples and their spicing are exactly the same. Here are a few of our recent pastry experiments – an extraordinary series of savory and sweet combinations which would be virtually impossible without the power of the whirling blades to combine all kinds of ingredients that resist mixing by hand.

First, a basic crust dough which you can then change with the variations listed on the following pages . . .

BASIC GENERAL-PURPOSE PASTRY DOUGH FOR ALL KINDS OF SAVORY OR SWEET PIES

(for two 9-inch pie shells)

We think that this kind of pastry dough – good for dozens of different uses – ought to be one of the staples stored in every refrigerator. You can pull a small or large piece off it at any time for all kinds of odd little uses to dress up even the simplest dish at the most informal meal with a buttery-hot, golden crust. Then, as we shall show in the later recipes of this chapter, you can vary this basic mix by adding to, or subtracting from it.

Flour, all-purpose (2 cups)   **Egg yolks (2)**
Salt (⅔ tsps)   **Ice water (about ⅓ cup)**
Butter, chilled (½ lb)

Active Preparation in About 3 Minutes – Plus 15 Minutes of Baking
See the previous recipe on pages 86 and 169 for the detailed dis-
cussion of techniques. Spread around the bottom of the Cuisinart
work bowl: the 2 cups of flour and the ⅔ teaspoon of salt. Whirl the
steel blades for just 1 second to mix and sift. Then drop in, in small
chunks or thin slices, the ½ pound of butter and whirl the steel blades
until the butter is amalgamated to the "niblet corn" stage – usually
in about 4 or 5 seconds. Lightly beat the 2 egg yolks, put them into a
½-cup measure and fill it up with ice water. Start the steel blades
whirling again and pour in a steady stream through the cover chimney
the egg and water mix. As soon as the dough rides up in a ball on
top of the blades, stop the machine, the job is done. Depending on
the temperature and the weather, it usually takes about 6 seconds.

Transfer the ball of dough to a lightly floured pastry board, knead it
for a couple of minutes with floured hands, then roll it back into a
ball, cover it with a plastic bag and store it in the refrigerator as your
basic dough supply. Half of this amount can be rolled out into a pie-
shell and baked by the standard technique into a golden crust at
400°F in about 15 minutes.

Variation 1 – with Sharp Cheddar Cheese for an Apple Pie: Fit the grating disk to the bowl of the Cuisinart and finely grate ¼ pound of
quite-sharp Cheddar cheese. Take it out of the bowl and hold it.
Then make the pie dough by the basic recipe, above, adding the
cheese with the butter. This will give you a pie crust with a delight-
fully sharp cheese flavor.

Variation 2 – Herb-Flavored Pie Crusts: Put into the Cuisinart bowl,
with the flour and the salt in the basic recipe, 1 tablespoon of a
chopped fresh herb, or 1 teaspoon of the dried version. Or you can
add a mixture of several compatible herbs to a total of 1 tablespoon
fresh, or 1 teaspoon dried. For savory pies, try basil, caraway or celery
seeds, dill, oregano, rosemary, tarragon, thyme, etc. For sweet dessert
pies, cassia buds or mint leaves. You can get a most attractive crunchy
effect by including coarsely cracked seeds of allspice, cumin, or
toasted sesame seeds. The possible combinations and variations are
almost unlimited.

Variation 3 – Delicate Cream Cheese Dough: You will get a very light and soft pastry if you add to the basic recipe, at the same time as the butter, 6 ounces of cream cheese in small chunks or slivers. The machine will work it into the flour in exactly the same way as the butter, but the dough will be very soft and will have to be chilled for at least 3 hours before you can work it. Even then, it is best and easiest to roll it out gently between sheets of waxed paper.

ALMOST-INSTANT GRAHAM CRACKER CRUST

(for one 9-inch pie)

Or, you can, for an entirely different variation, throw out altogether the standard, flour, butter and egg pastry, switching to the Cuisinart almost instant method of chopping different kinds of cookies and crackers into smoothly workable, measured amounts of crumbs – all precisely graded to the degree of coarseness or fineness you want. Your first, simple experiment might be the Cuisinart technique for the ubiquitous graham cracker crust, which, it hardly needs to be said, can either be baked into a crunchy shell, or used unbaked and just chilled.

Graham crackers, quartered (12)   **Butter, chilled (7 Tbs)**
Sugar (4 Tbs)

Active Preparation of Dough in About 5 Minutes – Plus 8 Minutes of Unsupervised Baking
Spread the graham crackers around the bottom of the Cuisinart work bowl, then whirl the steel blades until the crackers are quite coarsely chopped – usually in no more than 3 or 4 seconds. Now add the 4 tablespoons of sugar and the 7 tablespoons of butter, in small chunks. The old method of first melting the butter and then gradually working it in is now entirely eliminated. The whirling steel blades, in a second or two, will simultaneously work in the sugar and butter to a fairly firm, smooth melange. It can, immediately, without further chilling, be pressed with your fingers into a 9-inch pie pan. This shell can then be baked in an oven preheated to 375°F and will usually be brown and crunchy in about 8 minutes. Or just wrap the pie pan and its shell in a large plastic bag and chill it in the refrigerator for 2 or 3 hours. Then put in your filling.

Variation 1 – Chocolate or Vanilla Wafers: Replace the graham crackers in the above recipe by 54 chocolate or vanilla wafers (about 8 ounces), chopping them in the same way for about 5 seconds, adding the same amounts of sugar and butter and, finally, baking or chilling them as before.

Variation 2 – Gingersnaps: Replace the graham crackers by 30 gingersnaps, running the blades in the same way for about 6 seconds, adding the same amount of sugar and butter, and baking or chilling as before.

Variation 3 – Bran or Grape-Nuts Flakes or Other Flaked Cereals: Replace the cracker crumbs in the above recipes by 3 to 3½ cups of a good, firm, nutritious cereal or breakfast Granola, using the machine in the same way for 6 to 7 seconds, adding the same amounts of sugar and butter, and baking or chilling as before.

Variation 4 – Graham Crackers and Walnuts: In the basic graham cracker crumb recipe, above, first coarsely grind in the Cuisinart enough shelled walnuts to fill one cup. (You will usually need to buy about ½ pound of shelled nuts, or about double that amount if they are still in their shells.) Then reduce the number of graham crackers to 9, chop them in the Cuisinart separately from the nuts, then combine the cracker crumbs and the chopped nuts, add the same amounts of sugar and butter and bake or chill as before. We think that this shell makes a particularly good marriage with a filling of coffee custard cream.

ALMOST-INSTANT CRUSTS OF ALL KINDS OF OTHER NUTS

(for one 9-inch pie)

You can easily make all-nut crusts from one particular kind of nut or from a combination of several kinds. As the steel blades chop and churn the nuts, it extracts so much oil from them that no extra butter need be added to make a workable crust dough. Try the following nuts, either alone or in combinations: blanched almonds, brazil nuts, filberts, hazel nuts, walnuts, among the more oily types. Put a total of about 1 pound of nut meats into the Cuisinart work bowl, then start and stop the steel blades in 1-second bursts until the nuts are fairly finely chopped – usually in about 4 to 7 bursts. After that, you can whirl the steel blades continuously until you have a quite fine grind – usually in about 7 to 10 seconds longer. (Almonds may take a bit more time.) You must finish up with exactly 2 cups of ground nuts. Combine this, in the work bowl, with ¼ cup of granulated white sugar, continuing to whirl the steel blades until you have a smooth, workable paste – perhaps 5 or 10 seconds more. Now, with your fingers you can press this nut paste into a lining shell for a 9-inch pan. This can be baked to a marvellously crunchy crust in an oven pre-heated to 375°F for just about 10 minutes. Excellent with a fresh fruit filling.

ALMOST-INSTANT MERINGUE AND NUT CRUST

(for one 9-inch pie)

Egg whites (4)
Cream of tartar (½ tsp)
Salt (⅛ tsp)

Sugar, fine grind (1 cup)
**Nuts (see previous recipe
(2 cups)**

Active Preparation in About 5 Minutes – Plus
About 10 Minutes of Baking

Put the 4 egg whites into a copper bowl and stir in the ½ teaspoon cream of tartar and the ⅛ teaspoon salt. Beat by hand with a wire balloon whisk, or use an electric beater, until the egg whites hold a stiff peak, but are not yet dry. Then start beating in tablespoon by tablespoon, the cup of sugar. The mixture should remain thick and smooth, like marshmallow. Now grind the 2 cups of nuts with the steel blades in the Cuisinart work bowl (as in the previous recipe) and, at the point where you would previously have the sugar added now put in half the meringue, then whirl the steel blades for not more than a couple of seconds to blend meringue and nuts together into a stiff melange. If it is not quite stiff enough, spoon in more meringue, whirling the blades for 1 second each time to mix in the addition. Finally, line the lightly greased pie pan and bake it, as before.

ALMOST-INSTANT CRUNCHY COCONUT PIE CRUST

(for one 9-inch pie)

If you can get a fresh coconut and break it open, so much the better. Once you have skinned the inside meat, the Cuisinart will chop it in a second or two to any grade of coarseness or fineness you need. When fresh coconuts are out of season, you can, with a small compromise in quality, use the packaged, processed, coconut flakes.

Coconut, fresh or packaged,   **Butter (3 Tbs)**
   chunked or flaked (1⅓ cups)

Active Work (Apart from Preparation of the Coconut) About 3 Minutes – Plus About 25 Minutes of Baking
Put into the Cuisinart work bowl the 1⅓ cups of coconut, with the 3 tablespoons of butter in small chunks, then whirl the steel blades until both are fairly finely chopped and completely amalgamated into a firmly workable paste – usually in about 3 or 4 seconds. Press this with your fingers into a 9-inch pie pan and bake it in an oven preheated to 300°F until it forms a firmly crunchy, golden shell – usually in about 20 to 25 minutes.

Variation 1 – Coconut and Coffee Pie Crust: In the above recipe, add with the butter, 2 tablespoons of very concentrated and strong black coffee. After the machine has worked it in, you will have a quite definite coffee flavor and color to your crust.

Variation 2 – Coconut and Chocolate Pie Crust:

Chocolate, unsweetened, cooking   **Sugar, confectioner's (⅔ cup)**
   (2 standard squares)   **Coconut, chopped or flaked, see**
Butter (3 Tbs)   **previous recipe (1⅓ cups)**
Milk (2 Tbs)

Active Work (Apart from Preparing the Coconut) About 10 Minutes
In a saucepan over very gentle heat (or, if you feel safer, in a double-boiler) melt the 2 squares of chocolate with 2 tablespoons of the butter, stirring continuously with a wooden spoon. In a small mixing bowl, lightly beat together 2 tablespoons of milk and ⅔ cup of confectioner's sugar. The moment the chocolate is melted, begin working the milk-sugar mixture into it, but very carefully, tablespoon by tablespoon, thoroughly incorporating each tablespoon before the next is added. Put into the Cuisinart bowl 1⅓ cup of chopped or flaked coconut, as in the recipe above. As soon as the chocolate mixture

is ready, remove the pusher from the cover chimney of the Cuisinart and, with the steel blades whirling the coconut, pour the mixture from the saucepan, in a steady stream, into the bowl. The moment everything is thoroughly amalgamated – usually in about 2 or 3 seconds – you should have a workably stiff paste. Press it and shape it with your fingers to form the lining of a previously greased 9-inch pie pan. This should not be baked, but, instead, wrapped in a plastic bag and chilled in the refrigerator until it is completely firm. After you have filled the shell, perhaps with chunky fruit, and chilled again, you should let it come to room temperature for about 15 minutes before attempting to cut it. Otherwise the shell will be too crackly and hard to cut.

15

The Proper Ending for a Meal (or a Cookbook) Is a Memorable Dessert

In every part of the world, some of the most delightful and popular of desserts are the simple purées of the freshest of fresh seasonal fruits, sometimes slightly thickened with a whip of heavy cream and chilled till they are pure ice-cold velvet on the tongue, with a sparkling balance of sweet-sour refreshment. Across the United States I have loved, again and again, our farmhouse-made apple sauce, spiced with cinnamon, clove and lemon peel. In England, in the Spring, there is the exalted Gooseberry Fool (the word comes from the French, *fouler* – to pass through a sieve). In France, they have a *mousse* of every fruit in season. In homes across Russia, there is *kissel*, a slightly thickened purée of each fruit that comes into the market in turn. All these dishes have always involved the laborious work of rubbing the fruit through a fine sieve to achieve the smoothness of texture. Now it can all be done by the Cuisinart blades.

These same blades also help us to achieve absolutely the smoothest ice creams and sherbets we have ever made. If you will learn the basic principles from the recipes in this chapter, you will be able to translate any standard recipe to the Cuisinart technique.

KISSEL OF FRESH STRAWBERRIES

(for 4)

For the definition of *kissel*, see above.

Strawberries, fully ripe, hulled and washed (2½ lbs)

Sugar, preferably unrefined cane or fine-grind white (about 1½ cups)

Lemon juice, freshly-squeezed (a few squirts)

Dry white wine (about ¼ cup)

Arrowroot, ground (about 3 Tbs)

Heavy cream, for whipping, optional (½ pint)

Active Preparation in About 25 Minutes – Plus Several Hours of Chilling

Put into the Cuisinart work bowl the 2½ pounds of strawberries, in batches of not more than 2 cups each, then whirl the steel blades until the fruit is coarsely puréed – usually in about 5 to 10 seconds. You may have to stop and restart the blades once or twice to insure even chopping. As each batch is done, transfer it to a saucepan over fairly gentle heat. When all the batches are combined, let them bubble gently, stirring them often, to boil off the water and concentrate the strawberry flavor. After about 10 minutes of this, the strawberries should taste much stronger. Measure the purée and return it (in 2-cup batches) to the work bowl. Now use the machine to incorporate precisely the right amount of sugar, according to the natural sweetness or tartness of the fruit. A good starting rule is ⅓ cup of sugar to each cup of purée. Mix in the added sugar by whirling the steel blades for a second or two. Taste and add more sugar, if needed. The trick is to balance the acidity of the fruit without drowning out the fresh flavor. We also add, at this point, a squirt or two of lemon juice. When the flavor is dead right, whirl the steel blades again until the purée is perfectly smooth – usually for an extra 2 or 3 seconds.

The traditional Russian method of slightly thickening the *kissel* is with a mixture of ground arrowroot and dry white wine. For roughly this amount of fruit, we mix in a small bowl about 3 tablespoons of arrowroot and just enough wine smoothly to liquify the powder. Hold it. Now transfer the strawberry purée back to the saucepan and again heat it up to gentle boiling, stirring it continuously to dissolve the sugar and again concentrate the flavor. After a couple of minutes of bubbling, turn off the heat, give a final stir to the arrowroot mixture, then spoon it into the fruit purée, teaspoon by teaspoon, vigorously stirring in each addition. Before you have added all the arrowroot, the purée will show the first signs of thickening. Stop adding the arrowroot, turn on the heat and bring the purée back just to gentle bubbling, stirring it continuously with a wooden spoon and scraping the bottom and sides of the pan as the purée increases in thickness. Let it all bubble, still stirring, for 2 or 3 minutes more, then finally adjust the thickness, either by working in more arrowroot, or by thinning it with a dash or two of the wine. Let it cool, then pour it into a covered storage dish and refrigerate it until it is completely chilled. Serve it ice cold, with or without whipped cream, as you please. This works in the same way for all soft fruits, such as blueberries, peaches, pears, plums, etc. If you use raspberries or blackberries, you will have to sieve the mixture once to get rid of the gritty pits.

ENGLISH FOOL OF DRIED APRICOTS

(for 4)

In its simplest form, an English Fool is a purée of fresh fruits with cream and nuts. (See the definition of the word in the Introduction to this chapter.) It is usually made with fresh spring or summer fruits, strictly by the seasons, but here is an unusual recipe made with dried apricots, which are available all the year round.

For a result that will wow your friends, there are two demands that you must remember to satisfy. First, you MUST get the best-quality apricots, entirely free from additives or chemical preservatives. This type can usually be found at health food stores. Second, you should cook the apricots by our "secret method" of slow baking in an oven, rather than quick boiling in a saucepan.

Apricots, dried, best-quality,
  see above (½ lb)
Sugar, natural or fine-grind white
  (about 4–6 Tbs)

Heavy cream (½ cup)
Blanched almonds (⅓ cup)

**Active Work of Preparation About 10 Minutes,
but Pre-Soaking of the Apricots Overnight, Plus About an Hour
of Unsupervised Baking**
Put the ½ pound of apricots to soak in cold water in the refrigerator overnight. Stir them around a couple of times. Cover them. In the morning, cook them in their soaking water. Preheat your oven to 325°F. Transfer the apricots and water to a lidded oven casserole. Do not add any sugar at this point. Set the casserole, uncovered, on top of the stove and gently bring the liquid just to the bubbling point.

At once turn off the heat, put on the lid and set the casserole in the center of the oven to bake for just about 1 hour, a little more or less, as you please.

When the timer rings, strain the apricots from the juice (reserving the liquid) and put them into the Cuisinart bowl. Whirl the steel blades until the apricots are perfectly smoothly puréed – usually in 4 to 6 seconds. Now add the sugar, the amount depending on the sweetness or tartness of the apricots. We usually sprinkle on 4 table-spoons first, amalgamate it with a single 1-second burst of the machine, then taste and add more sugar, teaspoon by teaspoon, as needed. If you oversweeten the apricots, you will mask their refresh-ingly tangy flavor. Now add the ½ cup of cream and amalgamate that with a single, 1-second burst of the blades.

Finally, adjust the thickness to a smooth not-too-stiff cream by working in some of the juice from the baking. Spoon the fool into handsome tall wine glasses and set them in the refrigerator to chill for an hour or two. Rinse and dry the Cuisinart bowl, then put into it the ⅓ cup of almonds. Start and stop the blades in 1-second bursts until the almonds are fairly coarsely chopped – usually in 3 or 4 bursts. Just before serving the fool, sprinkle the top surface in each glass with a good spoonful of the chopped almonds.

A MAGNIFICENTLY SMOOTH FRESH LIME CHAMPAGNE SHERBET

(for 4)

We have adapted this recipe from one given us by a brilliant young chef of France. His Cuisinart method is quite revolutionary and it gives an extraordinary result. You do not need to use an expensive, sweet Champagne. A medium-priced average California, French, or New York State sweet sparkler will do very well, and the sweeter the wine, the less sugar you should add. The natural grape sugar has a far better flavor and is much more healthful than processed white sugar crystals.

Sweet champagne, see above (1 bottle)	Maple syrup, pure (about 3 Tbs)
	Salt to taste
Limes (8)	Gelatin, granulated, unflavored
Sugar, see above (about ½ cup)	(1 envelope, or 1 Tbs)

Active Preparation About 10 Minutes – Plus 5 or More Hours for Chilling, Freezing and Ripening

Start the day before. At least 2 hours before you begin the preparation, set the bottle of Champagne to chill in the coldest part of your refrigerator. Also, set in your freezer an empty, 1-quart flat-bottomed, tightly lidded stainless steel casserole or saucepan. (The metal is an essential part of the "secret trick.") You are going to use the juice of all 8 of the limes, but first pick the 4 with the best skins and, with a sharp potato peeler or a French "zest scraper" sliver off the thin, green, outer rind. Mince the slivers, in the usual way, in the Cuisinart chopper-churner. In a 1-pint saucepan combine ½ cup of the sugar, 3 tablespoons of the maple syrup, ½ cup of the Champagne, the minced lime rind and a pinch of salt. Separately, in a small mixing bowl, stir together another ¼ cup of the Champagne with the envelope of gelatin until they form a thick paste. (At once, of course, recork the Champagne and set it back in the refrigerator.) Gently heat the saucepan, stirring its contents continuously, until the sugar is completely melted, then begin spooning in, teaspoon by teaspoon, the gelatin paste. Press out any lumps with the back of the spoon against the sides of the saucepan. You do not have to bring this mixture to the boil. As soon as everything is melted and completely smooth, turn off the heat and let it cool.

Now we use our steel blades to beat and aerate the sherbet mixture. Squeeze the juice from the 8 limes. They should give you slightly under 1 cup of juice. Put it into the Cuisinart work bowl. As soon as the mixture in the saucepan is about at blood heat (touch it with the tip of your finger), add it to the lime juice in the work bowl. Also add 1 more cup of the Champagne. At once whirl the steel blades for a full 25 seconds. There will be an almighty frothing. This is the secret of the extraordinary feather-lightness of the finished sherbet. Taste and add more sugar and maple syrup if needed. The moment you turn off the machine – before the frothing subsides – pour everything into the metal casserole from the freezer and, contrary to all the standard instructions, cover it and set it on the floor of the freezer, so that the sherbet will set as quickly as possible – usually in 1 to 1½ hours. Also set in the freezer at the same time the work bowl of the Cuisinart, with the steel blades, and the container of whatever type of ice cream machine you are going to use.

As soon as the sherbet is fully set, but not yet rock hard, it will have developed all kinds of unpleasant ice crystals and hard lumps. Never mind. The French "secret trick" takes care of those. Now work very fast. Set the chilled work bowl with its steel blades back in place on the machine. Scrape into it the hardened and lumpy sherbet. Whirl the blades until the sherbet is perfectly smooth – usually in 4 or 5 seconds. It will probably turn into a syrupy liquid. That's O.K. At once pour it into the ice cream machine container, stick in the dasher and turn it according to the requirements of your particular machine until the sherbet is completely set. With our new air-suction, electric freezer machine it usually takes from 1 to 1½ hours. Finally, as always, you have to spoon the sherbet into a tightly lidded freezer container and let it ripen and solidify in the freezer for a few more hours. This, to us, is the smoothest sherbet we have ever tasted. One of the nicest ways of serving it is to put a scoop or two per person into tall, chilled wine glasses with some of the remaining Champagne poured in to fill up the glass.

A VARIATION OF THE PREVIOUS RECIPE – SHERBET OF FRESH PEACHES

(for 4)

This is virtually the same recipe, with the limes replaced by fresh ripe peaches, so the basic method should be taken from the preceding text.

Peaches, ripe (7 or 8, according to size)	Gelatin, granulated, unflavored (1 envelope or 1 Tbs)
Lemons (2)	Champagne, sweet, pre-chilled,
Sugar (about ½ cup)	see previous recipe (1 bottle)
Maple syrup, pure (about 3 Tbs)	

Active Preparation About 20 Minutes – Plus About 5 or More Hours for Chilling, Freezing and Ripening

You will need 2 cups of peach pulp. This usually requires 7 or 8 peaches. Skin them and remove their stones. Work fast, or they will quickly turn brown. Chunk the flesh into the Cuisinart work bowl and add at once the juice of the 2 lemons. Whirl the steel blades until the peaches are smoothly puréed – usually in about 3 or 4 seconds. Prepare, exactly as in the previous recipe, the sweetening mixture of sugar, maple syrup, gelatin and Champagne. When it has cooled, add it to the peaches in the work bowl and churn for about 3 seconds. Add ½ cup of the Champagne and churn again for about 20 seconds. Taste and add more sugar and maple syrup if needed. From this point on, follow precisely the procedure of the previous recipe.

SMOOTH LEMON-CREAM-WITHOUT-CREAM IN TALL GLASSES

(for 4)

You might say that this is a cross-breeding between lemon curd and lemon jelly. It is refreshingly tangy and, in a tall glass with its bright color, it looks very handsome on the table.

Gelatin, granulated, unflavored	**Sugar, fine-grind (about 6 Tbs)**
(2 envelopes, or 2 Tbs)	**Egg yolks (4)**
Dry white wine (2 cups)	**Madeira or dry Sherry (6 Tbs)**
Lemons (2 large)	

Active Preparation About 15 Minutes – Plus About a Couple of Hours of Chilling

Put into a 1-quart saucepan the contents of the 2 envelopes of the gelatin. Stir in ½ cup of the wine and leave the gelatin to dissolve into a paste. Sliver off the thin, yellow, outer rind of the 2 lemons and, if necessary, mince it finely in the Cuisinart. Transfer it to a second saucepan, of about 1½ quarts capacity, then add to it 6 tablespoons of the sugar (or more, to your taste) and 1½ cups more of the dry white wine. Heat it all up, stirring to dissolve the sugar, but do not let it boil. Now, stirring vigorously all the time, begin working it into the gelatin paste in the other saucepan. Make sure there are no gelatin lumps. Let it all heat up very gently, but do not let it boil. Meanwhile, squeeze the juice from the 2 lemons into the Cuisinart work bowl, adding the 4 egg yolks and the 6 tablespoons of Madeira. Whirl the steel blades until the eggs have been thoroughly churned and everything is amalgamated to a smooth cream – usually in about 4 to 6 seconds. Measure ½ cup of the hot mixture from the saucepan, restart the blades and, through the cover chimney, pour in the hot stuff in a steady stream. The moment it is all in, stop the motor, turn off the heat under the saucepan and slowly add the egg whip to the hot saucepan, stirring constantly with a wooden spoon. When it is all in, turn on the heat to a very gentle temperature and, continuing to stir all the time, allow the eggs slightly to thicken the lemon cream. Get rid of any possible lumps by passing everything through a fine sieve into a mixing bowl, continuing to stir while the mixture cools slightly. Spoon it into 4 tall glasses and chill them in the refrigerator for at least a couple of hours. The lemon cream should not be fully set to the consistency of a hard, rubbery aspic, but should be soft and creamy, tangy on the tongue and not too sweet. If it gets too firm in the refrigerator, let it soften again at room temperature for a few minutes.

A SUPREME PARTY DESSERT OF ARMAGNAC-BRANDIED PRUNES WITH ICE CREAM

(for 4)

This magnificent concoction requires substantial advance planning. At least 1 month ahead, you must lay down your prunes to soak in the Armagnac brandy, according to the recipe on page 209. Only when you have a solid supply of the prunes can you start making the ice cream.

Brandied prunes – see following
   recipe, page 209 (22)
Egg yolks (5)
Sugar (½ cup)

Light cream (2 cups)
Heavy cream (¼ cup)
Armagnac – see following recipe,
   page 209 (about 14 Tbs)

Active Preparation About 30 Minutes – Plus About 5 Hours or More for the Freezing and Ripening of the Ice Cream
Put into the Cuisinart work bowl the 5 egg yolks, then whirl the steel blades until the eggs have been completely disintegrated and are frothy – usually in about 3 to 5 seconds. Now sprinkle around on top of the eggs the ½ cup of sugar and again whirl the blades until the two ingredients are completely amalgamated to a smooth cream –

usually in about another 2 to 4 seconds. Add the 2 cups of light cream and the ¼ cup of heavy cream, then whirl again to amalgamate – usually in 2 or 3 seconds. Transfer this custard to a large, heavy saucepan and heat it up gently, stirring continuously with a wooden spoon, until the mixture is thick enough to coat the spoon. Of course, never, never allow such an egg custard to boil. When it is exactly thick enough, transfer it to a covered storage dish and cool it in the refrigerator, taking it out now and then to give it a good stir.

Choose 10 of your largest prunes that have been soaked in Armagnac, drain them thoroughly, pit them, if necessary, then mince them not too finely in the Cuisinart bowl, usually in 2 to 4 one-second bursts of the steel blades. Add to the bowl 10 tablespoons of the Armagnac in which the prunes were soaked. Whirl the steel blades for a second or two just to amalgamate the mixture. Now thoroughly blend this mixture into the cooling custard.

When the custard is completely chilled, freeze it to ice cream in the standard way in whatever ice cream machine you normally use. (See the previous recipes for some of the details.) Finally, ripen the ice cream in the freezer for a couple more hours and then serve scoops of it in handsome glasses, each serving garnished with three more drained and pitted Armagnac prunes and a teaspoon or two of the Armagnac itself dribbled over. This is a splendid party dessert if ever there was one!

PRUNES MARINATED IN ARMAGNAC BRANDY

(3 dozen prunes, a basic supply)

For this recipe, be sure to get "softened" prunes. Some people call Armagnac, which is distilled in the southwest of France, the second greatest brandy after Cognac. Others consider Armagnac quite the best in the world! It always comes in a flat flagon.

Softened prunes (3 doz)   **Armagnac (2 flagons)**

Active Preparation 5 Minutes – Plus at Least 30 Days of Marination
Thoroughly prick each prune with a fork and put them in a 3-quart

jar with a tightly fitting lid, then cover them by pouring in 2 flagons of Armagnac. Let them stand, in a cool place, but not in the refrigerator, covered, for at least 30 days. Gently stir them with a wooden spoon once every day. Those that are left over from the ice cream of the previous recipe may be eaten as a dessert on their own, with whipped cream. It is slightly dangerous to eat more than 6 of these prunes at one sitting. Armagnac, after all, is a brandy for heroes! None of it should be wasted. The remaining, prune-flavored marinade makes an excellent and healthy after-dinner liqueur.

INDEX